HOLE

Kidnapped in
Georgia

PETER SHAW

Published by Accent Press Ltd – 2006
ISBN 1905170726
Copyright © Peter Shaw 2006

Printed and bound in the UK

Cover Design by Ed Talfan – Squint Films Ltd
Cover image supplied by Empic

The publisher acknowledges the financial support
of the Welsh Books Council

To Tim and Jackie
– for everything

Acknowledgements

Thank you, people who helped and supported and who do not necessarily appear in this narrative – in no particular order:

Michael Boyd (Executive Chairman of Landell-Mills and Director of DCI Group) and Tim & Jackie Hammond, without whom this attempt would never have been made; Denis Corboy (Former Head of European Commission Delegation in Georgia and Special Envoy for the European Commission), without whom I would not be here; Jane Corboy – his charming wife who supported Denis throughout in his efforts; Dr Garret FitzGerald, Lynda, Baroness Chalker of Wallasey, Trevor Bowen (Directors of DCI Group) for their superb networking abilities; Peter Sutherland (Chairman of British Petroleum and Goldman Sachs), Bono (U2), Richard Miles (US Ambassador in Georgia) and Paul O'Neil (US Treasury Secretary), for their willingness to be networked and take action; Detective Superintendent David Douglas and Detective Inspector Ron Holmes at New Scotland Yard, for travelling to Georgia, for supporting my family in the UK and for all subsequent efforts; Chief Superintendent Bob Evans, Superintendent Colin Jones and Chief Inspector Chris Parsons of the South Wales Police who provided comfort to my family when they were most in need; Michael Mgaloblishvili (MD of Agro-business Bank of Georgia), for years of insight, foresight and support in Georgia and the UK; Chris Patten and his colleagues Anthony Carey and Patrick Child; Neil and Glenys Kinnock, Pat Cox, Cornelus Wittebrood, Per Eklund, Reinhold Brender, Hugues Mingarelli, Robert Liddell, Dino Sinigallia, Albert Russell, Maya Draganova, Paul McGregor, especially Giuseppe Angelini (for going out on a limb) and many others at the European Commission and European Parliament in Brussels, and Elio Germano, Torben Holtze, Jerome Cassiers, Jacques Vantomme, Patrick Daubresse, Julian Schulman, Kate Whyte and Emmanuel Anquetil at the European Commission Delegation in

Georgia. Rob Macaire, Dominic Schroeder, David Drake, Chris Clarke, Norma Reid and Sally Moody at the FCO in London; Ambassador Deborah Barnes-Jones, Stuart McLaren, Mike Seaman and Eilidh Kennedy – a very special thank you – at the British Embassy in Tbilisi; John Dexter and Tony Bishop – the communicators; Paul Craig and Mike Gutteridge (MD and Director of Agrisystems), Nigel Peacock, Charlie Keane, (Directors of Landell-Mills and ICC Bank respectively), and George Shonia (Deputy Minister of the Economy in Georgia) for long-term support and refreshment in Tbilisi, Baku, London, Washington, Bath, Aylesbury and Dublin; First Minister Rhodri Morgan, Ministers Jane Hutt, Jane Davison and Rose Stewart at the Welsh Assembly Government for family support and the "welcome home"; John Smith, my Member of Parliament, for making every effort in Georgia and Wales; Martin Flint (Risk Analysis) for wise advice to the FACC group; Colin Adams (Chief Executive of BCCB) for innovative thinking; Dr Lesley Permann-Kerr for confirming my "normality"; David Burrell (British-American Tobacco) for giving me the first chance; David Black, Mike Lloyd and Tim Attridge for Vilnius and Baku; Dr John Channon and John Kennedy, my first colleagues in Georgia; Norman Matthews for getting me there; Anna Bradshaw and all others at LML; Tim Hooper, Gerry Morrisey and Michael Brennan – fellow consultants in Georgia; the Welsh media – BBC Wales, HTV, S4C, Real Radio, Red Dragon FM, Bridge FM, *The Western Mail* and *South Wales Echo* – for launching the campaign; my dear Georgian friends and former colleagues in Georgia – too numerous to mention individually, and my many friends in Wales and elsewhere in the UK, past and present, with whom I shared my prayers; the many hundreds of well-wishers from whom I received messages on my return and who prayed for me from all over the world. The prayers worked. And finally, those who remain closest, my family – my mam, Mair, Lisa and Gavin, Rod, Pip, Diana and Danny and the hundreds who extend from them in Wales, England and Georgia.

FOREWORD

Before reading Peter's account of his kidnap, I jotted down a few notes about this ebullient bundle of Welshness. The first thing that came to mind was: 'Peter Shaw is a strong man'. Towards the end of the book, it was no surprise to find the self-same conclusion expressed by Sasha, the leader of the kidnap gang, in their final meeting. Peter's response on the character of Sasha, immediate, honest and to the point, spoke of a man who against all odds was able to preserve his sense of self – *intact* – through a harrowing and terrifying ordeal; bravely compromising physical safety in the service of psychological well-being.

Peter writes often of his family and although I know little more of his early years it is clear that his birth family gave him the precious gift of himself – nurtured and loved. From those steady hands and warm hearts so Peter grew his own strong and dear families and a highly robust inner core that might be broached but never destroyed.

More than this, his survival is consequent on something vital and fundamental lodged within that strength – a kind of entrepreneurial self-preservation mechanism – the intelligence and the talent to use whatever is presented and to see possibilities where little possibility objectively exists. From the start he took an active part in what was happening – followed his instincts – continually soaking up information and assessing his situation – sustaining hope and control in a myriad of ways.

This incredible and moving first-hand account of survival is a gift and should be required reading for us all and certainly for anyone at risk of kidnap. It is not possible to give a list of 'dos and don'ts' because every situation is different but what we can do is learn from survivors and find ways to develop those qualities within ourselves.

Peter also gives us the opportunity to know a little of Georgia and of Georgians who do not make headlines. Happily, we learned of Diana, Danny and her family but also Peter's work colleagues and the people he encountered in Tbilisi. Against pressures of corruption and deprivation were people living their everyday lives well and so our lasting image of a place and a people Peter obviously still holds dear is dappled with light.

A couple or so years ago, I had both the joy and the misfortune to follow Peter speaking at a security conference. As I remember he was on his feet for two hours, speaking without notes and holding the audience of businessmen and women enthralled. Not only that but he (unwittingly) upstaged everything that I had to say about surviving kidnap and the survivor personality. Oh boy!! But with kindness and grace, he rushed forward and thanked me for confirming that he had done things correctly!!

Not only is Peter a strong man but he is also a very special one. This is a story from which we find the most precious truth of all is to be true to oneself above all else.

Dr Lesley Perman-Kerr CPsychol
St Albans September 29th 2006

PREFACE

The people of Georgia are warm, welcoming, spontaneously humorous, intelligent and naturally gregarious. They are famed for their ability to organise feasts for their guests – the ubiquitous Georgian 'table' – and eventually bore the pants off them by the interminable rounds of toasts delivered by the ever-present *tamada*, the Georgian toastmaster. Participants at the tables invariably end up enjoyably inebriated. Georgians have long been labelled by their Russian neighbours as incorrigible liars, cheats and rogues, and they are rather proud of that. This is not meant to be a criticism of the Georgian character, simply components of the survival techniques imposed upon them by the economic and social environment in which they have had to live. They are also proud of their culture – they are great singers, dancers, musicians, poets and artists – their language, and their independence. During my time in Georgia, they were not sure from whom they wished to be independent – the West or Russia – or how to achieve it. They simply knew it was out there somewhere and they wanted it – urgently!

There was no real infrastructure in Georgia, at least not as we know it in the West. During the winter, schools closed because there was no heating. There was no heating because there was no consistent electricity or gas supply, and even if there were, the radiators within the schools may well have been removed and sold as scrap metal. Officially, Georgia's biggest export was and is scrap metal. Salaries to teachers, police, judges, and government ministers were paid, at best, sporadically. The police existed by taking money from drivers who paid up rather than risk being thrown in jail. Judges thrived by taking bribes – the highest bidder won the court case. Government ministers existed by stealing money from international donor organisations. Teachers had no chance and depended upon family support, and direct international aid, as did surgeons, doctors and nurses. University degrees and driving tests were easily purchased.

I spent six years working in Georgia, living in the capital city of Tbilisi, and working under contract to the European Commission. I was Project Team Leader for four and a half years of my time in Georgia – with intermittent responsibilities in neighbouring Azerbaijan – the last three years of which were spent establishing and helping to manage the Agro-business Bank of Georgia. With the financial and technical support of the European Commission, the bank was dedicated to providing credit to the privatising agricultural sector of Georgia and its associated rural agri-businesses. In other words, the bank provided basic financial services to small farmers, processors and traders when no other bank in Georgia would. It had been very difficult to establish and thereafter to manage, but nothing prepared me for what was to come a few days before I was due to leave Georgia at the end of my contract.

The Pankisi Gorge

The Pankisi Gorge – where I was held captive for most of my incarceration, although I did not know it at the time – is a 40km-long, hook-shaped river valley in the north-east of Georgia, from which numerous mountain passes run north and east to Georgia's border with the Russian republics of Dagestan and Chechnya. Average elevation in the valley is four hundred metres rising to more than three thousand metres in the mountain ranges to the north. Vehicle access to the valley is almost impossible, apart from the main road from Akhmeta. The surrounding dense forests further isolate the area. Once out of the valley itself, the terrain quickly becomes inhospitable and virtually impossible to traverse.

Following the outbreak of the second Chechen war in 1999, as Russian forces pushed to the south, groups of Chechen refugees fled across the border into Georgia. Some eight thousand refugees were thought to have taken up residence at that time in the Pankisi valley. The refugees were taken in by the seven thousand local Kists – Chechens who settled peacefully in the Pankisi at least two hundred years ago. With the refugees came a number of Chechen fighters who saw Georgia as a convenient rear-retreat position. From that time until the present, they have used Georgia for rest and recuperation and as a base for their logistics support networks. The Pankisi area, already in 1999 a criminal hotspot seen as beyond the powers of the Tbilisi Government, and home to their Kist cousins, represented an ideal bolthole for Chechen fighters. A census in 2002 put refugee numbers at about four thousand. The refugees refused to return to Chechnya while the Russian armed forces remained there. The Gorge was also home to a small number of Arab facilitators who were thought to have provided logistical, financial and technical support for the fighters in Chechnya.

It is estimated that, since 2000, several hundred anti-Russian fighters have come to live in the Gorge. These militants are thought to be dispersed in among the refugee population, and to the north of the Gorge within seasonal settlements. Russia has brought concerted pressure to bear upon Georgia to eliminate the rebels harboured on its territory, further aggravating the difficult relations between the two countries.

At the same time, the Pankisi valley was home to a thriving organised crime community, specialising in anything from car theft to drug-trafficking and kidnappings. These criminal activities were most often thought to be carried out by Kist gangs, for financial rather than political gain. Weak central government control, prevalent throughout the whole country, had all but disintegrated in the Pankisi, leaving the gangs free to act with impunity. Between the refugees, the Kists and corruption within the Georgian security bodies, the Pankisi Gorge became a lawless area in which criminality was virtually unchecked. Added to this was the Georgian Government's fear that any attempt to bring order back to the Pankisi Gorge would result in a violent Chechen backlash, which it could not control.

I wouldn't recommend a holiday in the Pankisi Gorge.

Chapter One

It was 6.00pm on Wednesday, 18th June 2002, an unusually wet and windy day for that time of the year in Tbilisi, Georgia, but I was a happy man. Having worked in Georgia for six years, I was going home for good on 20th June. A wonderful prospect!

All preparations had been completed. My partner, Diana, had packed the accumulated debris of our time together and had successfully negotiated with local contractors to fly out seven crates of domestic accoutrements to arrive in South Wales somewhere near to our own arrival date. That was no mean feat, given the dislocated and confused nature of customs administration in Georgia. The final pieces of the logistical jigsaw had been put into place over the past few days, including the transportation of three of our pack of feral cats to the UK by Austrian Airlines. There were many tears shed over the ones we were going to leave behind, but so it had to be.

Following a lot of hassle involving the payment of various "fees" to the airport and customs officials, by 9.30am on the morning of 18th, Blacky, Whitey and Panther were finally on their way. My last telephone call from my office in the Agro-business Bank of Georgia a few minutes earlier had been to Phil Morgan, the "cat man", who confirmed that he was *en route* to meet them at Heathrow Airport and would then transport them to his quarantine centre at Bridgend.

I had enjoyed and survived a series of farewell parties given by my friends and colleagues in Georgia, and all that remained was to attend a final party organised by the local Delegation of the European Commission. This was to be held at the home of the Senior Counsellor at the Delegation, Jacques Vantomme, on the evening of 19th June. I hoped the weather would improve as I knew the intention was to dine *au sauvage* in his splendid garden just outside Tbilisi. It'd be a pity if the weather led to another postponement: we'd already changed the date because of an unexpected trip that Jacques had to make to

Armenia. I'd immediately agreed to delay my departure from Georgia from the 18th to 20th June in order to fit in with Jacques' amended timetable. It seemed churlish to refuse, given the support I'd received from the EC Delegation during my time in Georgia. All that remained for today was to leave the office in a few minutes' time and link up with a couple of colleagues for a final pint of local lager in the Toucan Bar on the way home to the apartment I shared with Diana and Danny, our son.

As I closed my laptop for the penultimate time, I looked around for the diminutive figure of George Kalandarashvili, our Head of Credit. He was not at his desk, but on inquiring with George Kankava, Head of Public Relations and a fellow director of the bank, he assured me that Kalandarashvili would meet us in the bar shortly. He was simply interviewing a customer at nearby business premises. I offered Kankava a lift in my car but he was already striding purposefully toward his own ancient Lada and confirmed with eager anticipation that we would meet in the bar in fifteen minutes' time. Great, I thought. I could do with a pint.

As I nodded my farewells to the security guards who opened the door to let me out, I cast a glance around the front office of our modest little premises, and made a mental note to ask Eka to tidy up the papers surrounding her desk the following morning, a request I would not have to repeat. As I crossed the road toward my aging Skoda Octavia, I noticed a white mini-bus pulling slowly from the kerb about one hundred metres down the street from the bank premises. As I opened my car door, the mini-bus stopped. When I retraced my steps to pick up the local English newspaper I'd forgetfully left behind on my desk, the vehicle had come to a halt in the middle of the road. On re-emerging from the bank with my newspaper, I was surprised to find that the mini-bus had returned to its original parking place. Strange, I thought, but no more than that, as I settled into my car and buckled up. I really fancied that pint.

Chapter Two

I have always been rather proud of the fact that I was born in my granny's parlour at number 11 Church Street, Maesteg in South Wales.

My father was called Ron and, like me, was an only child. He was a native of Sheffield and had spent his formative and early adult years in the coal mining village of Langold, Nottinghamshire. My birth certificate describes his occupation as a colliery blacksmith at Firbeck Colliery, Langold. I suppose he was, but he was a quiet man and never mentioned that part of his life to me. He did tell me that he was a bit of a sportsman in his youth. He played tennis and soccer and was captain of the Sheffield Wheelers Cycling Club. Until his death in 1989 his full-time occupation in Wales was wagon repairer at the Steel Company of Wales at Port Talbot, just over the hill from Maesteg. His real enthusiasm however, was music. He was an accomplished pianist and in his early life obtained a degree at the Victoria College of Music in London and seriously considered pursuing a career as a professional pianist. His aspirations were, fortunately for me, thwarted by his meeting my mother during the pre-war years – an introduction made by a family friend who had himself migrated from South Wales to the Nottinghamshire coal-fields in the 1930's. This meeting led to an extended courtship and ultimately marriage in 1942. My father's musical ambitions were thereafter partially fulfilled by playing piano with various local dance bands in the South Wales valleys. No doubt, to him, a reasonably enjoyable means of augmenting the family income. He could certainly make a piano bounce.

My mother is the eldest of four sisters – there was also an older brother – and was born and raised in the coalmining village of Caerau near the top of the Llynfi Valley. A neighbour was the grandmother of Kylie Minogue. The family eventually moved down the valley to Maesteg. The valley was then, and remained throughout my early life, a community dependent almost entirely on coal and the steel works at Port Talbot. There were seven working deep mines in the Llynfi valley in those days and virtually every family had a male member who worked either in the coalmines or in the steel works. The Davies family was no exception. My maternal grandfather was a collier, as was the only son, Desmond, until the outbreak of war from which he returned minus one arm and one eye. During the war, my mother worked in the munitions factory – the "arsenal" – at Bridgend. She is still quite proud of that.

Following my parents' marriage, there was apparently an abortive attempt to make a home for themselves in Nottinghamshire. They tried for a short while, but my mother's homesickness won out, as did her very natural desire to have her child born in Wales, close to Mam. My father had no choice but to up-sticks and move to Wales.

In those days home ownership was not a venture entered into lightly by a working-class family in the South Wales valleys. Usually the only choice was to live with Mam and Dad. And so it was that my childhood was most happily spent living in a large, comfortable rented house with four bedrooms, a huge scullery, a living room, middle room and parlour, and a large back garden in which my grandpa kept chickens, and which had direct access to Maesteg's cricket field and the river Llynfi. Ours was an extended family consisting of my grandpa and granny, my mam and dad, Aunty Nance and Uncle Tom, Aunty Iris and Aunty Shirley; the latter only fourteen years my senior and more like a sister than an aunt.

I had an idyllic childhood punctuated by the occasional "clip" handed out to me by that member of the family who happened to be in closest proximity to my most recent misdemeanour, and by the frequent visits of cousins from their nearby homes. My memories are of happy schooldays at Plasnewydd Primary School, big, boozy Christmas parties shared with similarly large neighbouring families at which we all had to do a "turn", of festive Guy Fawkes' bonfire nights – my grandfather was a council employee in his later years and was able to collect old tyres which made a terrific blaze, of Sunday nights in the parlour where my father played piano and the family took turns to sing. I spent a lot of time with Shirley, who encouraged in me her love of cinema, film stars and numerous boyfriends, with whom I often shared the back seats of local cinemas.

I don't think we were a poor family. All male members of the family were generally in full-time employment – the pits were going full swing after the war – and my mother worked at nights as an usherette at the Plaza cinema. I think I saw every film for many years at least once and without ever having to pay. I've loved old films ever since. At an early age, my father indoctrinated into me a lifelong love of music, particularly jazz.

Gradually, and inevitably, the family split up. Shirley went off to university at Cardiff; Iris married a posh fellow and moved to Cardiff; Tom and Nance moved house, initially just up the road to number nine Church Street, and subsequently to Cymer, a colliery village over the mountain in the next valley. Some years later, following a horrendous colliery accident which my Uncle Tom survived, suffering very severe burns, they returned to Maesteg on the back of the compensation monies paid out by the National Coal Board. At forty years of age my uncle never worked again.

When I was about nine years old, my parents finally decided to leave the family home at Church Street and move to a new council house at Turberville Estate, a few miles down the valley from Maesteg town. I remember that there was a difficult settling-in period. My mother in particular was not happy living at this distance – about four miles – from her mam and dad. My father was in his fifties before he bought his first car and we lived some distance from the nearest bus-stop. After a few years, we moved again to a council house at Maesteg Park, within walking distance of Church Street and across the road from Maesteg Grammar School. I attended that school after passing the eleven-plus examinations in 1956.

By this time, Shirley had completed her degree course at university and had successfully landed a job teaching at

Maesteg Grammar School. Iris had divorced and returned, temporarily, to the family home, and my father had become an established member of a local dance band and was happily undertaking two or three gigs each week at local clubs and dance halls in addition to his day job. It was the nearest he got to Ted Heath. During the whole of this period, the entire family – including Shirley until her marriage – always came together at the family home, eleven Church Street, every Saturday night. There my granny and grandpa would provide acres of food and lakes of bottled beer, and welcome any passing friend or acquaintance to join in the weekly celebrations. My grandfather, a successful amateur boxer in his time and a boxing referee thereafter, had a large number of drinking friends – he was a bit of a character – all of whom were very happy to take advantage of the free hospitality. The address was well-known in Maesteg for many years as "Fred's half-way house". It was a very good place in which to grow up. Later I played a bit of rugby for Maesteg Youth, cricket for Maesteg Wednesdays and, with a friend, Clive Lewis, came runners up at the Welsh under 16 doubles tennis championships at Neath. I really had a smashing childhood in the heart of a large and loving family.

Chapter Three

I moved slowly away from the kerbside and noticed that the white mini-bus was also moving very slowly away from its parking place. Proceeding down Budapeshti Street to the road junction at the street end, it moved at a snail's pace. A little odd, but people drive in strange ways in Tbilisi, either like lunatics or geriatrics. I hesitated for a second, and overtook the mini-bus before halting at the junction for the usual busy flow of traffic to pass. I then proceeded across the junction to continue the short trip to the pub.

Within a few metres of crossing the junction, a policeman stood on the pavement to my left with a whistle to his mouth, poised and ready to blow. Damn, I thought, just my luck. Being stopped by the police for no reason is a common occurrence in Georgia. There were seventy thousand uniformed police in Georgia, the vast majority of whom had received no salary – around seventy US dollars per month for the traffic police – for many years. Their only means of remuneration was stopping and demanding money, normally around five or ten Georgian *lari*, from motorists entirely innocent of any misdemeanour.

True to form, the policeman blew his whistle and stepped purposefully onto the road and walked toward my car. The thought occurred to me to do a runner and simply ignore the instruction to stop. This I had done on many occasions in the past, but normally outside the city, where there is a better chance of avoiding police reinforcements. In the city centre of Tbilisi, clogged with traffic at this time of day, there was little chance of evading the multitude of police officers who would be lining my route to the pub.

I stopped the car and opened the window. "What's the problem, Officer?" I asked as the policeman drew alongside my car twirling his baton. Usually, on hearing a foreign language, the police are inclined to walk away and allow the vehicle to continue in the knowledge that foreigners do not cough up. On this occasion, however, this gentleman's response was to hit me hard with his fist below my left eye, as he shouted, in English, "You are the fucking problem!"

I realised immediately, despite being stunned by the blow, that I was in very serious trouble. I had on one occasion some years previously witnessed an attempted kidnap in Tbilisi, and I had a nasty feeling that this was now happening to me.

Everything was a blur. First, the mini-bus, which unnoticed had followed me across the road junction, screeched to a halt immediately behind my car. In the rear-view mirror I saw, in a daze, three men jumping out of the back of the mini-bus. They were wearing balaclava-type black masks and full military uniform and they brandished Kalashnikovs, which they fired in quick bursts into the air as they ran toward my Skoda. At the same time, a police car came from nowhere and slewed to a halt at a forty-five degree angle to my off-side front wheel, thereby preventing me from making any forward progress. Three men dressed in police uniforms disembarked, two of them jumped into the rear seat of my car and one into the passenger seat.

I'd managed to bowl over the police officer who'd initially stopped me by slamming the driver's door into him. The three policemen in my car tried forcibly to extricate me from the driver's seat and lift me into the rear seat of the car. The fourth officer – who'd picked himself up off the ground and was clearly not amused – was trying to get behind the wheel. There was a mêlée of fists and elbows; my shirt was torn open; I felt blood coming from my nose and my eye began to swell.

One of the "officers" in the back seat was using some kind of stun-gun which he pressed against my neck. I clearly felt some kind of electrical impulse coming from the gun but the charge was insufficient to knock me out. Electricity was a problem in Georgia. Despite repeated applications of the gun I remained conscious and pretty bloody mad. The "policemen" were having great difficulty getting me out of the front seat and into the back seat, partly because I was still wearing a seat-belt – not a common practice in Georgia where it is considered unmanly to do so. Despite their efforts with the stun-gun and their fists, I remained stubbornly pinioned to the front seat.

My overriding emotion was anger. I knew what was going on, and I was extremely hacked off that this should be happening to me now after six years in Georgia, and only hours before my intended final departure from the country. I am not a big man and, at fifty-seven years old, way past my physical prime, but I was bloody well pissed-off! I guess I put up a pretty good fight.

I was conscious of the noise of the guns and the shouts and curses of people around me. Crowds of pedestrians in the street were yelling and gesticulating as the Kalashnikovs were fired, but there was no attempt to help me – I couldn't understand it. This made me more angry, and as I struggled, I yelled and cursed at the bastards who were still pummelling me as they tried to extricate me from the seat belt and into the rear of the car.

In the midst of the struggle, I saw through the windscreen another police car scramble to a halt directly in front of mine. Three roly-poly policemen jumped out and ran purposefully, brandishing pistols, toward the fracas.

The police in Georgia are all armed, but frequently sell their ammunition in order to raise money. As these three "real" policemen rushed toward my vehicle brandishing guns which were noticeably silent, the hooded guys in military garb who'd been firing their weapons noisily into the air throughout, now turned their attention to the newcomers and began to shoot in earnest over their heads. My three rescuers came to a halt and beat a hasty retreat back to the safety of their vehicle, which then reversed with tyres smoking, and took off in the direction whence it had come. There was nothing in the least humorous about this at the time, but, with hindsight, it was just like a scene from a Keystone Cops silent movie. Only Fatty Arbuckle was missing. No cavalry coming over the horizon for me.

I continued to struggle and yell, but I was tiring and the policeman who had initially stopped me eventually managed to get into the driver's seat, the police car blocking my vehicle moved away, and the driver of my car executed a U-turn and took a right in the direction of the main Tbilisi/Gori road.

I was covered in sweat and blood. I smelled the sweat of the two guys holding me in the rear seat, and felt their limbs trembling as they struggled to hold me down. They were shouting instructions to the driver who was frantically trying to weave his way through the dense traffic. We were followed by the police car and the mini-bus containing the military gentlemen. Although both my arms were pinioned by the men on each side of me, I extricated my legs from under theirs and with one foot kicked the back of the driver's head, repeatedly, and with the other, sounded the horn of the car intermittently by stamping the centre of the steering wheel.

It must have been one hell of a sight as the car careered through the busy streets with the horn blasting, and the driver screaming in Georgian at his colleagues to keep me quiet. This they tried to do by continuing to press their stun-guns to the side of my neck and by punching me on my face and head. Despite the obviously crazy progress of the car, the very visible signs of struggle in the rear seat and the blare of the horn, there was no pursuit and no attempt by anyone to intervene.

Gradually I became exhausted. My struggles weakened. My jacket was ripped, and my shirt torn all the way down the middle. Blood oozed from my nose onto my chest, and sight rapidly disappeared from my left eye. At the same time I knew very well in which direction we were heading.

I was being driven toward Mstkheta, the ancient capital of Georgia, near to which is the eleventh-century monastery of Djvari. We had picnicked there, Diana, Danny and I, almost every Sunday during the summer months. A scene flashed through my mind of Danny gurgling happily on the primitive old swing, the wonderful smell of wood-grilled *shashlik*, greasy potatoes, the tastiest tomatoes in the world, and the smell of the pine trees which shaded us from the hot sun. We once found a tortoise living happily in the forest. I wondered for a long time afterwards what became of him. We usually bought some ice-cream on the way home.

But what was happening to me now? My memories of the kidnapping are quite clear and the impressions imprinted are those of noise, particularly gunfire, constant and loud, the shouts and snarling curses of my kidnappers, my own yells, and the screams and cries of the dozens of pedestrians who witnessed the event but felt unable to assist; and the smell of sweat, pain, fear and anger.

As I was being driven toward Mstkheta, I tried to calm myself, gather my thoughts and to remain aware of what was going on around me. Don't panic. No point in continuing to struggle in a moving car. Conserve your energy. Stop panting. Take stock.

Chapter Four

I had left school at eighteen years of age in 1963 with three good "A" levels and nine "O" levels. Much to the chagrin of my family, I elected not to pursue a university education but to get a job. Why not? My friends were all working and had money in their pockets, and I hadn't. So I made the somewhat impulsive decision to join the Midland Bank; a decision made one Saturday morning when I happened to be passing the local branch in Maesteg, and popped in to ask if there were any jobs going. Within weeks I found myself struggling to balance *batches* on an adding-machine at Midland Bank in Queen Street, Cardiff. I remember vividly hearing of the assassination of President Kennedy toward the end of a particularly trying day during my traineeship.

I managed to forge a reasonable career within the bank, holding four managerial positions, culminating in the passably senior position of Corporate Banking Manager responsible for a lending portfolio based in Swansea and South-West Wales. At the age of fifty years I elected to take early voluntary retirement. The then Hong-Kong based HSBC Bank had recently bought out Midland, and was in the process of replacing established managers with their own people. It seemed a good idea to go, with lump sum and pension intact, and seek new horizons.

During a celebratory lunch at a local pub with a number of fellow early-retirers a few weeks later, it was mentioned that a former colleague had found meaningful employment as adviser to a bank in Central Europe. Would I be interested in learning more about it? Why not? It sounded a bit more interesting than what I had planned to do. I received a telephone call a couple of days later and promptly accepted an offer to travel on a look-see basis, all expenses paid.

And so in June 1994, I found myself sitting on the banks of the Danube in Budapest, quaffing a litre of Hungarian lager in the company of Peter Belward, an old friend and colleague who had himself, a year or so before, opted for early retirement from HSBC. He was working on a project involving the privatisation of the National Bank of Hungary; I was offered a position in a team working on the privatisation of the Kereshkedelmi Bank, a large state-owned bank based in Budapest. A new career had begun, completely without any planning on my part.

And very enjoyable it was too. Following a nine-month stint in Hungary, I found myself working on short-term banking projects on behalf of international donor organisations such as the European Bank for Reconstruction and Development (EBRD), the World Bank (WB) and the European Commission (EC). I moved on from Budapest to Prague; then on to Lithuania, Belarus, the Ukraine, Estonia and Azerbaijan. I was lucky. I enjoyed the travelling, meeting new people and trying to understand their culture. I found the work immensely challenging and thoroughly rewarding; I was also being well paid and somehow managed to find plenty of contracts. I was never unemployed for longer than a few weeks.

In early March 1996, I found myself in Tbilisi, Georgia. This too was meant to be a short-term contract – I signed on with the EC for three months initially, but it turned out to be a much longer affair: much longer than I'd planned.

Chapter Five

My introduction to Tbilisi, the capital city of Georgia, in March 1996, was of course via the airport. Not the spanking new marble-floored edifice that exists today, but a typically smelly, soviet-style labyrinth inhabited by fat, slovenly, unshaven military types, chewing gum, clutching their Kalashnikovs to their chests with one hand and holding out the other for baksheesh. I, with my co-travellers, was corralled behind a fenced area for some hours while airport staff played football with our luggage. If anything valuable fell out, they kept it. Fortunately, I was met at the airport by my team leader and spared the onslaught of the scores of taxi drivers, also no doubt extremely keen to deprive me of my luggage, and whisked off to a local guesthouse.

The following morning, I was driven to the Ministry of Agriculture – an uninviting, malodorous, stone block-house – and introduced to the Minister, one Bakur Gulua, a Khrushchev-like scowling figure with the limpest hand-shake in the world, a number of deputy ministers, and the ambiguously titled Head of Foreign Relations Department. I was given an office on the fifth floor of the Ministry, a tiny box containing a table, chair and a computer with no lead, and told to get on with it. I had arrived. I quickly learned to avoid using the lift – electricity was intermittent and people had been known to be stuck between floors for days – and the toilets. I spent my pennies in the yard behind the Ministry – a bit public and a long toil up and down stairs but the much better option.

I quickly familiarised myself with Tbilisi, which, during the spring and summer months is a strangely attractive city. It seldom rains between May and October and July and August are extremely hot and uncomfortably sticky. Tbilisi has a population of some one million two hundred thousand people, easily the largest city in Georgia, and is delightfully situated in a long narrow valley, overlooked by the huge metallic statue of

Mother Georgia and the brooding ruins of its eleventh-century castle. Georgia is full of castles. On a clear day the distant snow-covered Caucasian mountains – the highest in Europe – can be glimpsed, and the city contains many green parks, complete with lakes, where the locals play and picnic at weekends. The main drag is Rustaveli Avenue, a mini-Champs-Elysées, broad and lined by plane trees and a multitude of small shops, cafés, and restaurants. Beggars then abounded, and the old in-tourist multi-storied hotels in the city centre accommodated thousands of refugees from the Abkhaz and Ossetian wars, their depressing hovels, one room per family, made colourful by draped bed-linen aired from the balcony railings. I familiarised myself with the Old Town, which although collapsing from lack of maintenance, remained an intriguing stroll along old cobbled streets and alleyways occupied by small ghettoes of Russians, Armenians, Jews and Kurds.

At its bottom end and running parallel with Rustaveli, are a series of narrower streets, the main one being Perovskaya Street. This is the Montmatre of Tbilisi. Every building incorporates a bar or restaurant of surprising variety and variable quality; this is the area frequented at weekends by the small contingent of ex-pats who make Tbilisi their home in the short or long term. I was no exception. The street also contains the house in which the infamous Comrade Beria was born. The birthplace of Comrade Stalin, his boss, is the town of Gori – where he continues to be idolised – an hour and a half's drive west of Tbilisi.

The first president of Georgia following the collapse of the USSR was Gamsakhurdia. He died in mysterious and perhaps sinister circumstances, and was succeeded, some say by force, by Shevardnadze in 1993. President Shevardnadze, as Foreign Minister of Russia, had achieved fame and kudos, at least in the eyes of western democracies, as one of the architects, with President Gorbachov, of "Perestroika" – the unravelling of the Soviet Union. To the West he brought the promise of stability in Georgia – interrupted by internal wars with Abkhazia and

South Ossetia – and to his countrymen, at least initially, he brought hope. This, despite misgivings regarding his disastrous first term as President of Georgia when part of the Soviet Union, and his infamous links with the KGB.

Unfortunately the "Old White Fox" over the years, failed to deliver, and the economic recovery of the country was blighted by a combination of self-interest and, particularly surrounding Shevardnadze and his family, avarice, a paucity of management skills, cronyism, and political and Governmental corruption. The people, quite justifiably eventually lost all faith in their leader and his political team, and Shevardnadze and his clans were deposed in November 2003, a year after my time in Georgia, by the bloodless "Rose" revolution. He was replaced by Michael Saakashvili, a young well-educated firebrand with huge ambitions to democratise the politics of Georgia and bring long-awaited benefits to its people.

My initiation to driving my initial mode of transport – a Lada Niva – in Tbilisi was an exciting experience. You had a choice: avoid the potholes in the roads, or other vehicles – it was difficult to do both. The result was a constant stream of edgy motorists driving ancient cars, wrestling frantically with their steering wheels in their efforts to make progress and remain intact. Traffic lights, if they worked at all, were largely ignored and the police constantly badgered motorists in order to extract money for imaginary offences.

The dilapidated buildings reflected decades of neglect, but Tbilisi still exuded a certain old-world charm and dignity which I found immensely appealing and attractive. History and culture abound. I learned early on that the average Georgian could proudly recite volumes of ancient and modern poetry and recount the exploits of *King* Tamuna and her descendants at the drop of a hat. Almost every home contained a piano which at least one occupant knew how to play – loudly, enthusiastically and well. Music, Georgian folk and Western pop, blared out of bars and cafés. Conversation inside was difficult unless the proprietor was paid a few *lari* to lower the decibels. The food served in these establishments was generally good, particularly the Mingrelian variety from west Georgia. The local beer and vodka was strong and cheap, if somewhat inconsistent in quality and taste. I spent many a happy weekend in and around Perovskaya Street – a mere stone's throw from the apartment I eventually called home.

I quickly appreciated that Georgian hospitality is legion and feasts mandatory, at which a *tamada* – toastmaster – is appointed and leads the proceedings by expounding a series of ritualised and strictly ordered toasts after every other nibble. Frequently, the burden of continuing the theme is passed to another, usually a guest, by way of *Alaverdi*. Any failure on his or her part to maintain the composition of that particular toast is punished by having to drink two rams' horns of wine without pause and, *bolomde,* "to the bottom". The horns are always hung on a wall in very close proximity to the dining table in anticipation of a guest's aberration. The outcome is inevitably a bevy of drunken guests, much to the obvious delight of the Georgian hosts.

I learned to try to avoid the *Georgian tables* during my many treks around Georgia visiting rural customers and their businesses. They had no money but certainly knew how to make wine and vodka and imbibe it with enthusiasm. Refusal to partake was always difficult and caused offence on occasion, but it had to be done in order to keep one's health reasonably intact.

Quite early on, I met up with a delegation of councillors from Bristol City Corporation – Tbilisi is twinned with Bristol – who came to Georgia full of good intentions and with a wish to bestow a not inconsiderable amount of money on their opposite numbers in order to contribute towards an improvement of the infrastructure of the city. I met them bleary-eyed and hung-over at the airport on the day of their departure. They had been blitzed by a series of *tables*; conversation and discussion had been impossible owing to the constant intrusion of the *tamada* and his toasts. They returned home hung-over, tired, but happy, and with cheque-book unopened.

I gradually learned that Georgians are inherently generous people; the average Georgian will give you his last *lari* if the cause deserves it and never speak of it again. Georgians are also great liars, which is more a reflection of the way of life imposed upon them than a criticism of character. They have to lie to exist. They see no problem with this. They are also superb actors and entering into a discussion with a Georgian about, say, a request for a small loan, involves all kinds of verbal acrobatics and flights of fancy. A determined Georgian farmer can almost make you believe that growing potatoes in the desert is a truly viable proposition.

I once spent a very happy hour in a Tbilisi bar with an aged Georgian academic of impeccable professorial credentials. Like me, he was a jazz fan and had once attended a concert in Tbilisi given by the famous Benny Goodman orchestra which toured the former Soviet Union in the early 1960s. He recounted the story of the leading trumpet soloist in the band, Roy Eldridge, a brilliant black musician, who was found urinating in the river Mtkvari which runs through Tbilisi, in the early hours of the morning. He was arrested by the local police and accused of taking samples of the river water for analysis by the American CIA. My professor friend really believed that Eldridge was a spy: a spy who faked playing trumpet on stage and was certainly not a jazz-man! A more unlikely spook I cannot imagine. In any event, he must have got away with it because the tour continued with trumpet section intact.

I learned also that behind the bravely affable countenance of the majority of the people lies real pain. More than fifty per cent of the population live below the poverty line. Schools and colleges, as we know them, do not really exist in Georgia. Glass in windows is removed and sold; radiators and plumbing are stolen and sold as scrap-metal. Even where plumbing is left intact, the heating system doesn't work because, certainly during my time, there was virtually no power in Tbilisi during the winter months; two or three hours per day if you were lucky. The supply of electricity to Georgia was determined by Russian oligarchs; Georgian politicians joined in the corrupt trade, lining their own pockets in the process. Very few in government cared about the average Joe. Those who were able to afford them bought generators, but fuel prices increased by at least one hundred per cent in the winter, and the supply of fuel was controlled by a few families, politically and governmentally well-connected.

I managed, during my early weeks in Tbilisi, to heat my apartment mainly with a mix of kerosene stoves and propane gas heaters, and to light it with a combination of kerosene lamps and candles. A few people had natural-gas heating systems that occasionally worked. The more fortunate of us, ex-pats and a few wealthy Georgians, were able to graduate to a generator which, in my case, was chained to the balcony railings of my second-floor apartment, resting on an old tyre. I was never quite able to figure out how to use this complex piece of machinery. The process involved revolving valves in coordination with pulling a series of electrical switches in correct order inside the apartment.

But my neighbours helped. They showed me how to rig up a lead from the generator into their apartments, thus giving them each power enough to light at least one bulb per family. If I had to sacrifice the use of the fridge, or a hot shower in the morning, then so be it. It was very worthwhile and it had the dual effect of engendering a little kindly disposition toward me while preventing the generator from being constantly nicked. My generator was stolen on only two occasions during all of my time in Georgia. A record, I think, for an ex-pat.

Despite there being hardly any power, there were plenty of petty officials who made a living from pretending there was. A collector would call at the apartment at least once each month with an electricity or gas bill to be settled. The vast majority of Georgians didn't pay any bill and simply paid the collector a small amount of money – far less than the amount of the bill – to go away. The cost to an ex-pat was, in any event, considerably higher than that levied upon the locals. Similarly

19

the cost of a propane gas *ballon*, and heating fuel generally, increased enormously during the winter period. Naturally, any price increase had an even more outrageous impact on *inostrantsi* – "foreigners".

As I travelled around the country, I learned that away from Tbilisi, in the provinces, the situation was much worse. The peasant population scraped a living by subsistence farming. They sold any modest surplus at local markets and proceeds had somehow to carry them through the winter months. Many desperate people drank themselves into oblivion, manufacturing lethally impure vodka with home-made stills. A sizeable proportion of the rural population died of alcohol abuse.

Initially, my trips through the countryside in the summer of '96 provided an illusion of a rural idyll. Tractors and agricultural implements less than twenty years old were not common. The main form of transportation and propulsion remained the horse or donkey. In the summer sun, the countryside still looks very pretty and unspoiled, dotted with castles and ancient fortifications. Wordsworth would feel at home here. The reality is far harsher. It's a very tough life in the Georgian outback; almost medieval and certainly tribal. In Tbilisi I know of two examples of young women being kidnapped by men who, having forced them to have sex, then invoked a form of *droit de seigneur* and approached the parents to formalise a kind of marriage. In both instances, the parents conformed. In the sticks, this form of union is not uncommon. Family vendettas and inter-village rivalries are frequent, often resolved by blood-letting. These are seldom reported to the police or in the media: they are not important enough.

To my knowledge, there are no official statistics on suicides; they are, however, quite commonplace. The difficulty is in differentiating the real suicides from murders. I knew of several examples of murky deaths, ranging from the "suicide" of a high-profile bank president who managed to shoot himself in the head while shaving one morning and then throw the gun away – it was never found, to a well-known Georgian journalist whose obvious murder was presented as a suicide by a huge police-led media campaign. A young girl of seventeen, whose family I knew well, committed suicide by jumping off her sixth-floor apartment balcony in Tbilisi; her family swore that she was thrown off by the local police with whom she had declined to share the proceeds of a drug deal. Another young lad who lived a few miles from Tbilisi and who was an enthusiastic member of a dance group, sponsored by the bank I helped to form, did a similar thing. It was well known locally that the police were actually responsible – apparently another drug-related murder.

And yet, generally, the average young Georgian man or woman in the streets of Tbilisi exuded a carefree and vibrant attitude. In contrast to the older people, most of whom looked backward to a time when all were equally poor, when life had more security and a defined beginning and end, the younger population appreciated their freedom. Sure, hope faded little by little, over the years, as the Shevardnadze regime constantly failed to deliver on repeated promises and the much-vaunted wealth of the West never materialised in Georgia. The oil pipeline was delayed; housing decayed while large mansions were built for officialdom in the superior suburbs, no electricity, no gas, contaminated drinking water; no jobs, no pay, no pensions, disease and poverty; civil war, rampant corruption… And yet, for most of the six years I spent in Georgia, the mood, especially among the young, was of hope and optimism – an amazing reflection of the strength of character of its young people.

Chapter Six

So, what was my job in Georgia? During the early nineties, the European Commission, among other international donor institutions, had provided the newly independent Caucasian countries of Armenia, Azerbaijan and Georgia with food aid, mainly in the form of wheat and other cereals. By way of a Memorandum of Understanding dated October 1993, signed by the EC and the government of Georgia, it was mutually agreed that an accepted proportion of the food aid was to be given in the form of money, and the resulting "Counterpart Fund" utilised in fulfilment of certain reforms to be undertaken by the Georgian government in the agricultural sector.

The total amount realised from monetisation of food aid in Georgia amounted to some forty-two million US dollars, the bulk of which was to be used to assist in funding the privatisation process of important state institutions operating in the bread-production industry of Georgia. Having initially kicked off the credit component of the project in Baku, Azerbaijan, the European Commission asked me to transfer my activities to Georgia.

My particular role involved lending the local currency equivalent of nearly nine million dollars through selected Georgian commercial banks into the agricultural sector, with particular emphasis on financing small cereal farmers, millers, bakers and traders. The chief overall project objective was to assist Georgia in becoming less dependent upon imported food aid. In the context of my credit component there were particular objectives. These were:

Firstly, to test the efficacy of the Georgian banking system in its ability to lend and to recover credit from the extremely risky agricultural sector. No existing Georgian banks were lending into this sector. Secondly, to test the efficacy of the Georgian legal system recovering debts from defaulters. This depended on the enforceability of charges on assets, taken as collateral.

And lastly, to test the ability of the person or company given loan to use the credit for the designated purpose and to achieve a benefit in helping the business become profitable.

Not too tall an order, you might think. But this was to be undertaken in a country which, although economically largely dependent upon agriculture, had no tradition of debt repayment in this sector. "Grants" had been provided in abundance, but never "credit". There was no working legal system, no history of enforcement of assets taken as bank security, no insurance safety net, and the concepts of privatisation, market economy, competition, profitability and, in particular, non-interference in the private sector by government, were simply words written in text books which only a few enlightened academics had ever bothered to read or understand.

I quickly realised that simple things became big problems. For example, there is no word in the Georgian language for "loan" or "overdraft", simply credit – "crediti", and there were huge difficulties in differentiating this word from "grant" or "gift".

Then there was the on-going issue of who actually owned the Counterpart Fund. After all, if the European Union had granted the food aid to the government of Georgia, why then should not the resulting monetisation proceeds also belong to the government of Georgia? What right did the EC have in dictating how the Counterpart Fund should be used? The fact that the government of Georgia had been party to the original Memorandum of Understanding, which set out the terms of the agreement, had no bearing on this. After all, the Minister of State who had signed that document had long since been dismissed from his post. The new guy would never have signed it!

I was introduced to my translator during my first few days at the Ministry of Agriculture in Tbilisi. This plump, puce-complexioned, five-by-five figure wobbled down the corridor in my general direction, grabbed my hand firmly in both of his and pumped away, bellowing, "*Gamarjobat*, I am Ilia, the best bloody translator in the whole of Georgia." Holding my face firmly in his hands, he kissed me wetly on both cheeks and beamed. This was the beginning of a beautiful friendship which lasted for the whole of my time in Georgia.

Ilia had been for many years the translator for the *Patriarch* – the head of the Georgian Orthodox Church in Tbilisi – and, as such had travelled extensively in Europe. He'd met two Archbishops of Canterbury and the Pope, as he was wont to frequently remind me. He was a superb mimic, and during his frequent trips to the UK had picked up a famously plummy English accent which he was keen to demonstrate at every opportunity, much to the confusion of our American friends. Over the following months, he developed the happy knack of *simultaneous translation*, and often pre-empted what I was about to say in a meeting, by a sentence or two with amazing accuracy. He was also able to emulate the emotional content of any conversation I had, particularly with government officials, copying the rise and fall and inflections of my voice unerringly while small rivulets of perspiration dripped off the end of his nose. I'm sure he eventually came to speak Georgian with a Welsh accent, a lovely man with a superb sense of humour – absolutely essential – and never-ending affability. He became irreplaceable, and we, inseparable.

Lisiko (Liz or Liza) Koiava became a permanent member of my credit team at a very early stage. Aged about twenty-one years with long auburn hair (not common in Georgia, except in the far west), ever-active, strikingly attractive with alabaster skin and pale green eyes; quick and clever, extremely keen to learn everything she possibly could and intelligent enough to do so. She blushed profusely when we first met, and stammered out a "pleased to meet you", before hunching herself behind her computer screen in an effort to become invisible. As the weeks passed, her shyness dissipated and she began to confide in me. She had, a couple of years earlier, won a scholarship to an American university following her graduation in Agricultural Engineering from a Tbilisi university, but couldn't stand the home-sickness and returned home after a few weeks. A common Georgian trait, I learned. Her father was in business, but unsuccessfully, while her mother was a doctor of medicine who had not received her salary for over two years. Liz was the sole bread-winner and supported two younger sisters, both in university, and an aging grandmother. She eventually became the brightest member of my team, keen to accept responsibility and accountability – not a common Georgian trait, I discovered – and a loyal friend and colleague.

Liza's best pal in the team at that time was Eka. She was as pretty as a picture, tall, dark, languid, quiet and shy, but she habitually worked until late in the evenings without complaint before returning home to her one-bedroomed apartment shared with her chronically sick sister and two nephews. She too was the only bread-winner in her family.

When I first arrived in Georgia there were fifty-eight commercial banks in existence. This was a reduction from well in excess of a thousand banks in 1990. I well remember musing over this fact when I first arrived in Tbilisi. How on earth could a population of around four and a half million people, ninety five per cent of whom had no bank account, sustain this ludicrously high number of banks? These were not, of course, "real" banks in the context of western European understanding but were simply the tools of the state, individual governmental officials and a few oligarchs. There are obviously very sinister, not to mention illegal, purposes for which a bank can be used.

As the project progressed, as part of the selection process for participant banks, I met a large number of bank directors. They were a mixed bunch. Most were around sixty years of age and overtly corrupt. Their numbers were leavened by a few young, bright and eager bank directors who had attained that status, no doubt, by way of family connections, but who were nevertheless anxious to learn Western banking practices and to progress beyond the nefarious self-seeking activities of their Soviet-style peers. One of the most striking examples of the "new breed" was Misha (Michael) Mgaloblishvili, Vice-President of one of the better banks in Georgia at that time. Misha broke the mould. He was then twenty-four years old and had graduated from a Tbilisi university with a degree in

Economics at a very early age. He subsequently studied in the Netherlands and received a Batchelor of Arts degree from the University of The Hague. He was an imposing figure, well over six feet tall, powerfully built and genuinely handsome in a typically dark Georgian way. The ladies thought so too: he was never short of female admirers. Misha supervised his bank's activities in the context of our credit programme and his bank repaid every loan, on time and without deviation. His bank's achievement, coupled with that of a few others blessed with young, energetic management, set an example to the remainder and demonstrated that the project could work and provide a real benefit to all levels of participants.

There were of course consistent attempts to hijack the project on the part of the Ministry of Agriculture, usually in the form of pressurising local project staff to provide credits to *preferred* customers, relatives or political cronies. Of course, these "loans" would never be repaid. These political ploys needed to be constantly thwarted, and local personnel were sifted until only those who were able to demonstrate resistance to such pressures, and a good track record of loan recovery, remained in place. In the meantime, I signed on for a further three months in Georgia, and ultimately for a total of eighteen months, which was the proposed duration of the project.

By early 1997 the project was in full swing. Credits were being disbursed and recovered at a substantial rate of knots. Despite having to constantly repel government boarders, the positive output of the project was receiving unanimous official approval from both the government of Georgia and the European Commission. Everything was tickety-boo. Not so, however, in Azerbaijan.

There, the credit component had failed to take off, largely because the Ministry of Agriculture wanted to "manage" it their way. In other words they wanted to select beneficiaries of credit – friends, relations, and colleagues. The Commission asked me to work with the EC Project Manager, who travelled from Brussels to Baku, in an attempt to revive and re-establish the objectives of the project in Azerbaijan. This was not easy, but we got there in the end, and after three weeks of determined persuasion, working from the Prime Minister down, the project was re-started. We even prevailed upon government ministers in Azerbaijan to travel to Georgia to see how it should be done! The Georgian government loved that.

The project lasted three years, at the end of which my Georgian team had increased to twenty-something and had revolved the Counterpart Fund nearly four times, achieving a ninety-five per cent repayment rate. This was pretty good going. My bosses in Brussels were delighted, as was, officially, the government of Georgia.

Chapter Seven

My first accommodation in Tbilisi was at Manana's Guesthouse, up the hill from Rustaveli Avenue. Manana was a rotund little lady in her early fifties who bombarded her guests with conversation – she had learned English by listening to the BBC World News on the radio – and food, in equally abundant proportions. She was the epitome of Georgian hospitality, a relentless gossip in semi-comprehensible English, and deservedly quickly became a legend among the ex-pats of Georgia. Reluctantly, after a couple of months of prime pampering, I moved into an apartment at Barnov Street, Tbilisi – just around the corner from Manana's.

This was a spacious, slightly seedy, second story, two-bedroom affair situated in a quiet cul-de-sac – superb acoustics for my neighbours' pianos, the sounds of which reverberated around the walls – within easy walking distance of the restaurants and bars of Perovskaya Street and the Babylon Supermarket. There, every Sunday afternoon I did my weekly shopping while the young female shop assistants fluttered their eye-lashes and gleefully ripped me off. I learned to charge my Lada Niva through the streets of Tbilisi with the best of them, and became as adept as the locals at avoiding pot-holes, policemen and prostitutes, all equally dangerous in their own particular way.

My life settled into a routine: three or four days each week in my office at the Ministry, sanctioning, monitoring, coaxing, cajoling and bullying loan repayments out of dilatory banks, inevitably culminating in a visit to their premises and a quiet confrontation which usually yielded results. On one or two days each week, I visited customers – sometimes a twenty-four hour journey over very rough roads – at their farms, mills, timber-works or bakeries, in the sticks. I learned to appreciate their way of life – immense poverty, no electricity, no gas, no drainage, water from a well or river – but plenty of home-produced food and drink, pressed upon their guests with immense generosity and gusto. Long rambling conversations, taxing Ilia's patience to the extreme, usually ending with a selection of regional folk-songs sung in gorgeous polyphonic harmony, much kissing and back-slapping and inevitably a request for more money as we departed.

I worked each Saturday and Sunday morning, catching up and writing reports, but, invariably, Friday and Saturday evenings were spent in a bar or restaurant in the company of my Georgian colleagues and friends, and ex-pats from the EC Delegation in Georgia. These were heavy drinking affairs at which the political activities of the week were discussed and re-interpreted according to the views of those present. I never ceased to be amazed by the political awareness and enthusiasm of the young people of Georgia. I sensed a desperate need to express opinions and to grasp each of the convoluted events of the week and work out what was actually going on rather than what had been reported by the media. Television stations and newspapers in Georgia were owned by politicians or political parties. This keen interest was in stark contrast to the young people in the UK who generally cared not a jot for politics. But these were turbulent times in Georgia. Great events were taking place; revolution was in the air in the late 90's. The conversation was frequently interrupted by the *tamada's* toast which often included the threat to *Shevardnadze Mogitkhan* – "Fuck Shevardnadze".

Of course I missed Wales immensely. I missed my family, my friends and my old way of life. True, I had by this time worked abroad for some years and had become accustomed to a somewhat nomadic way of life. But I still missed home.

Mair and I had divorced some ten years earlier, but nevertheless we'd remained good friends and met up frequently to discuss family affairs whenever I returned to Wales. Mair was my childhood sweet-heart. We'd started "courting" when we were both sixteen years of age, had married at twenty-three and had been together, through thick and thin, for over twenty years.

Our three children, Lisa, Rod (Rhodri) and Pip (Philip) had all done well academically and were settled in good jobs in the UK. Lisa, a qualified solicitor, but now a dedicated housewife, and mother of my two grandchildren, Megan and Manon-Haf, lived only a few miles from my home in Cowbridge. Short, darkly attractive, bubbly but determined, very much her father's daughter and happily married to Gavin, also a solicitor. Rod, a chartered surveyor and associate partner with a large firm in London, an ever-smiling maverick, single but playing the field vigorously, and Pip, an insurance executive living in Cardiff and working in Newport, more introspective and quieter by nature, also single but well settled in a long-term relationship. They were then aged thirty, twenty-nine and twenty-five respectively, and I was immensely proud of them all. We'd remained a close family.

I'd made a lot of friends in Georgia, including the then President of the National Bank and a few, not too many, enlightened government ministers. Yet I travelled home frequently: initially for four or five days every three or four weeks, mainly to keep in touch, see my children and grand-children, and have a few pints with my mates, but also to return to normality and rid myself for a while of the stresses and strains of working this project in Georgia.

Gradually, my trips home became less frequent. I became more and more immersed in my work. I began to realise increasingly that the work the team was doing was important and significant. It touched the lives of people in Georgia and we could make a difference to those lives. I was certainly no crusader but as the project activities grew, and more and more people benefited, we all recognised, in Georgia and in Brussels, that we were making a success of it. I, a middle-aged valley boy, would never be able to undertake work of such meaningfulness in Wales. As the challenges increased in direct proportion to the level of our lending book, so did our determination to overcome the problems and stick at it. In short, I became addicted to my work, to Georgia and its people.

Chapter Eight

I met Diana in July 1996. I'd been invited to a wedding party in Tbilisi of a director of one of the largest banks in Georgia. The party was the usual Georgian mixture of excess food and drink, exuberant companionship and interminable toasts emanating from the many *tamadas,* one to each table making up the wedding party. At some point in the evening I tottered my way toward an outside bar to get some fresh air, and found myself standing next to a young, dark-haired, smiling woman who was also alone.

The first thing I noticed was that she didn't look typically Georgian. She didn't possess the thin aquiline nose or the high forehead of the archetypal Georgian female, attractive though those characteristics undoubtedly are. This woman had the dark Georgian hair, but a wide nose, oval eyes, voluptuous lips and very white teeth. I had not been exactly celibate during my first few months in Georgia, so, turning on my cheesy grin, I ventured:

"Hello there. Who the devil are you?"

Surprisingly, she responded in English with a wicked glint in her eyes: "I am Diana. Who the devil are you?"

Touché – and the ice was broken. We entered into a garbled and disjointed conversation. Her name was Diana Khorina. She lived in Rustavi, a typically Soviet high-rise ex-industrial city of around three hundred and fifty thousand inhabitants about thirty minutes drive south of Tbilisi, with her widowed mother and sister, and she earned her living by teaching modern dance and ballet. She was twenty-three years old, had no serious boyfriend and was at the party as a friend of the bride. We chatted animatedly for about half an hour and I suggested we go somewhere rather more private for a drink. She *was* very attractive. We both made the appropriate excuses to our respective hosts and ended up in my apartment.

There, over a bottle of Georgian wine, we listened to Sinatra and Ella Fitzgerald and I played the piano while she sang. She left late that evening, having given me her telephone number and we arranged to meet on my return from the UK, where I was due to take some leave. When I returned to Georgia after a week's absence, I wondered whether it was wise to contact her again, but I couldn't resist. By the end of that week we had arranged to meet again and we dined together in a converted wine cellar in the centre of Tbilisi.

I found her enchanting company and her background was intriguing. Diana's father, who had died six years earlier aged forty-eight, was a *Kozak* from the Don valley in southern Russia. Her mother and maternal grandfather were Armenian, and her maternal grandmother was a *Buretian* from the Lake Baikal region of Siberia. Goodness knows how the various strands of the family all came together – probably through the many population migrations initiated by Stalin – but the result, in the form of Diana and her sister, Elena (Lena), struck me as an amazing union of disparate geographic, social and cultural strands.

Diana was born into and brought up within the Soviet system in Rustavi: in her childhood a thriving industrial town. Her family's first language is Russian, and although they all have a good knowledge of the Georgian language, they see themselves as emphatically Russian and not Georgian. This is not unusual in Georgia, as well as many other countries of the former Soviet Union. Diana's education was typically Russian and, in contrast to that which now exists in Georgia, very thorough, with no short-cuts. Her descriptions of how she proceeded through the various stages of her dancing training illustrated the systematic and methodical routines which were part and parcel of the Russian educational philosophy at all levels. Unusually in Georgia, she was also totally apolitical. Although she could, of course, well remember the relatively comfortable lifestyle that she and her family enjoyed under the communist regime, she exuded no feelings of bitterness or revulsion to change. Like me, she despised the high level of corruption endemic within the Soviet government system inherited and augmented by Georgian politics.

She was extremely well-read. She could recite tracts of Shakespeare, having read some of his major plays and sonnets while at school. She also knew a lot about the English Romantic poets: Keats, Byron, Shelley and Wordsworth; and had a smattering of Victorian literature, particularly Charles Dickens. She talked at length about Renaissance art, literature and architecture, and chattered away animatedly about Picasso, Chagall and Braque. She was also heavily into music. When I first went to Georgia, I was surprised to find how popular the music of Glenn Miller was. It was played in almost every restaurant in town. Diana was able to give me a potted history of Tex Beneke, one of the lead singers with the Miller band in the forties, and Marion Hutton, another singer with the orchestra, who was the sister of Betty Hutton, the Hollywood actress. This was all highly unusual for a twenty-three-year-old who'd spent the whole of her life in a run-down, dismal, industrial city in Georgia on the seventh floor of an apartment block.

Little by little the relationship grew. I suppose a key element was, and still is, our mutual love of music. We also shared the same sense of humour, and she liked the fact that I could manage to dance a little, including a waltz, fox-trot and quick-step, skills not commonly acquired in Georgia even at my basic level. She had also never seen the "twist" attempted before, and although she equated my endeavours with those of Balou in Disney's *Jungle Book* as opposed to the Chubby Checker definitive version, she found my efforts highly amusing.

Chapter Nine

Before the end of the RARP1 project, the Commission had the bright idea of "institutionalising the methodology" used in the project to ensure its sustainability. Correspondence ensued between President Shevardnadze and Commissioner Van den Broek, following which it was decided to establish a bank – the Agro-business Bank of Georgia – which would continue to lend and provide financial services to the small farmers, processors and agri-traders of the Republic. The tendering process took place in Brussels in early 1999; I was given the job of Team Leader and told to get on with it.

It was very obvious from the outset that the establishment of the bank, using the remaining, and largely intact, Counterpart Fund as its seed capital, was going to be difficult. Despite the clear support provided by President Shevardnadze – Shevy would always want to be *seen* to be co-operating with the European Union – there were many people in government who were vehemently opposed to the utilisation of the Fund for the formation of a bank.

I remember well discussing the many and disparate problems with my boss, Albert Russell, who travelled periodically to Georgia from Brussels to keep an avuncular eye on the progress of the project. Albert was a gentle, pipe-smoking Irishman whose middle-name was pragmatism. We agreed there were no easy solutions. It was simply a case of battling on and hopefully winning some ministerial hearts and minds. Some governmental factions wished the Fund to become part of the Georgian State Budget. Year after year the budget forecasts, under the auspices of the Ministry of Finance, had failed to be fulfilled. Despite the annual ratcheting downward of targets, the yearly shortfall grew ever larger – an obvious barometer of corrupt practices. A windfall of some ten million *lari* into the budget would certainly help their balancing act.

Other ministers wanted to use the Fund for their own particular "priorities". These included alleviation of the never-ending energy crisis, or the annual drought, or strengthening the reserves of the National Bank, or resurrecting old defunct Soviet industries which had never been viable. There were a hundred and one so-called priorities, identified by as many ministers as were involved in the weekly economic crises which were constants within the crumbling economy of the country. There were very few government officials who truly cared for the well-being of the rural population, which depended for a tenuous living upon agriculture and related industries, including the Minister of Agriculture.

In fairness, the European Commission stood firm on this. The Counterpart Fund was to be utilised as the seed capital of a bank that was to provide access to finance for the rural population. That was to be the objective, no deviation. It was my job to make it happen.

There were a number of obstacles. The Georgian government decided that the Memorandum of Understanding – the definitive document signed by the government of Georgia and the European Commission upon which all agricultural projects were based – was now out of date. It was decreed that a new document which precisely defined, among other details, the structure, objectives and repayment schedule (of the Counterpart Fund to the Government of Georgia) would have to be drawn up. The Commission happily delegated the composition of this document to me. It took five months of abrasive negotiations with six ministries to finally achieve a document, the contents of which were, at least at that time, acceptable to all ministries concerned and to the European Union. The document was finally signed on 1st December 1999. Ultimately the structure of the ABG was agreed, in line with Georgian legislation and National Bank regulations, putting in place a Shareholders' Committee, a Supervisory Board and a Management Board.

It goes without saying that arriving at this final constitution was an extremely frustrating task. It involved a huge amount of in-fighting between the various political and ministerial factions of the Georgian government as to who should participate in the various committees. Their innate desire was not to form a composite body to fulfil the terms and aims of the banking institution, but simply to have a voice in directing credits to their "preferred" recipients.

The Georgians saw the role of the Supervisory Board as that of a sanctioning authority enabling them to veto lending applications, and to "suggest" individually those who should receive loans. The fundamentals of viability and repayment-ability were a million miles away from their thinking processes or their intentions. They had no wish to depend upon, or learn from, the expertise and experience of foreign consultants, but simply wished to hijack the capital within the bank. To be fair, they were totally transparent in promoting these objectives. As government officials, they viewed this function as their entitlement; and additionally they wished to be paid a princely sum for attending the meetings.

Clearly, a bank cannot be profitable, or thereafter sustainable, if the vast majority of its loans are not repaid. The European Commission quickly became aware that, in Georgia, very few of its loans would be repaid if government personnel were to be involved in the lending decision-making process.

The hierarchy in Brussels, as I had been repeatedly told, viewed the ABG as a barometer of the investment climate in Georgia. It was felt that if the bank could successfully lend, and obtain repayment, within the difficult agricultural sector, (thirty per cent of the Gross Domestic Product of Georgia) then foreign investors might be encouraged to chance their arm in Georgia. If the legal system would support the bank in enforcing repayment through the courts, whether by enforcing collateral or otherwise, then a "contract" in Georgia would be seen to be meaningful.

But would the corrupt courts implement the law? Were there enough potentially viable agri-businesses to which to lend? Would they repay? Could security in the form of an apartment, farm buildings or equipment be taken by the bank and if necessary, realised? Was there a means of valuing assets? Could newly privatised land be taken as security? Did it have a commercial value? Was there a market for agricultural land? Would the government interfere if it were to be sold at "market" value? Did the newly established inter-bank market work in Georgia? How effective was the supervisory role of the National Bank? There were a thousand questions to which the performance of the bank could, at least in part, provide answers. The donor community in general was very interested in the performance of the ABG.

Chapter Ten

Diana and I were keen frequenters, each Friday evening, with our gang of Georgian and ex-pat enthusiasts, of the nearest thing to a jazz club that existed in Tbilisi. This was in the cellar of the run-down and seedy former *in-tourist* Adjara Hotel. Musicians in Georgia are generally of an extremely high standard – part of the communist musical education and training ethos – and jazz musicians are no exception. The resident group at the Adjara was of stunning quality and could have held its own at Soho's Ronnie Scott's Club with no difficulty. The group was presided over by an Ella Fitzgerald sound-alike named Maya who had obviously spent a considerable amount of time listening to every Ella recording of the fifties and sixties. It certainly paid off because she was pretty damned good and didn't seem to be in the least put out by our energetic cavortings on the dance-floor. Diana was a helluva dancer.

Bit by bit Diana and I began to spend more and more time together. She was able to drive a little – driving tests as we know them didn't exist in Georgia: you simply paid one hundred dollars – and I bought her an elderly Lada for a thousand dollars which she used to commute to and from Rustavi where she gave her dancing lessons. For a few months I persuaded an English teacher to give her lessons at her home, simply to polish up her already impressive language skills. She also briefly attended a local university in Tbilisi with the objective of proceeding to a degree course in English. Unfortunately, there seemed little point in pursuing it through the winter months, largely because the normal components such as books, teachers, lighting and heating were just not in place. Instead, I bought her a desk-top computer which she quickly mastered in both Russian and English. She really was a helluva dancer.

We had a large and close circle of Georgian friends. Some were colleagues with whom I worked at our tiny bank premises at Budapeshti Street in the Saburtalo district of Tbilisi. Bright, young, loyal people, many of them had already worked with me for more than three years and were intensely committed to the success of the ABG – and to letting their hair down at weekends.

Misha Mgaloblishvili was eventually appointed Managing Director (designate) of the bank. Of course we had a very hard time in obtaining confirmation of his appointment by the Supervisory Board. Every Georgian bank and political party had their own nomination perfectly selected to serve the individual interest of the sponsor. But we got there in the end, and Misha was confirmed in his position in December 1999. He was a pretty good weekend boozer, a great raconteur and could cut a mean furrow on the dance floor.

There was Giorgi (George) Kankava, only a year older than Misha at twenty-six but again a relatively experienced Georgian banker, tall, suave, debonair, pragmatic and immensely persuasive. He was appointed as our third director and doubled up as Head of Deposits. The three Ks – Kalandarashvili (Goga), Head of Credit, diminutive, aggressive, on occasion dogmatic and stubborn, but sincere and brave; Ketiladze (Temuri), Head of Sub-branches; big and bulky, on the face of it indecisive, but his easy-going nature hid a sharply incisive mind and a keen determination to win; and Kashia (Dato), Office Manager, curly black hair with an impish smile that never seemed to fade even when the bank generator packed in and the water went off, which frequently occurred.

The two Tamunas – Head of Operations and Chief Cashier respectively – charming young women and truly dedicated, never allowing the difficulties of their private lives to detract from their commitment to their work. One desperately seeking to escape from an abusive marriage and supporting a large family on her sole income; the other deeply affected by her father's suicide, the depressing aftermath of the Abkhaz war, but never missed a day's work; Teona, Head of International Division, as pretty as a picture and ever-smiling. Her husband worked in the National Bank in their International Division and gave us the inside track on exchange rate fluctuations.

My Deputy Team Leader was Tim Hooper, a sixty-three-year-old veteran of a multitude of banking projects in some twenty-four countries;: an Englishman who had made his home in Sydney, Australia for many years. He was the archetypal steady-eddie who allowed nothing to faze him or to interfere with his diligence. Apart, that is, from his wife, Kim, a diminutive but formidable Singapore-Chinese of whom he was immensely in awe, and who allowed him outdoors only infrequently after seven in the evening. Fortunately for Tim, she was a very good cook. Tim's contract came to an end in the summer of 2000 and owing to budgetary restrictions he was not replaced.

My other "Western" support and enthusiastic co-frequenter of the jazz club and other watering-holes in Tbilisi was Tim Hammond. Tim is an agronomist who hails from the West Country and who undertook fifteen short-term missions to Georgia over the three-year term of the banking project. His main role was to supervise the targeting and utilisation of credits dispersed by the ABG, and to ensure the funds were used for the correct purpose and achieved the desired results. In practice, particularly following the departure of Tim Hooper, and as the bank expanded by opening more and more sub-branches in the provinces, Tim's input broadened into that of a trainer, guide and mentor to the young Georgian staff who shouldered the burden of being responsible "sub-branch managers", usually with little experience and minimal training.

Tim, blond-haired, stocky and blessed with infinite patience, would happily spend weeks in the outback of Georgia where hotels, electricity and tarmac roads do not exist at all and water is available only from streams or wells. He became totally committed to the successful operation of the bank and to the introduction of western European practices and procedures; in his case, by teaching small farmers and processors how best to benefit from this wonderful new concept called credit. We became, and remained, good friends and his opinions and

41

invariably sensible advice were always very willingly taken on board.

This then, with the omni-present Ilia, plus Liza and Eka, was our gang. The pack, invariably augmented by any ex-pat passing through Tbilisi having the remotest connection to our project, and any visiting dignitary from Brussels, would descend upon the jazz-club on Friday evenings and any favoured bar or restaurant in Perovskaya Street on Saturday nights, invariably culminating with a last drink at the Toucan Bar, presided over by the delectable Olga, and a rousing sing-song comprising Georgian folk-songs, Welsh hymns and the odd English, Irish, French or American contribution thrown in.

The Agro-business Bank of Georgia was inaugurated by President Shevardnadze, with all due pomp and ceremony, champagne and speeches, in January 2000. There was hardly enough room in our tiny head office to accommodate the Shevy entourage of security people, bodyguards, journalists and general hangers-on. The whole of the busy Tbilisi suburb of Saburtalo was blocked off by his "Special Forces" and masked snipers were sited on surrounding roof-tops. Senior ministers said nice things about the bank, which almost certainly they did not mean, and European ambassadors made long-winded speeches. We opened for business the following month.

Chapter Eleven

Solving problems and difficulties became part of the daily routine as we tried to make the bank function. It was tough to establish a bank in a country where the infrastructure had crumbled into a state of almost complete non-functionality; where telephones were unreliable and many roads impassable in the winter; where during the winter months, electricity functioned at best intermittently and where fuel costs for the essential generator increased four-fold during any particularly cold spell. Here, bank vehicles were regularly stolen despite being kept in a "secure" yard complete with guard; here, we had to build a steel case to accommodate our large generator in order to prevent its theft; here, computers went down two or three times each day owing to network failure; and here old ladies frequently jumped in front of a bank vehicle (with ABG logo) in order to claim compensation for injuries sustained.

I was very fortunate in having a series of excellent Heads of Delegation at the Commission during my time in Georgia. Initially, there was Denis Corboy, a charismatic and magnificently straightforward Irishman, about whom more later, followed by Elio Germano, a smooth, urbane and charmingly persuasive Italian. Their deputies were also top-notch. First, Patrick Daubresse, a Belgian whose military bearing and background belied an innate sophistication, followed by Jacques Vantomme, another Belgian, but of Flemish stock which underpinned his qualities of quiet determination and patience. At the Delegation, there was also the constant but emphatic presence of Emmanuel Anquetil – Manu – a still-young, but campaign-hardened Frenchman from the Basses Alpes – clear-sighted, always positive and consistently supportive.

With them and others who travelled to Georgia from Brussels, I was able to discuss the inherent difficulties of lending money into the agri-sector where the rural population had no concept whatsoever of formulating the most basic back-of-an-envelope business plan and where there was an inability, brought about by years of Soviet demand economy ideology, to differentiate between grants (non-repayable) and credit (repayable). It is difficult to lend money where interest rates are fixed arbitrarily at impossibly high rates by bureaucratic political committees, where there is no faith in banks – they go bust at a rate of knots because the shareholders (usually political or governmental) run away with depositors' funds; where there is no money market, where there is no stock exchange and where there are no centralised payment or clearing systems. I regularly received telephone calls from politicians requesting the bank lend money to named friends in exchange for a bribe – normally ten per cent of the credit. I also received monthly telephone calls from government ministries *suggesting* that the ABG made a contribution to the state budget to assist in filling the ongoing deficit. And then there was the politics.

The Ministry of Agriculture never really came to terms with the fact that they were no longer the only project partner. There was a huge amount of resentment about being involved merely as a member of a team of ministerial representatives. Each ministry thought it was its right to be able to place its people in key positions, particularly within the credit department, but the Ministry of Agriculture was the project recipient. That ministry had the paramount entitlement to run the bank! Initially the Minister, a young, English-speaking, extremely plausible gentleman who had replaced a red reactionary, blamed the EC for compromising the ministry's position. When he realised that there was no joy in going down that road, he blamed me. Every failing, imagined or otherwise, would now be laid firmly at my door.

It was common practice to financially reward certain journalists to write up erroneous stories in newspapers which would then be taken up by the television channels, owned by powerful politicians and their friends. Any disenchanted customer who had a loan request turned down was able to join in the fray. The objective was to denigrate the management of the bank to such an extent that the Commission would ask me to quit the project. With me out of the way, the ministry felt it would be able to access the bank and raid its capital. And so it began.

The media stories went along these lines: it was me, personally, whose idea it was to establish the bank – I had drawn up the new Memorandum of Understanding and was personally responsible for making many banks bankrupt under the former project. I had organised the tendering process of the EC, I was a wanted criminal, I had five wives and I was gay. That one hurt!

Of course the European Commission through the delegation in Georgia issued a series of rebuttals in the media. These were largely ignored, but so too were the accusations against me – at least by the vast majority; with great support from my Georgian colleagues, we all carried on regardless. Despite the difficulties, I continued to enjoy thoroughly the challenge of working in Georgia. The more pressure there was, the more determined I was to see the job through to a successful conclusion.

By the end of 2001, with the help of all my colleagues at the Delegation, and Tim Hammond in particular, I was able to report that the Bank had made well over one thousand loans and had achieved a ninety-seven per cent recovery rate. In order to ensure complete transparency of the activities of the Bank from its inception, one of the "big five" firms of accountants undertook independent quarterly reviews in addition to the annual audit. By the end of the first quarter of 2002, the Bank's accounts, prepared by Price, Waterhouse Coopers (imported from France at great expense in order to ensure no local chicanery) showed a profit of some five hundred thousand *lari* (about two hundred and fifty thousand US dollars); we had also opened nine sub-branches throughout the regions of Georgia. The numbers of staff had increased to forty-six people and Brussels had extended the term of the project by a further twelve months. Additionally, the Commission had agreed to launch a new tender toward the end of this term, the main thrust of which was to privatise the bank – in fact to make it into a co-operative bank. It wasn't hard to see that this was going to anger the Ministry of Agriculture, and the political faction it represented, even more. How would they ever be able to control a few thousand shareholders?

Chapter Twelve

Life with Diana was pretty damned good, although we were not at the time really living together. Diana had family and dancing commitments in Rustavi and we had a bit of fun in sorting out the priorities. I learned that if Diana were to move into my Tbilisi apartment, then her mother and sister would have to come too. This is common practice in Georgia, but initially I was having none of that. It took a huge amount of desperately diplomatic persuasion – a quality with which I am not well endowed – to ensure that the visits of the family remained just that: limited to once or twice each week, and didn't constitute an introduction to permanent residency. Still, we got along very well, both of us have a well-developed sense of humour, and we became dependent upon each other in all kinds of ways.

For example, Diana was a dab hand at dealing with the "gas-man" – the collector who called at least once each month and attempted to con a gullible foreigner into paying exorbitant amounts for largely non-existent gas. With Diana around, he now invariably left with a flea in his ear. She was also able to befriend the families that lived below, above and alongside us in a way that I was never able to do. Not only because of the obvious language difficulty, but also because she had the uncanny knack of being able to understand just when a particular family was in serious need of help. Often she would disappear during the evening with a packet of tea, sugar or aspirins; a saucepan of *borsch* or a can of kerosene to give to needy neighbours. She was adept at providing a line from our generator to a neighbour who couldn't afford kerosene, candles or gas. I received a lot more smiling *"gamarjobati"* – *"*how are you*"*, from relative strangers over the following days and weeks than I would otherwise have expected.

We were good for each other. I provided her with financial security, a warm and reasonably pleasant apartment – in contrast to the tiny flat she and her family had in Rustavi situated on the seventh floor of a tower-block where water had to be carried each morning from a communal well – and a few small luxuries like a generator and a television. She provided me with companionship, some protection from the tribulations that ordinarily beset a foreigner living and working in Tbilisi, and an increased circle of Georgian friends. The ABG sponsored her dancing shows and concerts in Rustavi in exchange for which my Georgian colleagues and I were given free seats. I well remember the surprise caused when I took my friend Nodar Javakashvili, then President of the National Bank of Georgia along to one concert at the old and smelly (it reeked of urine) Dom Kulturi – the Centre of Culture Theatre – in Rustavi. He was entranced by the skill, energy and enthusiasm shown by the young Georgian children, as we all were. We had a very long and large 'table' that night.

A few weeks later, one of the dancing group, a boy no more than fifteen years old, killed himself by jumping off the balcony of his apartment. The official verdict was drug-induced suicide.

In the yard behind my apartment in Tbilisi, there lived a couple of chickens, a few dogs and around twelve feral cats. They existed off the few scraps thrown out by my neighbours and the contents of rubbish bins which were only very occasionally emptied by the garbage collectors. I am not a cat-person – before embarking upon my travels I always kept two labradors at home – but took it upon myself to feed the cats each day. I think I was the only person who bought proper cat food from the Babylon Supermarket, naturally at a hugely inflated price, much to the bewilderment of my neighbours who could not possibly conceive how anyone could spend money on feeding cats. Naturally, the feline population of my part of Tbilisi grew enormously and pretty soon there was a morning and evening queue of cats at my back door, all waiting to be fed. My cat food bills increased in line, but I didn't have the heart to desist. Amazingly, the resident population of my back-yard did not increase markedly, disease and the winter months made sure of that.

Diana was even dafter than me with the cats. Inexorably, one or two of them managed to ingratiate themselves with Diana. Pretty soon, there was a "Tiggy-Tom" or "Panther" or "Blacky" waiting in the living room when I arrived home from work. She soon had them house-trained, and once in, they stayed in, and they were great company. Oftentimes, when Diana was in Rustavi and the power went off, I would sit for hours in semi-darkness trying to read a book by paraffin light, listening to the noise of the traffic passing beneath my window and the contented purrs of two or three 'wild' cats firmly ensconced on my lap.

Chapter Thirteen

And then Danny came along. This was not planned. Diana and I had talked about our relationship a lot and the theory was that when my contract in Georgia came to an end I would return to the UK and our relationship would have a natural ending. Diana's pregnancy obviously changed all this. I couldn't just walk away. We agreed that I would return as planned to the UK in due course and from there continue with my working life as a free lance consultant in other parts of the world, but at the same time, continue to financially support my little Georgian family. That was plan A… It never had a chance.

Danny was born in November 1998 in Aromyantsov Hospital, Tbilisi. There is of course no National Health Service in Georgia and as usual, despite Diana's interventions, the cost of utilising the very basic Georgian maternity services was around three times what would normally have been paid by a Georgian father. Extras included the bed, bedclothes and post-natal treatment. I was not allowed to be present at the birth – unheard of in Georgia – and received a severe ticking-off from the doctor in charge for even mentioning it. After the birth, which was not an easy one for he was a big bonny lad, I was subjected to the usual Georgian bureaucratic mindset with regard to severely restricted visiting hours, and ridiculously was made to wear a white hat, white gown, rubber gloves and a face-mask whenever I visited Diana, while the local cockroaches were permitted to march all the way down the filthy corridors to the bedside without interference!

My working hours were long. I arrived at the office by 8.30am each morning and never left before 6.00pm and usually closer to 7.00pm, or later. I also worked each Saturday and Sunday morning, despite the hangovers, so time spent at home was relatively short. When Diana and Danny stayed over, I invariably came home to a houseful of people, sometimes

Diana's family and sometimes her friends or our neighbours. This is typically Georgian and I got used to it and liked it. One particular neighbour, a widow, and her daughter named Anna were always around. They were very pleasant people and despite my clumsy efforts at speaking their language, we somehow managed to make ourselves understood and got along very well. My Russian and Georgian language skills certainly improved over time, but although I learned to understand quite a bit of their conversations, I was never confident enough to be able to participate properly.

As Danny grew, and my relationship with Diana crystallised, it became increasingly clear to me that I couldn't go back to the UK without them. I worried about the age difference between Diana and me, but that seemed to become more and more irrelevant. In the summer of 2000, Diana and Danny finally moved into my apartment and we became a family unit. It was not all plain sailing – Diana is a feisty lady and my work was stressful and all-absorbing. But the bond strengthened over time, and Danny was, and is, the glue.

He was a smashing little chap, fortunately the image of his mother, and, like us both, he possessed a mind of his own; a chunky, robust little guy who chattered away in Russian and Georgian with equal ease and quickly grasped the basics of the English language – with a Welsh accent. Each Sunday afternoon during the summer, we would picnic either at Turtle Lake, a large expanse of foul-smelling water on the outskirts of Tbilisi surrounded by little café-bars, or at a primitive *shashlik* restaurant in the hills overlooking Mstkheta, a few miles south of Tbilisi. There he would play for hours on a rusty old swing and see-saw, while the elderly proprietors fussed around him and plied him with the Georgian version of Coca-Cola. From the age of three, we enrolled him in an expensive (for Georgia) American-sponsored nursery school where he mingled with the kids of foreign ambassadors and diplomats and became pretty fluent in English, and no doubt taught his class-mates some Russian. In July 2000, Diana and Danny came to Wales for the first time, met my family and friends, and spent ten wonderful days on holiday in France with my daughter, her husband and my grand-children. My little Georgian family were welcomed with open arms and were very quickly integrated within the Shaw clan. They returned with me to Wales in December 2000 and for the first time experienced the delights of a typical Welsh Christmas. They were hooked.

Chapter Fourteen

By February 2002, the deluge of pernicious criticism in the media was finally getting to me. I'd had enough. I formally advised the Commission that I did not wish to be considered for any role in the future development of the bank after my contract expired in June 2002. Six years in Georgia was long enough for anyone and I wanted to go home.

A factor in coming to this decision was that, by this time, a new Head of the EC Delegation had arrived in Georgia – a Danish gentleman by the name of Torben Holtze. He quickly came under increasing pressure from the Ministry of Agriculture, and others of that faction, to allow their people to have a greater role in the running of the bank. Holtze was not made of the same stuff as his predecessors. He was not given to breaking furniture in ministerial offices, as had one of his predecessors, Denis Corboy, on occasion. Nor did he have the charm, subtlety and quiet qualities of persuasion of Elio Germano, whom he replaced. He simply wanted a quiet life with the minimum possible number of difficult decisions to make. I knew he would not continue to support the independence of Fortress ABG, and I've since wondered where the Vikings went wrong! In any event, it was time for me to go.

I'd done my job. The bank was financially secure, profitable, and independent, and, depending upon how the privatisation situation was handled, could and should be sustainable. Personally, I was proud of our achievements, and my Georgian team would certainly carry on, under new management: the key players would remain in place and continue to build upon our progress. For me, a final farewell to Georgia beckoned. Or so I thought.

Preparations to go home had commenced at least a month before the proposed departure date of 18th June. It's amazing how much domestic garbage can be accumulated over six years. The neighbours benefited from a huge bonus of superfluous clothing and rewarded me magnificently with mugs of home-made wine and vodka, enthusiastically imbibed in a series of 'tables' in our communal back-yard. The local company employed to transport our luggage finally got their act together and we managed to accommodate our worldly goods in various containers and sent them, in stages, to a warehouse near the airport in readiness for the great exodus.

Then there were the parties. Mega thrashes over a two-week period at the Old Tbilisi Restaurant in the Old Town, my favourite bar, The Toucan, and Ovatio Restaurant at Perovskaya Street. There were many emotional farewells to the Babylon Supermarket staff who had no doubt prospered during my stay, to a host of bar-maids and waitresses who had put up with my boozy weekend antics and to the hundreds of bank customers from all over Georgia whom I had grown to admire for their courage and determination. There were lots of tears in lots of beer.

It had been arranged that on 17th June I was, with my Georgian co-directors of the ABG, to give a presentation at a meeting of the various European ambassadors in Georgia at the office of the EC Delegation. The purpose of this was two-fold: the first to provide them with a detailed update of the performance of the ABG, and secondly to say goodbye. This was a pretty emotional occasion. All present were aware of the trials and tribulations through which we had battled to make the bank happen, and indeed most of them had provided a huge amount of support throughout the difficulties.

I'd learned how to live happily in Georgia. My habits were well known. I'd occupied the same apartment for four years, shopped in the same little supermarket for six years and frequented the same two or three watering holes in Perovskaya Street each weekend, almost without variation. I had a large number of Georgian friends and could walk into any bar or restaurant in Tbilisi at weekends and know someone, Georgian or ex-pat, with whom to have a chat and a pint. I was on first-name terms with the majority of the customer-base of the bank, and travelled regularly into the provinces to meet with our borrowers and depositors. They were always extremely grateful for the support the ABG was providing and showed it by their welcome and hospitality. I knew the majority of other bank directors and senior bank personnel in Tbilisi and had a cordial relationship with the National Bank President and his staff. I was an active member of the American Chamber of Commerce in Georgia, I knew personally almost every ambassador in Georgia and was on particularly good terms with the British Ambassador and her staff, and with her predecessors. In short, despite the difficulties of the job, I had very positive feelings about what we were doing in Georgia and my role in it.

Over the years, I'd come to love the country and its people. But the job I was doing meant that I was exposed by the media as being openly critical of corrupt practices, and vehemently so when they impacted upon the ABG. It hadn't crossed my mind that this could ultimately put me in danger. Nor did I make any attempt to adapt my lifestyle.

I'd decided to delay my official farewell to the staff of the bank until my last day in work on the 19th June. I knew that many of the sub-branch managers and staff were travelling long distances to say a final goodbye, and I wanted them all to be present on my last day. The farewells to Diana's mother, sister, relations and friends would be said at the airport just prior to our departure on the 20th. I knew this would be a very emotional scene and I wanted to postpone it until the very last moment. Although Diana and Danny had already been to Wales, it was still going to be one helluva wrench for them to say goodbye to their family. But we were finally going home. Just one more formal bun-fight on the 19th, then off to Wales. At least, that was the plan.

Chapter Fifteen

The car continued its crazy journey on the road to Mstkheta with me trapped in the back seat, still kicking and struggling, but forcing myself to stay calm and take stock. The drive must have taken only minutes but it seemed like hours. The car suddenly veered through a gap in the main road, headed briefly back in the direction of Tbilisi, and then turned sharp right in the direction of a small village I knew was called Didi Digomi. The driver turned abruptly left off this track and drove for about ten minutes down a rough unmade lane before coming to a halt in a cul-de-sac.

The "policemen" on each side of me had relieved me of my money, about three hundred dollars and some *lari*, and my two rings, birthday presents from colleagues in Azerbaijan and Georgia and of no real monetary value. They also took my mobile phone, cracked it open on the sill of the rear window and pocketed the SIM card. Surprisingly, they didn't take my watch.

As soon as the car stopped, I was quickly pulled out and handed over to the three masked military men who had followed closely behind in the mini-bus. A black balaclava hood was placed over my head and I was handcuffed to one of them and frog-marched through long grass for about ten minutes. As I was being pulled along, I swore at them. I was still angry; fear had not yet set in and I mouthed off constantly. They remained silent apart from "Faster, faster!" in a hoarse whisper from the one walking behind, who prodded me constantly in the back with the butt of his gun to emphasise his point.

The two holding me by the arm propelled me along quickly and held me up whenever I stumbled. Tired of being prodded from behind, I lashed out in temper with my foot. I must have caught one of them on the shin with the heel of my shoe. He was clearly not happy and responded by giving an almighty rabbit punch to the back of my neck. I went down and must have momentarily passed out.

I awoke to find myself being dragged by the armpits in a continual circular motion. I guessed this was meant to disorientate me. No point: I was disorientated enough already. After an interminable series of stumbles and tumbles over rough ground, my hood was taken off my head, the handcuff was released and one of them gestured to me to sit down on a rucksack he provided.

I looked around. Two of the military men were standing over me, hooded, with their Kalashnikovs pointing directly at me. The third was positioned a few metres away, crouched in the undergrowth, also hooded and staring fixedly in the direction from which we'd come. He seemed to be the leader. No words were spoken. The leader turned toward me, put his finger to his lips, and made a fist which he waved in my direction. I guessed this meant that I should remain still and quiet, or else.

I was in a tiny clearing in a small wood. It was raining heavily, I was very wet and my torn shirt and jacket were covered in blood. My left eye was now completely bunged up and the back of my neck hurt; I had a throbbing headache. I felt in my trouser pocket for a cigarette and lit up. No one said anything. I was very thirsty and made a drinking gesture with my hand. No one spoke but one of those standing over me indicated that I could drink the water retained by leaves of surrounding trees. He showed me how. This was reasonably effective. I chain-smoked, and when I ran out, the same one offered me a cigarette of his own, which I accepted. There was no attempt at conversation with me. When I gestured to be allowed to stand, a short shake of the head was the response. There was little conversation between them, and that in whispered Georgian which I was unable to understand. Eventually, one of them opened a rucksack and extracted some lint which he dampened with water from grass and leaves and used to wipe the blood off my face, and gently pressed against my eye. When I muttered a thank you, he placed his finger to his mouth and hissed.

Thoughts raced through my head. Where the hell was I? Not far from Tbilisi, clearly. I thought of doing a runner, but the Kalashnikovs kept pointing in my direction. Other thoughts whirled uncontrollably. What the hell was going on? What did these guys want? Money, or were they going to kill me? Why? This was not really happening to me, surely! My anger gradually dissipated and fear and confusion set in. I began to shake, first my feet, then my knees and finally my hands. I tried not to show them; I sucked hard on my cigarette and kept my head down.

We stayed there until it became dark, about four hours. As darkness fell, the leader approached me and placing his masked face close to mine, whispered menacingly in English into my ear, "Mister, you in Caucasus now." And waved his clenched fist under my nose. I recoiled involuntarily but tried to look impassive. Don't look scared! He gestured that I should rise, pulled me to my feet and handcuffed me to the wrist of one of his mates. It began to rain again, heavily.

As they led me away, I felt miserable, dazed and confused. What was Diana thinking now? If I was delayed I always telephoned. What the hell was going on here?

Chapter Sixteen

We left the clearing in the wood and crossed a rutted footpath. We then began to climb a mountain, initially quite gradually. As we proceeded, the climb became steeper and more difficult, until I was being virtually towed up the mountainside by the one to whom I was handcuffed while the second one held me upright and shoved me along. The third, the leader, followed behind. He seemed to be carrying the bulk of the equipment. His breathing became more laboured as we climbed. I stumbled, slipped and fell frequently, but was immediately yanked to my feet and made to continue. Eventually, I signalled that I had to take a rest; they allowed me to sit on the wet grass and gave me a cigarette. No one spoke.

I don't know why, but at this point I felt I just had to strike up some kind of conversation with one of them, the one to whom I was handcuffed seemed the most obvious. At least I'd discover how much English he spoke, if any. I was also desperate to know what they were going to do with me. I asked quietly, trying to control my voice, "Are you going to kill me?" at the same time making a gesture of my hand crossing my throat. He immediately answered, "*Ara, Ara*", "no, no," "*Puli, Puli*", – "money, money". He rubbed his middle finger against his thumb in that unmistakable gesture. This was of some comfort, if true.

The third guy, still standing behind me, remained silent and simply stared directly at me. I couldn't see his eyes, it was too dark, but I had the impression that he didn't blink. He stared stonily at me as if trying to make out what kind of man he had under his control. I tried to stare back but couldn't maintain the eye contact and reverted to shaking my head in bewilderment. After a short break of about ten minutes, I was pulled to my feet and we continued to climb ever upward, slipping and sliding on the wet grass. It continued to rain hard.

The outstanding landmark of Tbilisi, which is visible for miles around, is the television mast perched on a hill above the city centre. Incongruously, it remains lit up even when there is no power in the city. On several occasions, I tried to get my bearings by looking over my shoulder in an effort to spot the TV mast. Each time I did, I received a thump in the back from the butt of the Kalashnikov carried by the guy bringing up the rear, each blow accompanied by a whispered Georgian curse. Nevertheless, I was able to see the mast which was gradually disappearing from sight around the bluff of the mountain. Simply seeing it was somehow reassuring. I was not far from Tbilisi. Eventually it disappeared altogether, but I was able to glimpse instead, bit by bit, the flickering lights of the town of Mstkheta coming into view over my right shoulder. As we proceeded, they too disappeared from sight. I continued to glance behind me despite the bumps and thumps, but civilisation was slipping away. We stopped frequently at my request, to catch my breath and on each occasion the two men alongside me lit a cigarette and gave one to me. The one bringing up the rear didn't smoke.

There was a pattern to the journey in that we climbed directly upward for a time then moved diagonally to the right before heading straight up again. This zigzagging course was followed for at least four hours. Eventually we reached the outskirts of a thick deciduous forest. We skirted this for a few hundred metres, then turned abruptly to the left and proceeded again directly upward. The forest now was extremely dense and the climb almost vertical. The two alongside me produced axes from their rucksacks, and the one not handcuffed to me took the lead. Wielding his axe like a machete, he cut a swathe through the thick foliage.

He was an extremely powerful man. My already bruised and bloody face and chest were now lacerated by the branches of trees back-lashing from the blows of the one in front. We proceeded for at least another hour, tugged, shoved and pushed upward. No words were exchanged; the only sounds were those of heavy breathing, the thud of axe against timber, muffled

Georgian curses and the constant noise of heavy rain falling on the surrounding foliage.

Finally, I was pulled to a halt and stood exhausted, panting, with water streaming off me. A dynamo-operated torch was produced and a light shone on the shape of a camouflaged structure that appeared from out of the darkness. It was a tent, standing in a small flattened clearing on the side of the mountain. The leader came forward, fumbled with the entrance flap and disappeared inside. A light appeared from within. My handcuff was removed and I was pushed inside. The light came from a small paraffin lamp placed upon a tiny table at the far end of the tent. Although I was totally knackered, the adrenalin was still pumping and I was still reasonably alert. I was able to make out some features of my surroundings.

I was in a small camouflaged army tent measuring about three metres by two metres, the floor of which had been dug out of the side of the mountain and levelled. The back wall of the structure was an earth bank, and the frame of the tent consisted of gnarled and lopped trees that had been bent into a supportive structure over which the tarpaulin had been stretched and attached. The earthen floor of the tent was sodden and puddled. A steady stream of rain water dripped from the roof on to the muddy floor.

The leader gestured for me to sit on a metal-framed camp bed over which a sleeping bag was draped, and I was handcuffed to the slim trunk of a supporting tree next to the bed. Another cot faced me across the width of the tent. Cooking utensils, pots and pans were strewn over the floor near the entrance to the tent, and hanging from wooden pegs driven into the soil forming the walls of the structure was a variety of guns and rucksacks which, I later discovered, contained grenades and ammunition. They really had a small arsenal in there.

A whispered conversation – in Georgian – began between my three guards, but I couldn't understand what was being said. They unpacked their kitbags and hung the contents, mainly provisions, on wooden pegs. There were a lot of provisions; they'd clearly planned to be there for some time. The guards undressed and changed into fresh clothes extricated from their kitbags and hung their dripping uniforms on the pegs. My handcuff was unlocked and one of them gestured that I was to remove my shirt, trousers, shoes and socks. I was handed military over-trousers and socks, and given a black shirt that incongruously looked like a formal dinner-shirt complete with ruffs. The remains of my tattered tie and shirt were incarcerated in one of their kitbags and my torn jacket was hung on a peg. I retained my very wet underpants. My trousers and socks were hung on a peg behind my camp bed and my shoes placed under the cot. My right-hand wrist was handcuffed again to the tree trunk.

My guards poured water from a container into a large saucepan into which they emptied some macaroni and placed upon a small paraffin primus stove. A separate primus stove was used to boil a saucepan containing water, and eventually I was handed a mug of very sweet hot water laced with a few tea-leaves. I was also given a cigarette. At no time did my captors remove their masks or utter one word directly to me. I still couldn't believe this was happening to me. The whole situation was completely unreal. While the macaroni was coming to the boil, one of them produced a portable radio and fiddled around with the antenna and the tuning wheel.

Having spent some six years working in Georgia, I'd developed a reasonable understanding of elementary Georgian. I was never able to speak the language but could understand the basics. The time by my watch was now 4.00am.

The radio broadcast a news programme. The female newscaster announced that Peter Shaw, director of the Agro-business Bank of Georgia, had been kidnapped in the Saburtalo suburb of Tbilisi during the evening of 18th June. She then read out various witness statements and ended by stating that a communiqué had been received by a senior employee of the bank from the kidnappers, demanding an amount of two million dollars in exchange for my safe release. I clearly heard the phrase *"Ori millioni dollari"* – two million dollars. She added that President Shevardnadze was to hold a press conference at nine the following morning which would be broadcast live.

The effect of this broadcast on my captors was electric. They became very excited, shook each other by the hand, slapped each other on the back, exchanged kisses and one of them leaned over to me, grabbed my hand and shook it energetically, yelling repeatedly *"problem ara"* – no problem. There was no attempt now to speak quietly. They shouted loudly to each other in animated Georgian, all talking at the same time – too fast for me to understand – but the content was clearly congratulatory. They had pulled it off, and they were extremely happy about it.

I couldn't help but become affected by their mood. Here was I, sitting on a camp bed and handcuffed to a tree, extremely damp and up to my ankles in mud, listening to the drumming of torrential rain on the tarpaulin of a military tent in which I was being held prisoner on the top of a mountain. But I was aware that my kidnapping had been reported to the authorities, the motivation appeared to be financial – two million American dollars – which I knew wouldn't be paid, but my captors clearly believed it would. It seemed that I was not to be killed after all; I couldn't be too far away from Tbilisi, and I was at least almost dry and about to be fed. I drew in deep breaths and tried to affect a calm exterior. Inside, my heart was racing. The authorities knew, therefore my family would soon be aware of my situation. God give them the strength to cope. I hoped that someone would stay close to my mother. Diana and Danny would take strength from Di's family. Stay calm. Think.

Chapter Seventeen

I hadn't received, or expected to receive, any training from the European Commission, or anyone else, on how to behave in a situation like this. It was never on the agenda. But I had over the years read bits and pieces of Terry Waite's book on his experiences while held prisoner in Beirut. One of the bits that stuck in my head was the need to strike up some kind of personal rapport with my captors. It might help. I knew that one of them, apparently the leader, had at least a few words of English. It seemed to me that while they were obviously happy, it might be worthwhile trying to draw them into some kind of conversation. I tried a chat-up line while they busied themselves with the food.

I began by introducing myself. "My name is Peter Shaw – most people call me Pete." I told them that I worked for the European Commission, and that I was not English, but Welsh – "Welsa". This distinction seemed to grab their attention and this first attempt at a dialogue developed into my drawing a map on the mud floor of the tent. It was a map of the UK, clumsily illustrating the location of Wales in relation to England, Scotland and Ireland. This seemed to help to break the ice a little. Bit by bit tiny pieces of information began to be shared and I began to build up a picture of my captors on this, the first night of my captivity.

I was correct. The leader of the group was the one I had earlier identified. His name was Sasha, short for Alexander. He was tall: around six feet two inches, and under the bulkiness of his military uniform, quite slim and athletic. He was also fair-haired – the hairs on his arms were the giveaway – and had distinctive blue-grey eyes, not typically Georgian. He also had a long, thin face, an aquiline nose and prominent white teeth behind thin lips seen through the slit in his balaclava mask above the Nike symbol. He had a loud distinctive tenor voice, and a deep, gurgling laugh which, for the time being at least, he was exercising considerably. He was clearly accustomed to being in command and exuded an air of easy authority. Every instruction he issued, always in the Georgian language, was carried out without hesitation.

In discussing our various countries of origin during the first night of my captivity, he explained in poor, but comprehensible English, that his father was Serbian and lived in Belgrade, and his mother, now dead, had been Georgian. His father had re-married and he had a much younger half-brother who lived with his father in Belgrade. Sasha claimed to be twenty-six years old, but I think he was at least ten years older. He didn't smoke, and he told me he didn't drink – again not typically Georgian.

His number two also called himself Sasha. I will call him Sasha (2). He was built like the proverbial brick bog. About five feet nine inches in height and thick-set, he looked, and was, extremely strong and muscular. It was he who had taken the lead in hacking a route through the forest. He spoke no English whatsoever, but by a mixture of very basic Georgian and sign language, he told me he came from Tskinvali – the capital of South Ossetia. I'd been there on several occasions as part of an EC delegation team. It was a tumble-down town of about thirty thousand inhabitants; its infrastructure had not only suffered from the effects of civil war some eight years earlier, but also from a severe earthquake which had flattened the town. It had never really been rebuilt. Sasha's parents were both dead and he had no living brothers or sisters. He had a round face, a very dark complexion and black, deep-seated eyes. He claimed to be thirty-three years old, and, in addition to soldiering, had been a wrestler. Wrestling is a popular sport in the Caucasus and I had no reason to disbelieve him. Although his hoarse voice gave away a heavy smoking habit, he looked and was a very tough nut.

The third member called himself Serge, an abbreviation of the Russian Sergei. He was about six feet tall and slim. It was his black shirt that I was now wearing and which was at this stage uncomfortably tight. I had been handcuffed to Serge during the long, wet climb up the mountain to the tent, and it had been he who had sought to assuage my doubts when I had questioned the reason for my kidnapping. He spoke little or no English, and also had lived in Tskinvali. He was, he said, a Moslem, a *Mussulman*. In profile, he certainly appeared to be more Asian in appearance than the other two, with a straight nose and long thin face. Over the following days, as his beard grew around his mouth, the darkness and sallowness of his complexion became more apparent. At this stage, he seemed to be directly in charge of me as a prisoner. It was he who handcuffed me to the tree, or to his own wrist, and it was he who offered me cigarettes and food. I guessed he was about thirty years old, and he told me he had no living relations. All were dead. He also told me he was wanted by Interpol for murder; he seemed quite proud of this.

That first night of captivity was a huge mix of physical sensations and emotional swings. I was obviously in a desperately uncertain situation and was physically uncomfortable. It rained incessantly, the roof of the tent leaked directly above my camp bed, and the ditch which had been dug around the tent soon overflowed. The floor of the tent became a quagmire. Everything became sodden, including me. I was told to lie on the cot, and reluctantly did so, but sleep was impossible. My thoughts constantly drifted to my family and what they were experiencing. Following the radio broadcast, Sasha, the leader, was in a communicative mood.

He told me very slowly, in halting English, that I, Peter Shaw, had powerful friends in Georgia. He had received "good information" that the two million dollars would be paid by the bank within the following five days. After that, I would be freed. He used the words "no variant" after every phrase, making a cross-chest gesture with both arms to emphasise the truth of the statement. I came to loathe this gesture, but, at this stage, I hoped that he was telling the truth.

He explained at length that he and his colleagues were *warriors* and not bandits. The money was required to purchase arms for their *business* and not simply for personal gain. He told me that he and his colleagues were professionals who had fought in Kosovo, Bosnia, Sarajevo, Srebrenica and Abkhazia. When I explained that I was merely a working consultant and of no value, he simply laughed and, pointing to his Kalashnikov, snarled, "This is my consultant. I need no other. Georgia needs no other too. Georgia has no need for foreigners. Russia will never leave Georgia."

He continued in this fashion for half-an-hour, generally denigrating foreigners, and praising Georgia and particularly its neighbour, Russia. When he tired of his efforts to educate me, he indicated that he wanted to sleep, and so should I. They all three sat on the cot opposite me, turned out the paraffin light, and proceeded to carry out in the darkness a whispered conversation in Georgian.

I lay awake, trying to think. I tried to work out how the news of my kidnap would be communicated to my family. What would they do? What *could* they do? The demand for two million dollars was clearly preposterous. I knew that the UK government would never accede to any demand, nor would the EC, and the bank could simply not afford it. Even if it were able, the bank could not pay. There was no way I could explain any of this to my captors. I certainly didn't have the Georgian language skills; they couldn't really speak English and the explanation would be lost upon them: too technical. Was there something more behind this than simply money? I tried to think it through, but was too exhausted and confused to make any sense. Just stay calm. I had not been too badly hurt, and I was still alive.

Chapter Eighteen

I must have dozed off for a short while. When I awoke, it was daylight and I needed to urinate. I heard Sasha's voice talking to his colleagues in very clear Georgian, which I found I could understand. "We will have no trouble with this guy. Everything will be fine." Then he laughed. It sounded like water going down a drain.

I heard the whirr of machinery. There was a helicopter overhead. Were they looking for me? My heartbeat kicked into over-drive. Serge became excited and said something I couldn't understand. Sasha gurgled again and said in Georgian, "No problem. They have the whole of the Caucasus to search. Don't worry."

I opened my eyes and squinted around. No change: the same three people wearing masks. I sat up on the camp bed and said, loudly, "toilet". There was a murmured conversation between Sasha and Serge. Sasha demanded in English, "big toilet, little toilet?" I said, "little". Serge unlocked the handcuff, gave me a pair of boots and I was led out of the tent. He gestured that I should walk into the forest, which I did, followed closely by Serge cradling his Kalashnikov. We walked for about twenty metres then he stopped me. When I'd finished urinating, he indicated I was to return to the tent, pushed me on to the cot, handcuffed me to the tree and gave me a cigarette.

It had stopped raining. The sun was shining and it was warm; insects were buzzing around outside the tent. We were surrounded by trees, nothing else. Everything seemed perfectly normal; an ideal summer day. Inside the tent, Sasha (2) was fiddling with the radio. My watch told me it was 9.00am when the distinctive resonant and halting tones of President Shevardnadze boomed out from the radio. I found that I was able to understand the gist of what he said.

He was holding the promised press conference. I was able to hear the clicking of cameras and the murmur of voices in the background. He confirmed that Peter Shaw, prominent EC expert, known personally to the President, and director of the Agro-business Bank of Georgia, had been kidnapped in broad daylight in the district of Saburtalo, Tbilisi. He further confirmed that a ransom demand of two million dollars – *ori millioni dollari* – had been demanded for my safe release. He called upon all the security forces of Georgia, including his own special forces, to search for me and ensure my speedy and safe release. He denounced the *criminali* who had perpetrated this extremely serious offence, yet a further example of the efforts made by bandit gangs to target conspicuous foreigners and undermine the President's authority in Georgia. He also indicated that the British Embassy in Georgia had offered a reward – unquantified – for any information leading to my safe release. A statement made by the UK Embassy was read out which emphasised that I had been due to return to the UK at contract-end, 20th June – tomorrow.

Other comments were made by various government ministers which I was only able to partially understand. These were largely descriptions of my activities on behalf of the European Commission in Georgia over a period of six years. All present hoped that I would be released quickly and returned safely to Tbilisi.

Again, the effect of this broadcast upon my captors was remarkable. General congratulations all round were evidently in order. Something had surely been said by Shevardnadze, either directly or in code, that told them the money would be paid. *Puli problem ara* – "Money no problem", they yelled, and leapt up to shake me vigorously by the hand. I tried to exude an air of resignation and indifference, shrugged my shoulders and hoped inwardly that they knew more than I did. A ransom, any ransom, was ludicrous, but two million dollars…!

Eventually, they settled down, re-heated the macaroni and tea and gave me my share. At no time had they removed their masks apart from when they ate. This they did in turn, each squatting with his back towards me, always ensuring there was no chance of my glimpsing their faces.

I was kept inside the tent throughout the day, handcuffed to my tree. They made food –more macaroni, in the evening – and allowed me water and cigarettes whenever I indicated the need. One of them remained, masked, in the tent with me at all times, seated on the cot opposite mine with his Kalashnikov cradled in his arms, sometimes dozing, but usually simply staring into space. They spent a lot of time cleaning their weapons. I had the impression they were showing off, like kids with toys. There was little conversation and then only with Sasha, the leader. He remained on reasonably friendly terms with me and told me of his fighting exploits in only just comprehensible English.

That afternoon he rambled on about the thousands of brave Russian troops still situated in Georgia. They would never leave. One of their largest camps was only a few kilometres away. The Russians still had, he said, more than one hundred thousand tanks in Poland ready to invade the West. He had been a junior officer in the Serbian army, and had no ambitions to become more senior. "They who lead, die," he said. He explained how the Americans (not NATO), in Kosovo had won only because of their superior air power. They had been frightened to face the Serbian *boyeviks* man-to-man because the Serbs were much superior soldiers. The Americans were cowards. He mockingly related how the Americans had demanded that ice-cream be part of their rations during the Gulf War. "Can you understand – ice-cream? They are penis!" A Russian soldier could survive on vodka and bread! He described how he had shot and killed a Croatian soldier at Sarajevo and on searching his body had discovered that he was sixteen years old and had parents and a sister. He had seen a photograph of them. He shrugged his shoulders and fell silent.

Two or three times during that day I heard the sound of a helicopter overhead. On each occasion, those guarding outside would quickly enter the tent. Once the noise had died away, two would return to guard duty outside.

On the second day of my captivity, I woke up in the morning desperate for a shit. I was provided with toilet paper and taken to a place in the forest to squat, again about twenty metres from the tent but in a different direction. My guard, Serge, moved a respectable distance away. I surmised that we were near the top of the mountain. I couldn't see through the thick forest sloping directly downward, but could hear the constant drone of distant traffic from below, and occasionally the sound of a train. I guessed we were only four or five kilometres above the main Tbilisi/Mstkheta road, parallel to which I knew was a railway line. I'd travelled that road many times, seemingly centuries ago. I could easily walk to Tbilisi, if only I could reach the road.

Later that day, I was allowed to walk in a small circle for half an hour to exercise, and then returned to the tent and handcuffed to my tree. The bees and wasps still droned away outside the tent; the mosquitoes found their way inside and bit like mad. I had to try to get away somehow.

I again requested to do 'big' toilet. I was not eating much but my stomach was genuinely in a bad way. I was taken by Serge to the same place. On our way back to the tent, I noted that Sasha (2) was not around. I assumed he had gone down through the forest to fetch water. Serge had dropped some distance behind me and Sasha, the boss, was squatting near the tent with his Kalashnikov on his knees, staring fixedly down through the forest. I noticed a shovel had been left leaning against the side of the tent. Presumably this had been used to dig out the floor of the tent and the ditches around it. If I could only grab the spade, I had the chance of bashing Sasha on the back of the head and making a run for it. I shuffled around behind him, grabbed the shovel and began to walk quickly toward his squatting figure. I didn't look behind me but assumed Serge hadn't yet noticed my movements. I ignored him and concentrated only on covering the few yards to within clouting distance of Sasha.

My intention was, having taken out the leader, to try and turn his gun on Serge. The fact that I had no idea of how to use

71

the gun hadn't entered my head. I had to try something and this was an opportunity. I was within a few feet of Sasha when Serge spotted me, shouted, and Sasha whirled around.

I was badly beaten that afternoon. Serge stood and watched as Sasha kneed me to the ground and beat me all over my body with the butt of his Kalashnikov. Then Serge took his turn to beat me with the handle of his axe. When they tired, I was dragged into the tent, flung on to my cot and handcuffed to the tree. Apart from a few grunts and curses, not a word had been said to me. There were no further conversations with Sasha.

Chapter Nineteen

A pattern began to emerge. Each night it rained heavily, usually thunder storms which caused the tent to flood, and the floor became a quagmire. Each day dawned bright and sunny. I was allowed to relieve myself each morning, fed and watered, and exercised by walking in a tight circle for about half an hour. Then I was handcuffed to the tree by the camp bed and not allowed to leave the tent. The entrance was kept tightly closed all day. Nevertheless, flies and mosquitoes found their way inside and nipped every bit of exposed flesh. When Serge was on guard duty inside the tent, he took to burning leaves and toilet paper in order to keep the insects at bay. I preferred the smoke to the bites.

On the third day of my captivity, I noticed that Sasha (2) was no longer with us. I suppose this put a greater burden upon my two remaining captors, who now had to guard me inside the tent for some twenty-three hours per day, as well as the approaches to the tent. None of us was getting much sleep, and while my thoughts at every waking moment were concerned with my family, and the slim possibility of the authorities finding me, or the chance of an escape, clearly these guys had their own problems. The helicopter flights over the area were becoming more frequent. Could it be that the authorities were closing in? Had Sasha (2) gone to negotiate with someone in authority? I sensed that the lack of sleep and the need for constant alertness was getting them down. The wet nights and hot, mosquito-filled days were fraying their tempers. I know not whether they were able to wash outside the tent, but the growth of beard around their mouths indicated they were not shaving. The skin on their faces must have been badly irritated, but at no time in my presence did they take off their masks, or place one on me.

There was now virtually no communication between us. Sasha was becoming more and more sullen. He would begin to talk for a few seconds, and then lapse into silence. Any attempt on my part to converse was met with an abrupt hiss, and a clenched fist under my nose. Sometimes he kicked me, hard. I tried to communicate with Serge. This took the form of translating simple words like knife, fork, spoon, kettle into Georgian, English and Welsh. It worked to a limited extent, but I could not maintain his interest and after a few minutes, I was invariably hissed into silence. In fairness, he kicked me only once.

On the fourth evening, I tried to explain that I had a stomach problem. I have genuinely suffered intermittently from indigestion for many years, which I've kept at bay by sucking my way through a tube of Boots indigestion tablets each day. I certainly had no problem with my stomach at that time, probably because I was not eating very much, but I thought it wouldn't be a bad idea to feign some sort of sickness. I had to do something.

So I moaned and groaned in my camp-bed and indicated, with circular motions of my hand, great discomfort in the stomach area. They paid no attention to me. I kept this up all night. No one had any sleep, and in the morning I pretended that I was unable to get out of bed. They muttered and gesticulated to each other for a few minutes, and then unlocked the handcuff and tried to help me from the bed while I writhed and yelled in pretended agony. Sasha tried to get to the bottom of the problem, and eventually came to understand that I needed a special prescription called "Boots" for my stomach malady. He shook his head and instead encouraged me to drink a mug-full of cooking oil. I took a few sips then threw the remainder away. I was re-deposited forcibly on the camp bed and handcuffed to the tree. No further attention was paid to any symptom of which I complained relating to my stomach, or any other part of my anatomy.

And so it went on from day to day. I had by now a fair growth of beard and I hadn't washed since the morning of the day of my capture. In sign language, I requested that I should have a shave and wash. Both were declined. My hands and face were badly bitten by mosquitoes, and I had noticed that my guards had taken to wearing gloves; I asked that I be allowed to share in this luxury. No chance. There was now a complete stand-off. My attempted escape had not endeared me to them and they were going to do me no favours now; so much for my attempts to form a rapport.

Chapter Twenty

Early on the morning of Sunday, my fifth day in captivity, we had some visitors.

I heard from my bed a repeated bird-call some distance away. Serge, whose turn it was to guard me inside the tent, jumped up and darted for the tent entrance where he was joined by Sasha. I then heard voices I hadn't heard before. A number of voices, two or three, all speaking in Georgian. The voices became louder and mingled with peals of laughter. I heard the clink of glass against glass; there was obviously some drinking going on. After about fifteen minutes, Sasha came bursting into the tent; he looked very pleased with himself.

"Ah, Peter," he shouted in English, swaying slightly, "you are bandit," waving his finger in my direction. "You have very good time in Georgia, no? Restaurants, clubs, uh? You know many girls in Georgia, uh?" I shook my head. He smacked his knee, laughed, and disappeared outside the tent. Serge appeared almost immediately, carrying a bottle of vodka and a glass. Smiling broadly, he poured out a large glass of vodka, handed it to me wordlessly, lifted his hand as if to toast me and left. The flow of excited conversation continued outside the tent for about half an hour before all became quiet again. Sasha and Serge returned to their cot carrying a large bunch of newspapers.

They both sat facing me, smiling, a little tipsy and obviously content with life. Sasha began to explain to me, haltingly, that they had received copies of many newspaper reports from his friends. "You are famous man," he yelled and tossed me a couple of Georgian newspapers. I wasn't able to read the words, but my photograph and that of Shevardnadze and various government ministers were plastered all over them. It took some time for him to explain, with obvious delight, that some journalists were accusing me of stealing large amounts of money, up to twenty-four million dollars, during 1996 and 1997 from foreign aid funds provided by the European Commission. I had apparently worked in collusion with the then Minister of Agriculture, Bakur Gulua, in amassing this fortune. The accusations were clearly ludicrous but my attempts at denial were mockingly derided. They were delighted by my obvious discomfort. Sasha then turned to my sex life.

"How many girls named Eka you know?" he asked.

I replied that I knew three. One, a long-standing colleague who had worked with me since 1996, the second a waitress who worked at Ovatio restaurant in Perovskaya Street, where I was a regular diner; and the third was a member of the staff of the Telavi sub-branch of the bank in eastern Georgia.

"Which Eka is good?" he enquired, moving his hips, simulating the sex-act and giggling uncontrollably. I shook my head and said I didn't know. He made a dismissive gesture with his hand and growled, "You have many girls, but you have wife?" I tried to explain that I was divorced and that the mother of my three children is named Mair and lives in Wales, and that I had a long-standing relationship in Georgia with a lady named Diana, and we have a son called Daniel.

He didn't seem in the least surprised by this, but immediately asked me to write down Diana's telephone number, handing me a biro ink-stem and a small piece of paper. I explained that I didn't know her number. This was true. I had never memorised it. The number was in my mobile phone that had been destroyed by the bogus policemen. Sasha spoke with Serge animatedly in Georgian for a few minutes. Turning to me, he demanded that I write down the telephone number of Mair. I saw no harm in this. It seemed those who had kidnapped me wanted to contact her. Mair and my family must by now be aware of what had happened to me. I assumed the authorities in the UK would also be aware and any contact made with Mair would be passed on. What harm could it do if she was contacted by my kidnappers? She would go to the police. It might help. I wrote down Mair's number in the UK and gave it to Sasha. He beamed, evidently satisfied, stuffed the paper in his pocket, and resumed his dialogue with Serge.

My captors' euphoric mood continued throughout the day while I became more and more despondent. Obviously I was being vilified in the Georgian newspapers. I was used to this, but somehow I felt hurt that this nonsense should continue even though I'd been abducted. Some political clique was clearly paying for certain newspapers to write this rubbish. This pointed to a motivation above that of simple financial gain. The politicians who had long wanted me out of the ABG were having their way. Had they organised the kidnap? Would they therefore make sure that I was permanently out of their way?

My captors fed and watered me that day as usual, allowed me my usual trip to the forest, and handcuffed me to my tree. True to form, it began to rain heavily from early evening into the night. The inside of the tent, as normal, became waterlogged and everything became very wet. The deteriorating conditions now had no effect on Sasha and Serge, who maintained their relaxed mood. Sasha, at one point, began to whistle, and the tune he whistled was Louis Armstrong's "What a Wonderful World." This tune was played frequently at Ovatio restaurant – one of a limited number of western popular tunes played at that restaurant. Why was he whistling this tune now? He hadn't before. Was there some connection?

At about nine o'clock that evening, I heard a bird-call. Sasha, who was inside the tent guarding me, jumped up, disappeared through the tent-flap and returned within a few minutes with Serge and Sasha (2). The latter had returned from his trip.

I'd come to realise during the past few days that my captors believed I could understand something of the Georgian language. On several occasions they'd entered into conversation within my earshot, which I believed I was meant to hear and understand. Sasha had made vague references to my being a member of the British security forces. They thought I was a spy! They'd also mentioned in their conversations the names of people they knew I would recognise; the names of people who worked in the ABG or at the EC Delegation. All three now began a long discussion in Georgian, speaking quite rapidly but clearly, and well within my ear-shot. I was able to pick up small snippets of information.

Sasha (2) had been to Tbilisi. He had toured the restaurants and bars at which I was known, he had even gone to the barber's shop at which I regularly had my hair cut. He related that there was a great deal of sympathy for me in Tbilisi. The Georgian authorities were very active in their search for me in and around Tbilisi but had no clue as to my whereabouts. There was, however, no problem at all with regard to the money being paid: the proper arrangements had been made. They then discussed the merits of moving me to Rustavi, where there was some gas and electricity. It seemed that Sasha (2) had already agreed the means of transporting me there. There was no problem.

Sasha then turned to me and laboriously explained in English that tonight we were all to descend the mountain. I would be handcuffed to Serge and I was to remain extremely quiet and co-operative, otherwise I would be killed. He made a motion of his hand passing across his throat. At the bottom of the mountain we were to be met by a vehicle and would be driven to Rustavi. The following day I was to be taken to Tbilisi and released. I would then go home. He made the usual motion of arms across his chest – "No variant." He handed me my still-wet trousers and jacket and a pair of army boots. He placed my shoes into his kit-bag, brewed some tea, and all three began the business of packing up.

I was confused and apprehensive. On the one hand, anything seemed better than remaining in this waterlogged tent, shackled to a tree for twenty-three hours each day. My stomach was genuinely playing up and I was suffering badly from mosquito bites. On the other hand, I didn't really believe that I would be released. Why had they discussed the power situation in Rustavi if they intended to release me in a day or so? It made no sense; nothing made sense. Nevertheless, I clung to the slim chance of being released. Was it possible? At some stage, they surely had to be telling me the truth. I determined that if there was any chance of making an escape I would take it, but the main thing now was to get off this mountain.

At about midnight, we began the descent. It was raining heavily and I was handcuffed to Serge. Sasha (2) took the lead, hacking his way through the forest with his axe, with the leader again bringing up the rear, carrying the bulk of the kit-bags and weapons. I have a fear of heights. Had it been daylight, I think they would not have succeeded in getting me down that mountain without knocking me out. But it was pitch black and they seemed to be following a pre-determined course planned beforehand by Sasha (2). This was apparently designed to provide the maximum amount of cover. Although it was pitch dark, they did not at any time use their torches.

The descent was horrendous. We slipped and slithered our way down steep mud-courses, gullies and ravines. On several occasions I was prevented from disappearing over the edge of a chasm only by the handcuff that attached me to the wrist of Serge. I fell frequently, and twice bashed my head against the boot of Serge. I was reminded that you really do see stars when your head receives a hard knock. Eventually Serge must have become impatient with my inability to stay upright and released the handcuff from my wrist. Instead, he held me firmly by the wrist with his hand as we continued our headlong descent. We stopped only twice for a breather. We were all quickly soaked to the skin and covered in mud, but there was no conversation, apart from the occasional murmured order from Sasha – "*Nella, nella*" – "Quietly, quietly," followed by a string of Georgian curses.

Despite my determination to take any chance to escape it became blindingly obvious very quickly that there was absolutely no way that I could do it. Simply staying on my feet was a huge challenge, and these guys were far fitter and stronger than me. I was very lucky not to break a leg, or worse, during that nightmare trek down the mountain. I caught a glimpse of the Tbilisi television mast in the distance through the driving rain, and the diminishing lights of Mstkheta. The rest of that journey down the mountain is a jumble of images of black wetness and pain.

After about six hours of purgatory we came to a railway line. I guessed this to be the main railway between Mstkheta and Tbilisi which runs for a short distance parallel to the main road. Images of Sunday picnics again flashed through my mind. Serge motioned that I was to crouch in the undergrowth with the two of them, while Sasha (2) carried out a recce. On his return, I was pushed over a barbed-wire fence, dropped down onto the railway track, across it, and pulled into and through a tunnel which ran underneath the opposite platform; then, a ten minute slide down a forested incline until I saw a small light in the distance. I was bundled in the direction of the light, my hand firmly clasped by Serge and my collar held tightly by Sasha. I could just make out a white vehicle, a mini-bus parked in a lay-by next to the paraffin lamp. It was pointing in the direction of Tbilisi.

My heart raced. Could it really be true that I was shortly to be released? A black balaclava was pulled over my head, and I was shoved roughly into a space in the mini-bus formerly occupied by a couple of seats. My face was pushed into the floor, a tarpaulin draped over me and a spare tyre was thrown on top; my three captors sat on the rear seats of the bus, directly behind me. I felt the pressure of their feet resting on the tyre. I was jammed tight and completely unable to move. A whispered conversation with people in the front seat, and the mini-bus lurched forward – in the direction of Tbilisi.

Chapter Twenty-one

Unknown to me, details of my kidnapping had been splashed all over the front pages of the Georgian press of 19th June. Unfortunately, they got it all wrong. They got my age wrong, the time and place of the kidnap wrong, they got my work experience wrong; they even got my name wrong. The reports of the kidnapping stated that an attempt to rescue me had been made by several policemen, but I had been forced into the kidnappers' car, which had made good its escape despite the great efforts of the police to pursue and apprehend my abductors. The police had several suspects, although no arrests had been made so far, but the motivation was definitely a ransom demand, and road blocks had been established at all exit-points from the city. Later in the day, the police reported that my Skoda car had been found near the village of Didomi, a few miles from Tbilisi. Another stolen vehicle used in my kidnapping was also found elsewhere in Tbilisi.

President Shevardnadze appeared on television and instructed the Minister of the Interior, the Minister of State Security and the Prosecutor General "to find the delinquents and release the British businessman, Peter Show (sic), in the shortest term possible." Otherwise, he promised to bring the law enforcement bodies to account. At the government sitting of 19th June, Shevardnadze expressed his deep concern over the abduction of the foreign businessman who had worked in Georgia for a long time. He said that this was not the first case by far, and kidnapping seemed to have become a fashion in Tbilisi. He upbraided the Georgian law-enforcement bodies stating that, "they cannot ensure proper control over the criminogenic (sic) situation in the country." Typically, the President added that, "Georgia is a small country in a difficult situation, but other countries, even strong ones like the USA have difficulties with their fight against criminality."

A statement criticising the government was issued on the same day by Fady Asly, President of the American Chamber of Commerce in Georgia. He pointed out that my abduction would "reverberate negatively on Georgia's investment climate and international companies' performance in the country," and called for this wave of kidnapping to be stopped. A business colleague of Fady Asly had been kidnapped and held for seventy-seven days a year earlier, shortly afterwards, Asly's business premises in the centre of Tbilisi had been hit and badly damaged by a mortar shell. No arrests were made in either context. During the afternoon of the 19th, the Delegation of the European Commission in Georgia issued a statement expressing their "grave concern" at my kidnapping. The statement incorporated corrections to the mis-information disseminated by the Georgian media earlier in the day.

The news hit the headlines in the UK on 20th June... "British banker kidnapped by gang after gunfight with police..." "Banker kidnapped in Georgia..." "Family's anxious wait..."

Many newspapers picked up the fact that a long-standing EC staffer, Mr Gunter Beuchel, had been brutally murdered in Georgia only one year earlier. No arrests had been made. Similarly, two Spanish businessmen had been kidnapped in Georgia and held for nearly two years before finally being released recently, following payment of a substantial ransom demand. This had been paid by their families. Again no one had been arrested. The *Washington Post* ran an article examining the security situation in Georgia making special reference to my kidnapping, the latest in a long litany of security scares, and examined the possible economic and financial repercussions on Georgia. A former colleague of mine was in Nepal working on a World Bank project when he heard of my kidnapping on the BBC World News. Another friend was in Kosovo at the time, and yet another in Beijing. It is strange to know that while I felt all alone and isolated, friends and family around the globe were thinking of me. And that they were doing everything they could to help me.

Diana Khorina – my partner:

Peter telephoned me from the bank at about 6.00pm on 18th June, to tell me that he was going for a drink with some friends. I said "Okay, I will go to Rustavi and take some of Danny's old toys and give them to my friends and neighbours, and say goodbye to some friends. See you tomorrow after work." We had no electricity in Rustavi during the evening of the eighteenth, so there was no television.

At about 9.00am on the 19th, I was at the apartment of my friend Lena in Rustavi when my mum telephoned me. Her voice was shaking and she couldn't say anything sensibly. Lisiko Koiava and Dato Kashia, colleagues of Peter who I knew well, were at her apartment. Lisiko took the phone and explained to me that Peter had been kidnapped. I said, "Are you sure?" I didn't believe that this could happen to Peter. Not to Peter. I went to my mum's apartment. She and my sister Lena were crying. Lisiko and Dato explained as much as they knew. Lisiko began to cry and said that she was ashamed that this could happen to Peter in her country. Dato told me that the police wanted to interview me in Tbilisi. I was at a loss, totally confused, but tried to stay calm and said "Okay, we'll take Danny and Mum to Peter's apartment and Dato can take me to the police station." They agreed.

I was at the police station from 10.30am until 7.30pm. They asked me questions about Peter's colleagues, friends, enemies, habits, everything. They wanted names of everyone he knew. I tried to help them. They were very aggressive to me and I was really frightened all day. When I got back to Peter's apartment that evening, my mum had put on the television and the news of Peter's kidnapping was being broadcast again. Danny, who was three years old, said in Russian, "What has happened to my Dad? Has he been killed?" I sat him on my lap and said, "No, he hasn't been killed. He's been taken by bad men." He said "I will kill them." Then, for the first time, I began to cry. I didn't know that Danny knew the word "kill." It really sank in then.

I went to the police headquarters almost every day that week. They told me on 20th June that they had found Peter's car. They wanted me to identify it, which I did. The police didn't seem to be doing anything very quickly or trying very hard. Everything was moving at a very slow pace. I was upset and very frustrated at that time. I stayed with my mum in Rustavi for the following few weeks, until Tim Hammond and the UK embassy organised an apartment for me in Tbilisi. Later, I began to receive strange text messages on my mobile...

The reaction of Mair on having the news of my abduction broken to her, in her words:

I knew that Peter was coming home on 18th June with Diana and Danny. He had telephoned me on the Saturday before and spoken about holiday arrangements. He had also spoken with Lisa, our daughter. We were all looking forward to his homecoming – always like a tornado descending upon us. Despite the divorce, we're a close family.

I'd been to a restaurant with some colleagues on the 18th and arrived home at about 10.30pm. The phone rang and there was a lady from the Foreign Office who explained to me that she had tried to contact me earlier, and that Peter had been kidnapped in Tbilisi. I just couldn't believe it, and she had to tell me the same thing several times. She told me the local police would be in touch with me tomorrow.

This could surely not happen to him. He had told me he worked in a dangerous place and of the kidnappings and other crimes that went on, but they didn't affect him. Not Peter.

I was confused and frightened; the first thing I did was to telephone Teresa, my best friend, who lived in Porthcawl. She was tremendously supportive and between us we worked out what to do: telephone the kids, telephone some of his relations, telephone his best friends, Ken and Phil and Bev. I didn't know what to do about his mother who was eighty-three years old and frail. I made the telephone calls. I also spoke to my boss and explained that I couldn't come to work for a few days. His first reaction was "That's a good one! Pull the other leg!" But the penny soon dropped. He was very understanding.

That night our two sons travelled home and Lisa, our daughter, who was heavily pregnant, came around. They were all incredulous, confused and numbed, but strong. This could not really be happening to their dad! We stayed up all night and drank lots of coffee.

The next day, Police Superintendent Colin Jones and Chief Inspector Chris Parsons came to the house. They told me what to expect in terms of possible ransom demands. They fixed something to my phone and left me a list of instructions. Detective Superintendent David Douglas called from Scotland Yard and told me he'd come and see me in a few days. The police were marvellous: very kind and extremely supportive. The Foreign Office was also in constant touch. Peter's friends came to the house. Everybody was kind, but no one seemed to know what to do. Just to wait.

Then the media people began to telephone me. I didn't know how to handle it. It was very, very difficult. Later that day, Michael Boyd and Jackie Hammond of Landell-Mills phoned me. Michael really then took charge of the situation and organised everything – thank goodness! It was a terrible time."

Michael Boyd was Executive Chairman of Landell-Mills (Management Consultants) Ltd., the company I had been contracted to for five and a half of the six years I spent in Georgia. Michael is also a director of the DCI Group of Companies based in Ireland, of which Landell-Mills forms a part. He is a dynamic character, full of energy, Irish charm and charisma, a marvellous persuader and a superb networker. These qualities were to become abundantly apparent later. In his words:

The first news of Peter's kidnap will last in people's minds for a long time. "Peter's been kidnapped!" "Oh, my God!"

"Where?" "Why?" "Why now?" "Poor Peter." I was on my way to America to a wedding at the time and turned back at Heathrow to get together with Jackie (Hammond) and see what we could do. It was a bad time and a first for all of us. We had no idea where to start.

The constant love and worry of those close to Peter, and indeed of many who did not know him, were very striking. Several people were outstanding in this respect – Mair, Peter's children, Gavin (Lisa's husband), Jackie, Misha (Mgaloblishvili), Denis (Corboy), Paul (Craig), John Dexter. They thought about Peter constantly; were very creative in what to do, and made sure that he was not forgotten. Many others – complete strangers – were moved by Peter's plight and prayed for a happy outcome.

We assumed that there would be a ransom demand – to the ABG, the firm or to the family. The decision not to pay was very, very difficult. It was based on UK policy, no insurance, absence of money and Peter's likely view. Nevertheless, we felt that we might be condemning Peter to death.

Misha identified early on that pressure on the Georgian authorities would produce the best result. That was the start of a continuous campaign with a simple plea to anyone and everyone who might have some impact, and to keep Peter's name in lights. We went very wide, and without shame, in who we approached...

Tim Hammond, colleague and friend, had worked with me in Georgia for many months. Tim's wife is Jackie, and they have a daughter, Ella, then three years old. Jackie had worked for Landell-Mills for many years before I was kidnapped. As the Desk Officer for the Caucasus, she had been my direct point of contact within the organisation for my entire term in Georgia and Azerbaijan, and had an intimate knowledge of the ebbs and flows of the Caucasian projects. She'd been immensely supportive at all times. During the period of my abduction, she worked as Personal Assistant to Michael Boyd. Tim Hammond's words:

Coincidentally, the first time I met Peter was in Georgia, back in 1996. Peter was working on the RARP1 project and came bouncing into the canteen at the Ministry of Agriculture with a hearty greeting, "Hello, my handsome boy" – a favourite greeting of his, "Everything tickety-boo?" Followed by, "Are you from Wales? No? Ah well, never mind. We can't all be born lucky." At this time, his arrival was a breath of fresh air in a typically depressing Soviet-era government building, damp, cold and uninspiring. Although on this occasion our paths crossed for only a short time, I still remember it well. He is one of the few people I can remember meeting for the first time. In September 1999, I joined Peter's team at the ABG and began a friendship based on respect for his professional capabilities, his inexhaustible dedication to developing a viable bank, and, above all, to his magnetic character. He does not suffer fools gladly, and is not afraid to confront those who don't share the same level of integrity and professional accountability.

The news of Peter's abduction came as a hammer blow to all of us. I can still remember the call from Anna Bradshaw (of Landell-Mills) to Jackie early on the morning of 19th June. "Oh shit, what are we going to do?" My first thoughts after the initial shock were, "What would Peter do if the tables were turned and it was me who had been taken?" In a strange way this gave me some comfort as I knew that Peter was an immensely strong character and would move heaven and earth, and bang on every door to instigate action. Then reality set in and our thoughts turned to "Where do we start?" Why was Peter taken, and why was it so close to his departure? Is there a link with the bank, possibly bank staff indirectly involved, or a disgruntled customer, or perhaps another bank, one of those which had gone bust during the RARP1 project? From my reading of previous kidnap cases in Georgia, I knew Peter was in for a hard time and his living conditions were going to be sub-human. I was asked on many occasions how I thought Peter would cope with captivity, and my greatest fear was that he

*might antagonise his captors. I knew he had the mental strength
to withstand hardship and extreme adversity.*

*The formation of the FACC (Friends and Concerned
Colleagues of Peter) team, so ably led by Michael (Boyd) was
an important factor, not only in galvanising ideas, but also
lifting the spirits of all involved, including those of Jackie and
me. It seems that all we spoke of was Peter and his plight, at all
times of the day and night. It consumed our private thoughts as
well. Underlying the main focus of the group was the thought
that Peter should not be forgotten by the powers that be, and we
should be constantly reminding them of Peter's predicament
and the appalling nature of the crime committed.*

*I also strongly desired to visit Georgia and see for myself
what was being done. There was of course the risk that I would
be the next one to be taken. It was a difficult decision for Jackie
and me to make. Although acutely aware of the risks, Jackie's
support for the trip was solid...*

Chapter Twenty-two

A few minutes, and the driver of the mini-bus executed a sharp U-turn and skidded round in the opposite direction to that of Tbilisi and Rustavi. My heart sank and my stomach churned. I knew that I was not going home. I was not going to be released. Sasha had lied to me again. Anger and frustration brought tears to my eyes. I tried to sit up and was booted back into a prone position.

There followed a drive of six or seven hours mainly over rough unmade roads, up and down steep hills heading generally in a westward direction, away from Tbilisi and freedom. For almost all of this time I was made to remain curled up on the floor of the vehicle, covered by the tarpaulin and the tyre on which my three guards rested their feet. I was soaking wet, shivering with cold and shock and totally knackered by the climb down the mountain.

The mini-bus stopped a number of times, the first about half an hour into the drive. The vehicle pulled over into a lay-by, one of my guards got out of the vehicle and I heard the rear door being opened and closed followed by the rustle of them changing their clothes. At one point I was hoisted into a sitting position and instructed, or so I thought, to take off my sodden jacket and shirt. It transpired that I was either mistaken or too slow in carrying out this instruction as I received a sharp blow with a fist to my head – again stars – accompanied by a Georgian curse, and was pushed back into my original position on the floor of the mini-bus. Wooden slats were placed over the windows of the vehicle making it totally dark within, and my blindfold was removed, the journey continued. I was excruciatingly cramped, cold and mentally scoured by a mounting sense of hopelessness and dread.

A few hours later the vehicle halted at some kind of control post, as I heard the driver talk to someone outside the vehicle and money evidently changed hands. The mood of my three captors changed immediately. Vodka and cigarettes were produced, and Sasha made a cynical comment in Georgian that only ten *lari* (about five dollars) was needed to "please the police." Laughter, chatter and a general mood of celebration ensued. Maybe I should have called out at the control post. On reflection, I don't think it would have been helpful; I'd just have had another beating. Once I tried to twist my body around so that I was facing my captors sitting on the back seat. I almost succeeded and tried to catch a glimpse of their faces in the lights of oncoming traffic. All three placed their hands over their faces, and were obviously aware of my intentions. As soon as the traffic passed they proceeded to boot me until I was forced to turn over and resume my original position.

The vehicle stopped later in broad daylight. I was masked and handcuffed again to Serge who pulled me out of the vehicle. It was hot and sunny and we were obviously somewhere in the mountains; I heard the roar of a rushing river, and smelled coniferous trees. The air was fresh and clean, in contrast to my miserable condition. Serge gestured that I was to "Shshsh," I was given a cigarette and made to stand still as they loaded the rear of the vehicle with jerry-cans of fuel. The clanging of metal and the smell were unmistakable. My clothes, although still damp, had dried out somewhat and I was no longer shivering, but I was very thirsty. The mood of the people around me was still self-congratulatory; they were excited and a lot of banter was being exchanged.

As I stood quietly listening, I received a number of slaps to my face and head. I had developed a technique of lifting the bottom of the balaclava mask above the level of my mouth, enabling me to inhale more deeply and to peek underneath the bottom edge of the blindfold. This was noticed, and the next thing I knew was that someone – I think Sasha (2) – was trying to tie some string around my neck, thereby preventing me from lifting the blindfold. He was stopped by Serge who simply said "Ara, ara" – "No, no." Sasha (2) stopped tying the string. I asked for water and was given vodka instead, which I spat out. I heard the voice of Sasha in English, "You want water, eh?" and freezing cold water was poured over my head. I started to shiver uncontrollably again. My three captors were showing off to the newcomers who had sat in the front of the mini-bus. Showing off is typically Georgian. I'd seen many instances in meetings of Georgian officialdom where a superior would verbally berate a colleague into abject submission. The point was to illustrate the power and control they exerted over me, while at the same time making me very much aware that I should behave and co-operate. I didn't appreciate their methods.

After about half-an-hour, I was bundled back into my space in the vehicle and the long drive continued. My blindfold balaclava was not removed. I was now frightened. This was a long journey, so was I being taken to Adjara? Adjara was a small semi-autonomous breakaway state in the far west of Georgia which was governed by a Papa Doc figure named Aslan Abashidze – no friend of Shevardnadze and his regime. Entrance and exit to and from Adjara were strictly controlled by the so-called Government of Adjara and I had heard of kidnap victims who had been taken there and hadn't been seen or heard of since. Was I destined to join those who'd been lost forever? All hopes of being returned to Tbilisi had been completely dashed. I'd been driven for many hours in the opposite direction, and the attitude of my captors toward me was becoming more abusive as their confidence, and sheer delight in their achievement, increased.

Chapter Twenty-three

A few hours later the mini-bus again drew to a halt. I was pulled out and handcuffed to Serge. My still wet blindfold was removed and a dry one placed over my head. No one spoke as I was led away from the vehicle, half-carried up some steps and through a door, dragged over a wooden floor, and pushed on to what turned out to be a small, soft bed. The handcuff was removed from the wrist of Serge, I was undressed down to my shirt and underpants and handcuffed by my wrist to the metal bed-frame. I heard the sound of a door closing and I was left alone.

I moved my head. This blindfold was different. Normally all is darkness save perhaps for tiny pin-pricks of light through the thick material. Now, as I looked around I could make out the shapes and forms of surrounding walls and furniture. But as my head moved, the shapes moved too, like wisps of smoke and mist in black and white. I felt a surge of panic. This was something I hadn't experienced before. I tried to tell myself that I was knackered, and not thinking or feeling right. Was I perhaps going mad? I carefully lifted the bottom of the mask, and caught a glimpse of tapestries on wooden walls and two other beds across a neat carpeted room. It seemed a pleasant room. Then a sharp pain and again I saw stars. I'd been watched, and someone standing behind me had given me a blow to the top of my head. I heard the voices of Sasha (2) and Serge as they entered the room; I saw in a diffuse cloud of shapes someone lifting what looked like a baseball bat and place it on my naked shins. The bat was lifted two or three times, each time it rested on my shins for a few seconds. They were going to break my legs!

I panicked and yelled to the person I instinctively thought might help. "Serge, what's happening?" He responded from behind me in English, "Fuck you." The shape holding the bat melted away and a voice said, in perfect BBC English in my right ear, "I'm awfully sorry about this," and chuckled. Footsteps moved away and a door closed again. A few minutes later, someone re-entered the room and, standing behind me, removed the balaclava blindfold from my head, walked away and closed the door.

What the hell was going on? I knew I was physically and mentally exhausted, very frightened and cold. I'd been traumatised by my forced descent of the mountain and by the horrendously long and cramped journey. I'd felt sick when I'd realised that I wasn't going to be released, and I still felt sick and wanted to urinate badly – a symptom of fear that I knew well by now. Where on earth was I now? Clearly a long way from Tbilisi, perhaps somewhere the authorities had no chance of finding me? I knew that I was knackered and that my imagination might be playing tricks on me, so I must be careful. I tried to reason that my kidnappers' purpose might be to frighten me; to deter me from trying something. Also, I could hear voices, muffled but distinct, ebbing and flowing as they approached the door of my room and moved away again. This house was inhabited by a family. I could pick out the voices of at least four people, including some elderly people. If the intention had been to frighten the shit out of me, they'd certainly succeeded.

Later that evening, I swear I heard English voices in conversation in the distance. One voice said in a plummy accent, "Have you heard anything about this hostage business?" I couldn't hear all of the response, apart from the words "but he seems to be secure." This made no sense at all. English voices – no way! Could English people be involved in my abduction? Surely my addled mind was playing tricks on me. Some minutes later, the voice of Sasha called out for "Eka." It occurred to me later that this could be the name of the lady mistress of the house, but at the time my thoughts turned immediately to Eka of the Ovatio restaurant and the tune whistled by Sasha in the tent the previous night. Could she, or her husband or boyfriend, somehow be involved in all of this? It was not possible surely; there were thousands of Ekas in

Georgia, but these thoughts and their ramifications returned to me over and over again. I began to shiver, whether from cold or fear I don't know. I looked around and tried to take stock of my situation.

I was in a little, neat bedroom that contained two other small beds in addition to my own. The walls, floor and ceiling were of pinewood, the floor partly carpeted and the walls covered in tapestries. There was a pine sideboard, the shelves of which contained tea-sets and crockery. There were two windows, one behind me and one above the bottom of my bed. Pretty floral curtains were drawn on both windows but, because the material was thin, some sunlight filtered through into the room. The entrance to the room was by a closed door behind my right-hand shoulder. I stretched as far as the handcuff would allow toward the bottom of my bed, and was just able to pull back part of the curtain and peek through the window. What a view! I saw a series of high, rolling hills under a deep blue sky; below was a pretty valley containing a small farm, with agricultural implements in its yard and a small attractive chalet next-door. It was a truly idyllic scene and reminded me immediately of the Jura Mountains near the Swiss border with France, where I'd spent many a happy camping holiday over the years with my family.

I guessed I was in the *Borjomi* region of central Georgia. I'd recently visited that area on a couple of occasions with a view to opening a sub-branch of the ABG in the main town there. Certainly the contoured hills and the steep valleys viewed through the window were very like those which I'd seen on my visits to Borjomi. Additionally, I'd often visited the family home of my faithful translator, Ilia, in Borjomi, and they'd made me feel very welcome in typical Georgian style. It was somehow comforting to feel that Ilia's family might be nearby. I crawled under the mattress for warmth and dozed off.

I awoke sharply. Someone had come into the room. It was still daylight and a young, slightly-built male, masked and wearing jeans and a T-shirt was standing over me. Silently, he held out his hand and I shook it, very cautiously. He moved away to the sideboard, collected some dishes and left the room. Soon afterwards, I heard the door open slightly, and felt, rather than saw, that someone was looking into the room at me. I tried to turn my head around, but the door was abruptly closed and footsteps moved away. I heard the sounds of a table being laid in an adjacent room, and smelled meat being cooked. I was hungry now and no longer cold. Soon, there were the sounds of people talking around a table and glasses clinking; the voices became louder as the meal went on, but I couldn't hear the words, though the language was clearly Georgian. I was able to make out one female voice and several male voices, including the distinctive tones of Sasha and the gruff tones of an elderly man. After about an hour, the boy returned wearing a mask. He deposited a bowl of potatoes and mutton on my bed together with a mug of tea, and left without saying a word.

I ate ravenously as darkness fell. Within a few hours, Sasha came in holding a torch and a chamber-pot, dressed in civilian clothes but masked as usual. Saying nothing, he deposited the chamber-pot under my bed, lurched onto one of the other beds and within minutes was asleep. I too fell into a deep sleep.

As I slept I dreamed. I dreamed of the trips that Mair and I had taken to north Wales on my motor-bike when we were courting as teenagers. On one occasion, we'd climbed Cader Idris and I remembered I was nervous. I was never comfortable with high places, even on the Welsh hills. On the way there, we stayed at a small hotel in Tregaron and had to sleep in separate bedrooms, which we could ill afford. Welsh Methodist tolerance didn't stretch to unmarried couples sharing a bed in those days. Next stop was a little B&B in Porthmadoc costing the princely sum of £4 per night for both of us – but again separate bedrooms. Years later, we honeymooned at the Royal Goat Hotel in Beddgelert. On the first night of our honeymoon I joined a male choir who were practicing in the hotel. By the time I got to bed, very drunk and very late, Mair was fast asleep. So much for romance! We couldn't afford to stay at the Royal Goat for the whole week of our honeymoon and half way through had to decamp to a cheaper hotel in the Llanberis Pass. From there we tried to walk up Snowden, but my nerve failed at the most precarious bit and I scurried back down the track. Mair was very understanding. After all, we'd known each other since we were both sixteen years old.

I awoke to the sounds of someone noisily hammering and a dog barking. Both sounds seemed to come from close-by outside the house. I glanced around, Sasha was not in his bed, so I tugged back the curtain of the window at the bottom of my bed; the same view, but no people in sight and no sign of a dog. Voices came from an adjacent room and within a few minutes Sasha appeared, masked as usual and wearing a tee-shirt and jeans. He was in good humour and seemed to want to talk.

"This good?" he asked, spreading his arms. I mumbled, "Yes," nodding my head vigorously. Taking advantage of his good mood, I tried to question him, slowly, using short, easy words, "When will I go home? Is there news from my family?" There seemed no harm in trying, Sasha simply repeated his stock response, "In four, five days, you go home. No variant." Arms crossed over his chest – the usual nonsense. Surprisingly, he launched into a disjointed outburst which had clearly been discussed and rehearsed beforehand.

His speech, long and laborious, was to the effect that he and his colleagues were well aware of the business of the European Commission in Georgia. They knew it was the intention of the foreigners to steal money from the Georgian people, as they had, he said, in Kosovo and all over the world. He and his friends were also aware of the bad business of the British aid agency, the *Know How* fund, and the desire of the British also to steal money from Georgia, all the time he was wagging his finger in my face, lecturing me. He then suggested to me, in a friendly manner, that I should appear on Georgian television, and tell the people of the real intentions of these institutions; explain how these thievings were being achieved with the connivance of the European ambassadors in Georgia and President Shevardnadze. He could arrange this without problem. I explained that I knew nothing of this. To the contrary, I said, the real intentions were to help the people of Georgia, and certainly not to steal; if he believed otherwise then he was misinformed.

That was a mistake. His mood changed, he slapped me on the face twice, hard, and left, slamming the door behind him. He talked loudly and angrily in an adjacent room, presumably explaining to his companions that I'd refused to co-operate. He returned within an hour to demand that I give him the telephone number of someone – *a big man* – in the European Commission in Georgia. I knew by heart the mobile phone number of Jacques Vantomme, number two at the Delegation in Tbilisi, and a personal friend of mine. I gave him Jacques' number. He seemed satisfied, nodded and left.

Later that day the hammering sounds ceased; Sasha (2) appeared, masked and wearing military uniform, and fed me, explaining quietly in Georgian each individual component of the meal to me. He gave me a cup of very weak tea and a bottle of water. He seemed friendly enough and keen to educate me in the culinary skills of our hosts. I thanked him and he left.

I was alone for the remainder of the day, handcuffed to the frame of the bed, and no one came to guard me that night. Before falling asleep I heard the sound of music from a room above me. An old Ella Fitzgerald album was being played. These people, whoever they were, had good taste in music. This was definitely one of the Ella *Songbook* recordings of the late 50's. My mind roamed back to the eighties when I had seen Ella live at Ronnie Scott's club in Frith Street, Soho. She was then a little past her prime and in ill-health; but she was still tremendously impressive. At the end of her first set she bowed to acknowledge the applause, blew a kiss to the audience and murmured appreciatively "Thank you, you're beautiful!" Someone in the audience yelled back, "No. You're beautiful!" and the place erupted. She sang like a twenty-five-year-old and brought the house down. My friends and I left the club that night knowing that we had experienced something very special. What a contrast!

Chapter Twenty-four

I woke up early the following morning with an urgent need for a shit. Fortunately, Sasha appeared without my having to call out and I explained I wanted to go to the lavatory. He shook his head and told me that I had been two days earlier. I demurred; I hadn't gone since we were in the tent. He sat quietly for a few minutes then left the room. About one hour later – it seemed like a week – he re-appeared with Sasha (2). They proceeded to dress me in military trousers and boots, and draped a military coat over my head and shoulders, pulling it down over my eyes. The handcuff was released and I was propelled from the bed, held tightly under each arm, through the door, over a wooden floor, down wooden steps and across a yard. The dog was barking loudly again from very close by but I could see nothing. It sounded like a little dog.

We stopped, the coat was removed from my head, some coarse paper was thrust into my hand, I saw a dilapidated timber building. Sasha gestured that I was to go inside, accompanied by Sasha (2) holding my arm. It was an old cow-shed with feeding troughs along the side of the wooden wall. Sasha (2) stood by the entrance while I proceeded to squat over a trough.

We returned the same way as we had come, and I indicated that I wished to wash my hands. As we crossed the wooden floor, I was led to a sink and a tap was turned on. The coat was again removed from my head, and I proceeded to wash my hands and dunk my head under the tap. This was the first real wash I'd had since my capture some two weeks earlier. I stole a glance around me; we were in a long pine-walled scullery with a stove to my left, above which, pots and pans hung on the walls. By Georgian standards, everything looked in extremely good nick. I was given a clean towel to dry myself, pushed through the door into my bedroom, handcuffed to my cot and left alone. Physically, I felt much better.

That night was strangely quiet. The hammering had stopped again, but the dog continued to bark sporadically. I had figured out, by listening to the voices in the rooms nearby, the inhabitants of the place. In addition to the two Sashas, there was a family of four, an old man and lady, and perhaps their son and grandson. The youngster I guessed was the boy who appeared in my room during my first day there, and had, apparently, good taste in music. Each day, a vehicle departed from the yard at about seven o'clock in the morning and returned twelve hours later. I wondered whether the son, the father of the young one, might have driven a mini-bus for a living, perhaps the one that had transported me there; or maybe he was simply driving to work each day. In any event, I heard no voices in conversation that first night, just Ella singing.

Then, without warning came the loud stamping of heavy footsteps up a wooden staircase, a male voice raised in excited interrogation and a loud response "Niet!" There followed the din of many people running on the wooden floors of surrounding rooms, some shouted instructions, and metallic sounds, which I recognised as guns being loaded, then an eerie silence. This silence lasted for about twenty minutes, followed by a babble of male voices breaking out in erratic loud conversations throughout the house. I couldn't make out which language they were speaking, but I certainly heard the Russian "Niet" and not the Georgian "Ara." Gradually the rumpus faded away and the building became quiet again. Ella had stopped singing.

I thought about these strange noises throughout the night. Could it be that the authorities were looking for me; had they been close to finding me, hence the alarm being raised? Had Sasha tried to contact Jacques Vantomme using the phone number I had provided? Had the authorities been able to trace the call to the locality in which I was being held? Were they now preparing for an armed conflict? It was impossible to sleep and my heart pounded away. Something was going on.

The following day all was quiet again. I was visited only once by Sasha (2) who brought me some rice pudding, tea and water and said nothing. I remained alone for the entire day and night, handcuffed to my cot. I heard voices in the distance, but there was no hammering now. There was no Ella either; the only noise was the occasional yapping of the dog.

Chapter Twenty-five

The next day, Sasha (2) appeared in mid-morning with rice pudding, an apple, tea and water. My request to have a shit was refused, and my attempts at conversation were rejected. I heard the voices of the family occasionally in a room nearby and the dog still barked in the yard. Otherwise, all was quiet.

That night, I was awoken by the two Sashas, both dressed in military uniform and wearing their balaclava masks as usual. My own tattered trousers, socks and shoes were handed to me and I was released from my handcuff to the cot. A large coat was draped over my head and I was taken again across the scullery floor, down the wooden steps and firmly guided across the yard, one to each arm. It was very dark. There was no conversation, just the barking of the dog.

A wooden door was opened, a short walk, then another door. Someone shone a torch, and I was deposited on a wooden cot, over which was draped some kind of material, and pushed down flat. I was handcuffed to something above my head, and I saw by the torchlight that Sasha had stretched out on a cot a metre from mine. Sasha (2) disappeared, the torch was extinguished and there was complete darkness. There was no conversation and my companion quickly fell asleep. I did not.

As dawn broke I was gradually able to see something of my surroundings. I was in a small wooden shed. The only light came from one window over which some sacking had been draped, but some chinks of sunlight percolated through. Both Sasha and I were lying on separate makeshift timber cots – hence the hammering I had heard earlier; I guessed they had been constructed over the past few days. Sasha had a mattress of sorts, I had an old anorak, there were no bedclothes, but I wasn't cold. I was handcuffed to a strut of timber leading to the roof, around which a chain had been passed, the handcuff had been inserted into a link in the chain. The walls of the shed were lined with wooden shelves on which were rows of jars and bottles containing a variety of preserved fruits. The floor was of timber and there was a wooden door facing the bottom of my cot.

I could stand up and move from my bed up to a distance of about one metre. Sasha heard me doing this and woke up. Glancing in my direction, he arose, went out and re-appeared with a bucket which he placed next to my cot. It contained a layer of sawdust on the bottom. This was my toilet. Sasha again went out, closing the door carefully behind him, but for a brief second I glimpsed an adjoining long room into which sunlight intruded through the roof and walls. This extension to the shed was also timber built and lengths of timber were stacked up alongside a narrow through-way leading to another door which I assumed led into the yard. I heard the second door creak as it closed on a latch and I was left alone.

Sasha (2) appeared a few hours later with macaroni, tea and water. Nothing was said, but he checked the handcuff, notched it on a little more tightly and went out. I was again alone.

This became the routine for the following four days. Each morning, one of the Sashas would enter the shed at about 11.00am and take away the bucket, which would be immediately returned duly washed and with a fresh layer of sawdust on the bottom. An hour or two later, one of them would bring me food, usually accompanied by tea and always with a plastic bottle containing water. Sometimes, one of them would stretch out for an hour or two on the cot during the daytime, but only once after the first night did one of them stay with me overnight. There was virtually no conversation: no response to my repeated questions.

I spent hours each day parading up and down within my one metre quadrant – about two steps forward and two steps backward. I also was able to exercise by doing push-ups on the cot – I got up to about one hundred per day – and around sixty squats per day. Flies and mosquitoes found their way into my small space and became a nuisance, but no more than that. In daylight hours I could see quite clearly my surroundings, and, now that the hammering had ceased, I could hear.

I picked up the sound of working machinery some distance away, and occasionally, particularly after rain, the sound of running water – a river. I surmised that the machinery might be dredging equipment used in taking sand or gravel for construction purposes from the river. This tied in nicely with my theory that I was in the Borjomi region; I'd seen these dredgers at work when I'd been there previously. I could also hear the sound, usually twice each day, of a train passing in the distance, but only very occasionally could I make out the noise of road traffic. I heard the diesel engine of the mini-bus starting up each morning and returning each night, but only very occasionally the faint drone of passing traffic, and then usually a tractor. I reasoned that wherever I was being held, it was a pretty isolated part of Georgia.

During my second night in the shed, a number of vehicles arrived in the yard and a number of male voices mumbled in conversation. As the night wore on, the voices grew louder, interspersed with bursts of raucous laughter. They were obviously drinking. Suddenly the door to my shed was flung open, and Sasha appeared, masked, holding his torch and gently swaying. He squatted near my cot and demanded that I give him the telephone number of my son, Rhodri, in the UK. This was a new demand. I explained as calmly as I could, that I didn't know his number, that he'd recently moved apartment in London, and that his new number was in my mobile phone, long since destroyed. This was true. He then demanded Mair's phone number again. I explained, clearly, that he'd already received this information. He waved his arms around impatiently and fisted me on the top of my head. I gave him the number. I saw no point in refusing. He disappeared, slamming the door loudly behind him.

My thoughts drifted inevitably to my family in the UK, especially to Lisa, who was due to give birth to my third grand-child in September. Would I ever see them again?

Sasha re-appeared late that night even more drunk than before and launched into a totally incomprehensible spiel. He had obviously been fired up by drink and the company he had just left, and kept repeating that he and his friends "well knew of the bad business that Peter Shaw and his friends from the European Union were doing in Georgia." He spat in my direction, shook his fist at me, fell on his cot and was immediately asleep. He slept until quite late the following morning and was awoken by the sound of my chain rattling as I undertook my limited daily walk. He stared at me wordlessly. Minutes later Sasha (2) appeared and they both left the hut and entered into a muted conversation in the yard. Later, Sasha (2) re-appeared with my food – macaroni and potatoes and a bottle of water. I indicated that the pressure of the handcuff had made my right wrist sore, and asked him to handcuff me by the left wrist. He did this, departed, returning shortly afterwards to take away my breakfast dishes. I hadn't heard the vehicles departing and assumed that my captors' friends were still around, probably sleeping off the excesses of the night before. The only sound was the constant yapping of the dog and the distant hum of working machinery.

I still had my watch on my left wrist. Amazingly, it still worked. Perhaps because of the watch, Sasha (2) had not ratcheted up the handcuff on my wrist as tightly as usual. Following an old rugby injury, I have the ability to bend back the thumb on my left hand. By wetting my hand and wrist with water, I could work the handcuff off my wrist. I did this a couple of times to make sure it wasn't a fluke, and then thought seriously about escaping. Could I really get away? The idea terrified me, but I knew I had to try.

The vehicles had still not departed, although it was now late morning. Sasha's friends must be around somewhere, or had they left during the night? Surely I would have heard them. Should I try and make a break for it now, and head in the direction of the machinery? The sound of it droned on temptingly in the distance. Or should I wait until darkness? But the operators would surely have gone by then. And what if one of the Sashas decided to stay in the shed that night? There was no way of knowing what they would do. The problem was always going to be the dog; but as the animal barked incessantly anyway, would anyone pay any attention to it? I had to do something. No point in sitting here. I decided to give it a go.

I opened the door – it creaked noisily – and walked on tip-toe along the narrow boardwalk of the adjoining timber shed toward the main exit. On both sides of me were rows of stacked raw timber, but plenty of light entered from cracks in the wooden walls and ceiling. I could see my way to the door. I peered through large cracks in the door and saw clearly into the yard. There was the door to the main house to my right, reached by the short wooden staircase. I couldn't see the end of the house, but guessed the yard continued past the door towards the road. I had to cross that yard to get to the road. I could hear but not see the dog, but I knew that when I opened the door it would make a creaking noise; I'd heard it. That would cause the dog to become excited and bark louder. I retraced my steps back to my cot and thought about it.

Logically, I knew I should wait for darkness, but there were too many imponderables. Also, I didn't know anything of the geography of the yard or roadway to the right of my exit door, so it had to be easier to make a run for it in daylight. At least I could see where I was going, and head in the general direction of the machines, still chugging away. I decided it had to be done now: no point in waiting for darkness. Opening the door again, I passed quietly through the main body of the timber shed. I worked the wooden handle of the main door very slowly and it opened surprisingly easily, making only a low groaning sound. Glancing to left and right, I saw three cars parked in the yard to my right, a gate beyond them, and then the road. There was no one in sight. The bloody dog barked but I couldn't see it.

I darted through the door and ran as fast as I could to my right without looking in any direction but straight ahead. I sprinted toward the long wooden gate and narrow road. The dog barked excitedly; its volume had increased but it wasn't chasing me and must have been chained somewhere in the yard. That was good news. I vaulted over the gate – a low one – and ran like hell down a narrow, badly made roadway that went initially alongside, then behind the house and into the valley below. I assumed this was where the river and the machinery would be. My legs felt like jelly and I could hear my heart thumping. Don't panic, don't think, just run. As I hurtled pell-mell down the lane I was conscious that I'd passed a gateway that led into a field on my left. Immediately afterwards, there was a hole in the hedge to my right where it seemed there may once have been a gate that led through a field back up toward the house. I don't know why I stopped running. I'd heard no sounds behind me, but somehow I knew that if I made for the river and the machinery, that would be too obvious a destination. When my absence was discovered, my guards would surely also head in that direction. It seemed logical. I had to do something different.

And so I stopped, retraced my steps, and worked my way through the hole in the hedge I'd previously noticed, and burrowed deep into the base of the hedgerow surrounding the field. There were no animals in the field, just long grass and shrubs on a steep slope leading to the rear of the house. As I lay there trying to collect my breath and my thoughts, I reasoned that the last place anyone would search for me would be near the house. They would surely assume that I'd try and distance myself as much as possible from them and the shed in which I'd been held. They would probably reason I'd gone down the road. They had vehicles and would definitely use them to search for me; they might not think of going on foot and looking close to home. There had to be somewhere in the vicinity of the house where I could hide for a few days. Then they might call off the hunt; I could subsequently approach the machinery men, or jump a train. But first I had to find somewhere safe to hide.

I lay there for a few hours. I knew I should wait until darkness fell, but I was too impatient. I couldn't keep still. I reasoned that as there was still no sign of my being missed, with a bit of luck they might not find out until the following morning. In the meantime, where could I hide? I felt too vulnerable under the hedge, so I began to crawl slowly through the long grass up the field in the direction of the house.

Amazingly, I didn't feel frightened, just exhilarated by my new-found freedom, and quite confident that I was following the right course of action. The trick was to find a good place to hide, and just be patient for a day or two. But I must do it quickly before I was missed; I had to take a chance that my luck would hold. I rose to my feet and sprinted fast for about forty metres toward the house and then dropped down into the grass again. As I ran, I could see the complex of timber sheds, in one of which I had been kept prisoner. The sheds were supported on this side by wooden stilts, and the covered area underneath the buildings was being used to store planks of timber and logs, the latter presumably used as firewood during the winter. This seemed to be a pretty good place to hide, but I'd best wait for darkness before making my final move – only fifteen metres to reach the shelter of the buildings. I lay motionless in the long grass.

Time passed very slowly; every small sound was magnified. I was restless and twitchy. Eventually, as dusk began to fall, I could stand it no longer, and without any attempt at subterfuge, I bolted for the timber-shed. The barking of the dog became louder but I ignored it and kept on running. I arrived safely. I was right: there was plenty of room to hide among the layers of timber and logs beneath the floor of the building. I wriggled deep inside, wedged myself in as tightly as possible and lay there panting for breath.

Darkness fell, and there was still no sign of my being missed. My mind raced, and for the first time the full enormity of what I had done came over me in waves of self-doubt. What would they do if they found me? At best I could expect a good hiding. Would they be angry enough to pop me off? Whatever, it was too bloody late now. All I could do was lie there, stay quiet and hope for the best. All the same, I was very frightened.

At about 11.00pm, I heard the sounds of male voices in the distance, and the scuffle of footsteps in the yard. Doors opened and were banged shut; people were entering and leaving the sheds; the dog yelped wildly; the gate was opened and closed continually; there were crunching noises of boots on the rough road. Gradually but inexorably, torch beams approached the space underneath the shed in which I was hidden; male voices speaking quietly were coming closer toward me. I wriggled myself deeper into the recess. One torch beam penetrated into my hiding place, and two hands grabbed my ankles and dragged me out.

They said nothing; the only sound was that of my own heavy breathing. A mask was pulled roughly over my head and I was yanked to my feet; two hands under each arm propelled me around the side of the shed and manhandled me roughly over a wooden fence, then into the timber-shed. I was thrown on my back on to the cot, handcuffed very tightly by my right wrist to the stanchion around which the chain and padlock was still attached, and my mask was removed. By the light of two torch beams, I made out the masked and uniformed figures of the two Sashas standing over me, still no words, just heavy breathing.

They beat me with their fists and feet over every part of my body apart from my face. It went on for what must have been ten minutes, but seemed like ten hours. They pummelled me on my back, legs, arms, head, buttocks and ribs. I must have yelled and struggled but I can't remember. All I remember is the pain, then nothing. I must have blacked out. I recall waking up, scrunched into a ball, unable to move or straighten my body, with a throbbing headache, and pain everywhere. I slowly checked my anatomy for any breakages, and struggled to sit up on my cot and take stock. My over-riding emotion was a deep sense of gratitude that I was alive. Strangely, I felt a lovely warm feeling inside. Also, I was alone, and the half-empty bottle of water was still on the floor next to my bed. Warm water never tasted so good. About an hour later, Sasha entered, fully uniformed and masked, glanced in my direction, waved his fist at me and lay down wordlessly on his cot. I pretended to be unconscious or asleep and simply lay there motionless. I don't think either of us slept that night, but I moved not a muscle for the following six hours.

I thought long and hard that night, on how they'd managed to find me as quickly as they did. It may have been the dog that alerted them, but I think not. I eventually concluded that I'd been seen by one or more of the gang as I attempted my escape – not surprising as I'd hardly tried to hide. They'd probably been unwilling to show themselves in broad daylight, openly pursuing me down the lane. I'd obviously chosen the wrong option: I should have headed for the sound of the machinery and sought help from the men who worked it. My captors must have been delighted when they saw my futile efforts to conceal myself in the field, and then saw me return stupidly toward the out-buildings to try and hide. They must have laughed their socks off as they watched me crawl under the shed, just across the yard from where they sat. But, strangely, I didn't feel as wretched as I ought. I'd tried and failed badly, but at least I'd tried. It made me feel better.

Sasha stayed with me in the shed all through the next day, leaving me only for a few minutes at a time. I heard the departure of his friends at about ten o'clock in the morning and the low murmur of voices bidding their farewells. The routine during the day was as usual, apart from the lingering presence of Sasha. I was fed and watered as normal, and allowed to walk – if you can call it that – within the compass of my chain. I felt as though I'd been run over by a bus. Every bone and muscle in my body was sore and my teeth hurt. I was becoming increasingly concerned about my teeth. I'd been able to clean them only with my finger and shirt sleeve since the day of my capture. I'd repeatedly asked both Sashas for a toothbrush, but both had refused. I hadn't shaved since the 18th June and, apart from swilling my head under the sink some days earlier, no other part of my anatomy had been washed. I was beginning to stink, but there was nothing I could do about it. For someone who is fastidious about personal hygiene, I'd become surprisingly pragmatic about such things. I'd come to terms mentally with the fact that, if I could do nothing about it, there was no point in dwelling upon it.

Off and on during that day I made several attempts to strike up a conversation with Sasha but to no avail. All he would say was "Shshsh" and wag his finger warningly in my direction and make a fist. He was obviously pissed off with me, which somehow made me feel a little better, but at the same time he was restless – he couldn't stay still – and I could see that he was worried and concerned. Good enough for him. I was pissed off with him, too!

During the late afternoon Sasha (2) returned, checked the handcuff was still tight on my wrist, and spoke quietly in Georgian with his boss. He spoke too quickly for me to understand, but I did make out the words *"Erte kwira"* – Georgian for "one week." They spoke for about ten minutes then both left the hut, leaving me alone with my thoughts. Sasha didn't return that night, and, surprisingly, I slept like a log. The following day followed the usual routine. I didn't see Sasha all day, but was fed and watered by Sasha (2) who also checked my handcuff. The only sounds were the drone of machinery and the constant barking of the dog.

Chapter Twenty-six

I dreamed a lot, or rather I had nightmares, the first of which occurred that night. I'd always had a real fear of heights. The Eiffel Tower in Paris or the big dipper in Blackpool were never for me, even as a child. As I grew older, this fear remained, but it had never prevented me from travelling by plane, or crossing bridges by car or train, or traversing high mountain passes in the Alps on holiday. I drew the line at skiing; I couldn't handle the ski-lifts. Now it seemed the longer I was kept in captivity, the worse my vertigo became. I experienced horrific nightmares in which I was being taken to the top of a tall building by my captors – sometimes being forced to climb up scaffolding – and then made to "walk the plank" blindfolded, and falling for ever into oblivion. I'd wake up in a panic, sweating profusely. Sometimes I was on top of the television mast in Tbilisi; another time being held by the legs from the balcony of my apartment in Tbilisi; yet again being pushed out of a helicopter, always accompanied by the three masked men in military uniform, forcing me to do something which genuinely terrified me. These nightmares are still with me.

I was awoken in the early hours of the morning by Sasha. He was holding a torch to my face, trying to tell me something I couldn't understand. He unlocked my handcuff and indicated that I was to put on my wet shoes and socks. He masked me, threw a coat over my shoulder and led me out of the hut and into the yard. A car engine was running; I was led toward it and pushed into the rear seat. Someone grabbed my arm as I got in; I recognised the smell of Sasha (2). The boss sat in the front passenger seat, and the car moved off.

The journey lasted about half an hour, straight and along a rough road before swinging left. I was aware that other vehicles were moving in front of and behind us, and that people holding torches lined our route; the sound of running water became increasingly louder. We stopped. I was led up wooden steps into a hut, pushed onto a bed and handcuffed to its metal frame, my balaclava mask was pulled off. I was in a small room lit by a paraffin lamp, with rough timber floor and walls. It contained my bed and some bits and pieces of basic furniture. The sound of rushing water was now very loud. I was near a river, apparently in full flow. People were clunking around in an adjacent room, the noises punctuated by male voices in animated conversation. Both Sashas were standing at the foot of my bed, uniformed and masked, staring at me. Sasha said in English, "Sleep, Peter, sleep. Tomorrow you go home. No variant." Arms crossed over his chest. I nodded, turned over on the very comfortable bed and hunkered down. More bullshit, I thought.

Of course, I didn't believe Sasha and I didn't sleep. I was being moved on yet again. Was this because the authorities were still trying to find me and were closing in, or had the occupants of the dacha been frightened by my attempted escape, and instructed my captors to leave pronto? Did the conversation between the two Sashas incorporating the words *"Erte kwira"* have some relevance?

As usual my thoughts turned to my family. How were Diana and Danny managing? Were they safe? How were they managing financially? Really I was the only bread-winner. What was happening to my family in the UK? How were my kids? How was my mam coping, if indeed she was aware that I had been kidnapped? Would my family try and hide this from her? I was sure they would. What was being done, if anything, about the ransom demand? What could be done about it? Who on earth were those responsible for kidnapping me? The usual suspects went through my mind: some disgruntled and particularly nasty customers whose loans had been declined: directors of banks who had blamed me for their banks' demise under the RARP1 project: political and governmental enemies who had long sought control of the ABG...the list of possibilities grew longer and longer the more I thought about it. But what would be the outcome? The ransom demand could not be met, so would frustration lead to my eventual death? But who would benefit then? There was no logic in any of this, but then there never was in Georgia!

Thoughts of my family kept on recurring: memories of our camping and caravanning holidays in the south of France where we drove every summer almost without exception for twenty years. Swimming in the Med – we made sure the three kids took swimming lessons almost from the time they could toddle.

When very young, they were totally fearless in deep water, even though Pip's snorkelling mask – too big for his face – would invariably fill with water. Oblivious to danger, he would carry on diving and search the rocks on the bottom for crabs. I was less certain. No problem until I looked down into a depth of twenty metres or so when my vertigo would kick in and I'd swim frantically to shallower water. The time when Rod, aged about five, got lost on Pampelonne beach near St. Tropez – three hours of panic until a tearful reunion; the time when Pip locked himself in the toilet compartment of the caravan for two hours and finally climbed out through the tiny window; the time when Lisa, aged thirteen, decided to become a vegetarian in the middle of the Alps and the ensuing long search for a suitable restaurant – not too many veggie dishes in those days; the time when I drove the wrong way down a busy one-way street in Bayeux, towing the caravan and provoking the French drivers' usual reactions – much to the delight of the kids. A thousand images passed through my mind: wonderful memories of times past.

The main thing now was to stay alive and look for the opportunity to escape. I went over the mistakes I'd made in my recent attempt. If only I'd made for the river. But then, I was very close to the river now, and the people occupying this hut seem to be in cahoots with my captors. Were the machinery operators also part of the gang? And so it went on in never ending speculation; one silly thought leading to another and ending with the inevitable realisation that I could do nothing about it. I eventually drifted into a fitful sleep.

I was awakened by someone shaking me roughly. I couldn't have been dozing for more than a couple of hours. The room was in darkness, but I could see the moving figures of the two Sashas using their torches to pack large kitbags with various pieces of equipment, including ammunition. They hauled me to my feet, the balaclava mask was placed over my head, and Sasha hustled me through the door, down the wooden steps, and dumped me into the back seat of a waiting car. Sasha (2) was already in the back seat. A short bouncing drive over a rough track followed, accompanied by the loud roar of the river in the background. I was hoisted out of the car, up some steps and rushed across a wooden bridge over the noisy torrent below. They were certainly in a hurry now. Then down some steps and dumped roughly onto the ground. My mask was removed and I was in darkness, sitting on wet grass.

It was too dark to see detail, but I was conscious that there was a third person around in addition to the two Sashas. I could see his silhouette, and hear his voice, he was older and much smaller than my two guards, a little, wiry man. He was not dressed in military uniform and he carried a long pole on which he leaned while carrying out a whispered conversation with Sasha. He wore the standard balaclava mask. After a few minutes I was pulled up to a standing position, Sasha (2) grabbed my arm, and we began to climb up a steep grassy slope. It began to rain heavily. The next four or five hours were among the most physically exhausting that I have ever experienced in my life.

I was dressed in what remained of my working sports jacket, trousers and underpants, socks and shoes and the black shirt provided by Serge, by now badly torn. My shoes – Marks and Spencer's of course – had done sterling service, but were finally beginning to disintegrate. The soles were coming away from the uppers, and provided no purchase whatsoever in the long wet grass. Although no longer masked, I could see virtually nothing. The little man seemed to be in the lead, Sasha (2) was pulling me upwards by the arm, while Sasha the boss, carrying the bulk of the kitbags, guns and an axe, brought up the rear. In minutes I was soaked; within half an hour I was struggling for breath.

The mountain-side was virtually sheer and devoid of any kind of foothold. The small man set the pace and the others were able to keep up. I could not. I fell and slipped continually and before long was forced to climb upward on my hands and knees. If I stopped to recover my breath, as I very often did, then Sasha prodded me from behind with the handle of his axe. As my halts became more frequent, the prods became whacks on my back and backside. When I failed to respond and lay down flat on my face, completely exhausted and gasping for breath, then Sasha simply laid into me with his axe-handle. Somehow I kept on moving. Eventually, the grass mountain became a muddy forested precipice through which the little man in front axed a route, while Sasha continued to beat me ever onwards and upwards with Sasha (2) pulling me by the arm. By now, I was completely out of it. I was stumbling, falling and crawling on hands and knees as if in a dream. I couldn't breathe and my brain had retreated into an inner recess. This was not real. Although I felt the blows, there was no pain: everything was numb.

Finally I could move no more. I simply lay down and remained immobile while Sasha pummelled me with his boots and axe-handle. One blow hit me on the head. I saw a blaze of stars and blacked out. I learned later that my skull had been fractured.

I awoke, lying on my back looking at a deep blue sky. Cold water was being poured over my head and face; I felt sick and had an excruciating head-ache. I attempted to sit up, failed, and fell backward. A few minutes later I tried again, this time succeeding in staying in a sitting position, but all about me was moving around. I sat still and waited for everything to settle down. My tattered clothes were soaked, and I was covered in blood which was still pouring from my scalp. Men were talking in a jumble of Georgian, and cold water continued to be poured onto my head while I shivered uncontrollably. I felt my clothes being tugged off down to my underpants, and I was wrapped in a blanket. Bit by bit I warmed up. I have no idea how long it took them to stop the bleeding. I learned later they'd used cigarette tobacco, which had the desired effect. Somehow they'd pulled, dragged and carried me up the mountain-side to the place where I now sat in a bundled heap. Gradually my head cleared, although the headache did not, and I was able to look around.

It was a warm sunny day and I was sitting in a small clearing in a forest. In front of me, only a metre or so away from my feet was an almost sheer drop. I could just see a small sliver of a river, a long way down, through a gap in the trees. The view had evidently been created by Sasha and his gang who'd cut down the obstructing foliage while I was unconscious. Behind me, the mountain slope continued upward covered by a thick forest. Facing me, across the valley, was a range of high forested hills, the summits of which seemed considerably higher than the place from which I viewed them. Directly behind me, the level of the clearing in which I sat had been raised by a platform of tree branches upon which Sasha (2) sat, cradling his Kalashnikov. He was staring straight at me, his piggy eyes mocking me behind his mask.

Directly behind him, out of the steep face of the mountain-side jutted a huge overhanging rock, about one metre wide and two metres long, under which the various paraphernalia of kitbags, sacks of food, guns, grenades and ammunition had been dumped. A narrow overgrown footpath led past the stone outcrop down the mountain-side, and continued in the opposite direction upward and out of my sight. Birds were singing loudly, and insects were dancing in the warm air. It struck me bizarrely that this would be a smashing place for a picnic. Sasha squatted a few metres away from me, staring fixedly down the mountain.

Every bone in my body ached, but I'd stopped shivering. I saw that my ragged clothes had been draped over branches of trees to dry out. Various sacks, held by the neck with string, which I later learned contained bread and tinned food, were also hanging from trees. The little man who had led us up the mountain to this spot was no longer present; only the two Sashas were now guarding me. No one spoke. I struggled to a standing position, and a wave of nausea passed over me; I vomited. Sasha strode purposefully toward me and said in English, "You, contusion." What a strange thing to say, I thought. He was trying to convey to me that I was suffering from concussion. This was true. "You sleep," he said, and digging a sleeping-bag out of a kitbag, he threw it onto the raft of tree branches. I struggled onto the platform, hauled up by one Sasha, and pushed up by the other. Somehow they got me into the bag, zipped it around me, and shoved an ammunition belt under my head to use as a pillow. "Sleep," shouted Sasha, and I did: like a baby.

Chapter Twenty-seven

When I awoke it was dusk. The two Sashas were squatting in the clearing, unmasked and with their backs toward me, eating. I tried to sit up, and the noise made by the shifting tree branches alerted them into immediately tugging on their balaclava masks. My head had stopped throbbing, but I still felt sick, and my limbs and trunk ached like a giant toothache. Sasha gestured in the direction of the food; I shook my head. Food had no appeal to me. He then launched into the longest attempt at a conversation since my first few days of captivity in the tent. He clearly had something to get off his chest.

"You think we animals. We no animals."

His theme, it became clear, was an attempt to justify the bash on my head that he had inflicted. Labouriously in a mix of English and Georgian, he explained that my refusal to move quickly up the mountain had placed them at great risk. Although, he said, he might respect me, this was business. If we had been seen while climbing the mountain, then we might all have been killed. He warned me several times that if ever again I placed their safety at risk then the consequences for me would be dire. I didn't need to be told this; I'd already received several hidings. "This is Caucasus," he repeated over and over again, smashing his fist into the palm of his hand. This was a man under pressure.

I thought over this outburst as they slept that night. Evidently I had been moved from the dacha because my captors felt threatened. They were clearly very nervous and on edge as we climbed the mountain, although the chance of anyone spotting us in pitch darkness and pouring rain in this desolate place must have been pretty remote. Nevertheless Sasha had been very keen to whack me into continuing exertion. He felt vulnerable. The relief he felt on arriving safely at their destination was reflected in his emotional outburst. No doubt we were miles away from anywhere, but I still clung on to the psychological comfort provided by my gut-feeling that we were in the region of Borjomi – somewhere close to Ilia's parents' home. Moreover, there were obviously a lot more people involved in keeping me captive than just the two Sashas and Serge – and I hadn't seen Serge since the first day in the dacha. I had sensed and heard a lot of people milling around over the past days. Logically, there must be a greater chance of someone breaking rank and snitching to the authorities to claim a reward. Despite my aches and pains, this made me feel a little better.

After they'd finished eating they chatted together quietly, squatting on their haunches, ignoring me completely until well past midnight. They then carried me bodily inside the sleeping-bag to the right-hand extreme edge of the protection of the overhang. Sasha (2) handcuffed me by my right wrist to an adjacent tree. They unpacked their kitbags, placing the contents, ammunition and Kalashnikovs against the cliff face well under the outcrop, and slipped into their sleeping bags, completely protected by the rock. Within minutes they were both sound asleep. I must have dozed intermittently during the night, but was awake at dawn well before my guards. It was a cloudless morning and the mosquitoes were biting with a vengeance. I burrowed into my sleeping-bag for protection until the Sashas awoke at well past 10.00am. Sasha (2) unlocked my handcuff, rummaged around in a kit-bag until he found a pistol, and indicated that I was to follow him down the muddy footpath. I put on the remains of my shoes and although my legs were still pretty well locked up, I managed to slither and slide in the mud after him.

About thirty metres down the track, we came to a spring gushing out of the mountainside. I took off my underpants and washed properly for the first time since the day of my kidnap. Sasha (2) even produced a bar of soap. I gestured to Sasha that I'd like to shave – by this time I had a long beard – but he shook his head, and simply said "Tbilisi." I wasn't taken in by this, but simply sat in the stream and splashed the clear cold water all over my body.

On returning to the clearing, Sasha was opening a tin of processed meat with a knife. He gestured that I was to eat. I certainly didn't feel like it, but managed to force a bit of tinned meat down with some bread and water, before returning to my sleeping-bag as instructed. Within a few hours my pants, shirt and trousers had dried out and I was allowed to dress in my tatters and sit on the stump of a tree that Sasha (2) had cut down apparently for this purpose.

The mosquitoes were hell. As the day wore on it became hotter and the mosquitoes more vicious. I broke off small branches of foliage to use as fans, but nothing would deter those little devils and, very soon, every exposed area of my flesh was covered in bites. It was extremely painful. My beard provided a certain amount of protection to my face, but I envied the Sashas who now took to wearing woollen gloves all day and, of course, their balaclava masks which gave complete protection to the face and neck. My only relief was to walk around intermittently in the limited space of the muddy clearing, always watched very carefully by at least one of the Sashas cradling his Kalashnikov, while the other dozed.

Before dusk, Sasha again used a knife to open a tin of processed meat which they ate ravenously with their single common fork and which they offered to me, with copious amounts of bread and unlimited water. I ate little, and was led to my sleeping-bag, handcuffed to the tree and told to sleep. They talked together loudly for some hours – there was no attempt now to hide their presence by muted conversation – and sometimes laughed uproariously at a joke or some shared experience of the past. They snuggled down in their sleeping-bags after midnight and were soon asleep. I was left to my convoluted thoughts, and to admire the patterns made by the myriads of fireflies that swooped around the clearing, and the sounds of small animals undertaking their nocturnal activities. Thank goodness, the mosquitoes disappeared shortly after dark.

In the early hours of the morning, it began to rain heavily. I was only partly covered by the overhang and within a few minutes, water was seeping through my sleeping-bag. The bottom end of the sleeping-bag was quite beyond any protection afforded by the overhanging rock and my legs and feet were soon soaking wet. Within an hour a torrent of water was rushing down the slope next to me, and found its way into my bag which quickly became saturated. The Sashas fared better, although they too awoke when it rained heavily. Of course, their munitions and guns took pride of place and had the maximum cover, but their torsos were also protected by the overhang, leaving only their feet vulnerable to the elements. By simply bending their legs, they were able to obtain complete protection from the rock above. Before long they were soon sleeping soundly again.

I lay awake all night, shivering with the cold and wet and longing for daybreak, warmth and the comparative comfort of being bitten by mosquitoes. After what seemed forever, dawn broke, the rain stopped and the mosquitoes dutifully began to bite. I hunkered down into my sodden sleeping-bag. By mid-morning the two Sashas were awake and active. My handcuff was removed and I was allowed to strip off, and hang my clothes and sleeping-bag over nearby tree branches. I was led to my morning ablutions – the toilet was a few metres past the spring on the edge of a small ravine – before returning to the clearing for breakfast of processed meat, bread and tea.

Chapter Twenty-eight

This became the pattern for the following eight days and nights. Invariably, it rained each night, usually severe thunder-storms during which lightning illuminated the mountains facing me, and thunder rolled and reverberated down the valley and into the distance. Sometimes it hailed, producing stones as big and as round as the alley bonkers with which I played as a boy in the school yard. Whether it rained or hailed, I received a good soaking each night. This was followed by the usual routine of sitting on my tree-stump for the first half of the following day; swatting away at the myriads of mosquitoes, wrapped in a filthy blanket, waiting for the sun to dry out my tatters. It was sheer misery. I'd never before imagined that mosquitoes could cause such intense discomfort.

The thought of escaping never left me, but there was really no chance. I was closely guarded at all times, handcuffed to a tree each night, and, even when washing each morning, Sasha (2) kept a pistol pointed very firmly in my direction. I resigned myself to watching and waiting. They couldn't keep me here for ever. My chance would surely come.

It was also extremely boring. Conversation was minimal. Only once did Sasha deign to speak to me at any length, following his first day soliloquy, and then in the absence of Sasha (2) who had disappeared on a scouting expedition up the mountain. He launched into a rambling spiel, which although very difficult to understand, seemed to be some kind of recitation of his life to date. He described his existence as a mercenary soldier as a drug – *opium* – to which he'd become addicted. He would always be a soldier. He loved the forests – his natural habitat he said, in which he and his friends lived like wolves. He made garbled references to his father in Belgrade and to his half-brother, and his intention to visit them when this *business* was over. He repeatedly referred to the strength of the Russian armed forces, reiterated his dislike of *Mussulmen* and mocked the US armed forces, which he described repeatedly as "soft penises". He was very fond of that phrase. He told me how much he envied his friends and colleagues who were now working as mercenaries in South America and Africa, training soldiers, and how, one day, he would join them. He referred to my kidnapping only once.

Sasha described his chief and the organiser of this *business* as a Georgian businessman who resided in France or Spain, and had strong links with the Georgian government. Sasha had never met this gentleman, but he knew that he didn't like him, or this *business*, the kidnapping business, which his chief organised all over the world. When I tried to push gently for more information, he simply said, "Police and government – the same all over world", and lapsed into silence. It was impossible for me to glean any more meaningful information from Sasha. On the few occasions he paid any heed to my repeated requests to shave, or to walk somewhere outside of the confines of the clearing, he would simply repeat the phrase "In five days, you go – no variant!" Any effort on my part to strike up any kind of conversation was met by this stock reply, followed by a snarled "Shshsh," accompanied by either his finger-to-mouth gesture, or a wave of his fist in my direction, depending upon his mood.

Clearly, this life in the great outdoors was not a comfortable existence for anyone. I was suffering, but so too were my captors. True, the two Sashas slept quite well, and were protected from the elements at night, and from the insects by day, nevertheless they were bored and morose. Their days were spent lounging on their sleeping-bags, dozing off in turn, but always ensuring that one of them was awake, or that I was firmly handcuffed to a tree-trunk. They spent a lot of time cleaning their weapons and taking pot-shots at empty meat-cans perched on the branches of surrounding trees. There was no attempt now to minimise the noise; they knew they were safe. Sasha was by far the better shot. He seldom missed his target, while Sasha (2) was far less consistent. Sometimes Sasha (2) amused himself by turning his gun in my direction and pretending to pull the trigger, imitating the sound of the rifle firing – "Boff, boff." He was disappointed when I failed to react. If instead, I showed fear and instinctively raised my arms for protection, he broke into hysterical laughter. On one occasion when Sasha was away for a couple of hours on a recce, Sasha (2) attempted to teach me the words of a Georgian folk-song. I learned quite quickly, and he co-operated enthusiastically when I responded by repeating the words of the Welsh national anthem. This unusual display of affability and curiosity came to an abrupt end when Sasha returned. They were always much more human when alone with me. It didn't happen very often.

By this time I'd lost a considerable amount of weight. I was still suffering the after-effects of the blow to the head and the beatings I'd received, and wasn't eating well. I couldn't keep much food down, and each time I ate, I vomited. My belt no longer held up my tattered trousers. This was noticed by Sasha (2) who substituted it for two pieces of wire which he threaded through the loops of my trousers and twisted, until the loops were drawn together. That belt – Marks and Spencer again – was later, much later, found and traced to me.

Chapter Twenty-nine

During the afternoon of the sixth day at the cave, we had a visitor. I heard a birdcall from somewhere down the track. Sasha (2) also heard it and gestured excitedly that I was to return to my sleeping-bag on the platform of tree branches. He handcuffed me to the tree, ratcheting up the handcuff as tightly as it would go. Both Sashas quickly disappeared down the track and left me alone for about twenty minutes before they returned. Nothing was said to me, but they entered into a long quiet conversation together during which Sasha appeared to be giving instructions to his colleague. They both then ate, as usual, squatting with their masks raised above their mouths and with their backs toward me. I was offered no food. The usual routine was followed during the remainder of the day and night.

The following morning, while sitting on my tree-trunk waiting for my clothes to dry, I again heard the birdcall. Once more I was pushed up on to the branch-platform and handcuffed to my tree while they both disappeared down the track. Within a few minutes they returned, this time accompanied by the little man who had taken the lead in the climb up the mountain. He was dressed in a check shirt with the sleeves rolled up, brown trousers and Wellington boots. He wore a balaclava mask over his head and carried a long stick and a small knapsack. He seemed very agitated. There followed a question and answer session in Georgian for my benefit – they over-rated my understanding of their language, but I got the gist of it.

We would soon be travelling to Tbilisi where I would be released. The little man, who was perched on the tree-trunk while Sasha questioned him in a loud voice, described the situation in Tbilisi as now quite normal; there was no risk to my captors of being nabbed by the authorities. The city was quiet and the hue and cry which followed my kidnapping had now abated. There were a lot of questions on this theme asked by Sasha, to which the newcomer responded with increasing assurances. There would be no problem in Tbilisi. I was to be provided with new boots to replace my dilapidated shoes and taken down the mountain-side. Then I was to be driven to Tbilisi to be released. This was to happen very shortly. The little man confirmed that arrangements had been made for the ransom to be paid. He repeated this statement several times, as though to make sure I'd understood it.

There followed a scene of general rejoicing. Sasha turned to me and shouted, "You go home. We go home," and with his Kalashnikov over his shoulder, arms raised and fingers snapping in the air, he began to dance, Georgian style, in the muddy clearing. He was joined by Sasha (2) while the little man yelled a tune and clapped his hands in accompaniment to the rhythm. It was a totally bizarre scene.

I really didn't know what to make of it all. I wanted fervently to believe what I'd heard, but I'd been so desperately disappointed before. I tried to appear relaxed and called in Russian to Sasha, *"Kogda?"* – "When?" He shouted back, *"Etoi nochu"* – "Tonight," and continued to dance joyfully in the mud. The little man produced a bottle of vodka from his knapsack and poured the contents into four tumblers and offered one to me. I sipped at it gratefully while the others downed theirs in one gulp, whereupon he replenished their mugs and, waving the bottle in my direction, indicated that I should have a re-fill. I declined, but continued to gaze with astonishment at the cavorting of my normally taciturn and unbending guards.

Slowly, they came down to earth. The little man shook hands with everyone, including me, and disappeared down the track. The two Sashas chatted together animatedly with much mutual back-slapping, but eventually, at a relatively early hour, prepared for bed and soon fell asleep. My thoughts raced.

Over the past weeks I'd tried to avoid imagining the joy of being re-united with Diana and Danny, and with my family in the UK. It hurt too much to think about it and made me very depressed. Now, for the first time, I allowed myself to anticipate the thrill of boarding the flight from Tbilisi to

Heathrow with my little Georgian family alongside me, and meeting up at Heathrow with my family and friends in Wales, of going for a pint with my mates, and of returning to normality in the comfort of my little cottage in Cowbridge. I was far too excited to sleep, and although at the back of my mind lurked the thought that the whole performance could again be a charade staged to ensure my co-operation, on the other hand it might this time be true. For now, I allowed myself the mental luxury of believing that it was, and conjured up wonderful scenes of happy reunions and joyful celebrations.

A thunder-storm began in the early hours and it rained non-stop throughout the night. Again I had no sleep, and this time my captors fared not much better. The noise of the thunder was so intense as to make sleep impossible. By morning I was soaked and freezing once again and bitterly disappointed that a trip down the mountain would be out of the question in these conditions. Judging by the surly mood of my guards, they felt pretty sick about it too, but it could have been their hangovers.

The day passed in the normal state of misery and discomfort. The two Sashas barely spoke to each other, and simply lounged on their sleeping-bags, dozing, or cleaning their weapons. Their mood hadn't lifted, and Sasha (2) snapped at me, accusing me of trying to see his face as he was eating. I hadn't, but he was looking for an excuse to lash out and punched my head enthusiastically. As further punishment – and for me much more traumatic – he took my wrist watch.

I depended on the watch to give me a sense of normality and a sense of myself. And, importantly, being able to accurately monitor the days and nights spent in captivity had kept me sane. Apart from what remained of my clothes, the watch was my only link with freedom and my former life. It was a damaging blow to my mental state to have lost it. I would have much preferred a beating.

That night, unusually, it didn't rain, but I still couldn't sleep. I was watching a family of mice scavenging only a few inches from my head, when I heard in the far distance the sound of three prolonged blasts of the horn of a car. Strange, I thought, but dismissed it as a trick of my imagination. A few hours later I heard the now familiar birdcall. Could I really be going home tonight? I nudged Sasha (2) who, as usual, was fast asleep under the overhang. Within seconds, both Sashas were awake and, within minutes, two figures appeared, struggling up the muddy track and into the clearing, carrying electric torches. Both were dressed in civilian clothes and wore balaclava masks. One I recognised as the little man, and the other, who was taller and bulkier, I hadn't seen before.

The clearing quickly became a hive of activity. I was released from my handcuff and pushed onto my tree-stump while the others quickly packed everything into their kitbags. They worked together quietly and efficiently. Within minutes, all had been completed and we were ready to go. My grotty shoes were handed to me – the promised boots hadn't materialised – together with the remains of my jacket, and I was given a long stick by the little man, presumably to provide support. Sasha thrust his masked face into mine, and wagging his finger he said, slowly and clearly in English, "You go home now. Come!" The new man led the way, followed by the little man and Sasha (2), then me, with Sasha bringing up the rear carrying most of the kit. We began to descend the mountain.

Chapter Thirty

It wasn't raining now, but the dirt-track was a quagmire. Quite soon, the track petered out and in pitch darkness the two in front began to hack their way through the forest. The descent was steep, and in places precipitous and my shoes finally disintegrated altogether as the soles came away from the uppers. Although the pole provided some support and I leaned heavily on the shoulder of Sasha (2), this didn't prevent me from slipping and falling frequently, much to the disgust of my guards. Sasha impatiently booted me onto my feet whenever I fell. I was quickly covered in mud, soaked to the skin from the fall of rain water from the trees, and my face was lacerated by the back-lash of branches bent forward by those in front of me. Fortunately for me, while under the canopy of the forest, my companions were prepared to stop frequently for a breather, and I managed to keep up with the pace set by the man in the lead. After some hours of painful but steady progress, the forest gave way to open field.

Although still very dark, the openness of the landscape clearly made my guards very nervous. My feet, by this time, had become very sore, and the two in front became increasingly impatient with me as I stumbled along, falling on them, and knocking them to the ground. Eventually, grabbing a leg each, they dragged me down the slope on my back. After an agonising couple of hours, we reached the bottom of the mountain. I was hauled over a small embankment and pulled and pushed over a timber bridge – the same one I imagine that I'd crossed several days before.

The river below was still full and noisy. Dawn was just about to break, and the sky was lightening slightly. As we came off the bridge, I could see the shapes of a number of vehicles with their boots opened, lined up behind each other. The ghostly silhouettes of four or five people moved around, loading the boots. A mask was hastily placed over my head; I was lifted by the legs and arms, and dumped unceremoniously into the boot of a four-wheel-drive. Someone joined me in the boot, and a few minutes later the vehicle moved off.

This was the start of a journey that was to last from dawn until the early evening of that day. The person who joined me in the boot was Serge. He'd finally re-appeared. He spoke to me in Georgian which I failed to understand, but gathered by his pushing and shoving me that I was meant to turn my body so that I faced the rear partition – between the rear seats and the boot – and that I was not to turn around and face him. He gave me a few fists in the back of my head to reinforce my understanding. The boot was cramped, my body was doubled up, and I was unable to stretch my legs. There was a strong smell of fuel, and I was bounced around between the lid and the floor of the boot as the vehicle gathered pace down a rough track. After about half-an-hour, the going became smoother and I assumed that we had joined a made-up road. This was confirmed by the sound of spasmodic traffic and gear changing becoming less frequent. On two occasions Serge offered me a few pulls on his cigarette, and I was allowed to lift my mask up to nose level in order to insert the cigarette into my mouth. Serge then held the back of my head in his hands to ensure I made no attempt to turn around. This wasn't necessary as I was masked and could see nothing. The driver of the vehicle frequently passed a bottle of water through a small flap in the partition which Serge shared with me. After a few swigs, the bottle was immediately returned. The vehicle stopped three times.

The first was about two hours into the journey when we pulled into a lay-by. The boot was opened very briefly, and just enough to allow Serge to get out. He didn't return. The driver's door was opened, and I heard a muted conversation and the engine noise of at least one vehicle parked behind us. The fuel tank was replenished and the vehicle moved on. With Serge gone, there was more room in the boot compartment. I was still unable to stretch my legs, and was tossed around a great deal as before, but at least I was able to move a little, and off the one side of my body. I could also lift my mask and peek through a small gap in the dividing partition. I could just make out the back of the head of the driver, clearly Sasha (2), with Serge now occupying the passenger seat. Loud Russian rock music was played on the radio.

As the sun rose, I judged that we were heading in a generally easterly direction, the direction of Tbilisi. My hopes rose. Perhaps this time I'd been told the truth and I was really going to be released. Also, we seemed to be driving on main roads and although there was a lot of stopping and starting as we zigzagged our way across road junctions, the general direction was easterly. With the departure of Serge, the supply of cigarettes and water ceased. My wet clothes began to dry out and I became very hot and thirsty. The smell of fuel added to the sensation of light-headedness.

The hours passed slowly and uncomfortably, but I was buoyed up by the hope that we were perhaps truly proceeding in the direction of Tbilisi. As time went by, I began to have doubts. Surely if we were driving over main, or even minor roads, it wouldn't take this long to reach the capital – if I'd indeed been kept in the Borjomi region. As my discomfort increased, so did my doubts. Where then, was I being taken? What did these people have in store for me now? As the surface over which we were travelling deteriorated into dirt tracks, the gear changing increased and our pace decreased, it became clear that the destination was not Tbilisi. I could see through the chink in the partition that we were passing lots of trees; we were moving through a forest. The track undulated, and steep climbs and descents became the norm. On one occasion the vehicle was brought to a halt on a steeply climbing U-turn and with the engine screaming the vehicle was manhandled around the bend. I clearly heard the sound of car doors closing behind us as those that had pushed our vehicle out of the mud returned to their own.

The second time we stopped was about five hours after the first. Although I had no watch now, I was occasionally able to glimpse the sun through the partition and from its position in the sky, roughly gauge the time of day. The vehicle came to a halt, the boot was opened wide, and someone immediately pulled at my mask to ensure that my eyes were completely covered. I was hauled out of the boot and immediately fell down. Two pairs of hands pulled me roughly to my feet, I was kicked in the backside and recognised the voice of Sasha (2) shouting loudly and cursing at me in Georgian. For a fraction of a second, I glimpsed from under my mask the shapes of people milling around, and at least two cars parked behind ours. I was pushed and pulled up a steep embankment and dumped on to my backside. Someone gave me water and a cigarette, and I heard from below the sound of fuel being poured into the tanks of the cars, and voices speaking quietly in Georgian. After about fifteen minutes I was dragged back down the slope, bumping into trees and stumbling over undergrowth, and bundled back into the car-boot.

As soon as the vehicle began to move, I pulled up the mask to breathe more easily and continued peeking through the gap in the partition. Suddenly, and without warning, the partition was pulled back from within the car, and I found myself staring straight into an unmasked face. The face was unshaven, dark, sweaty, swarthy and Georgian, but no one I'd seen before. The lips moved and sneered in perfect English, "So, you are Peter Shaw, the great financier!" His fist hit me hard just below the right eye. I fell backward, stunned momentarily, the face disappeared and the partition was replaced. The bastard, I thought.

We drove on over increasingly bumpy and undulating tracks. I was being shaken around like a pea in a whistle, my head bumped against the boot lid as the car lurched along. I tried to calculate just how far we had travelled on a guesstimate of average speed and number of hours spent travelling. We were still heading generally eastward but even making allowance for our much reduced speed over unmade tracks, we must surely now be somewhere east of Tbilisi. Where the hell were they taking me?

The vehicle stopped again after about three hours, the boot was opened momentarily, the mask secured over my face, and I was pulled out by two people, one to each arm, and, frog-marched over grass and through trees. Deposited roughly on the ground, I was given a cigarette and water and allowed to urinate. My mask was removed, and sitting next to me were Serge, and one other, who I didn't recognise by his build. Both were masked, dressed in military garb and carried the usual Kalashnikovs. I heard in the distance the sound of children's voices, laughing and shouting. It was still broad daylight and very warm. I wondered whether perhaps our convoy had come across a family picnic or a school trip into the forest. The idea leapt into my mind that I could make a run for it in the direction of the children's cries. Something in my body language must have communicated itself to Serge, as he immediately clamped the handcuff on to his wrist and mine. No chance of going anywhere for the time being.

We must have sat there for about an hour, interrupted only by a visit from Sasha who placed his finger to his mouth, and waved his fist under my nose. A string of masked men dressed in normal attire walked nearby, and stared at me out of sheer curiosity. Conversation was limited to the military gentleman on my right, who grabbed my chin, turned my head toward him and punched me in the eye. "That's for looking at my face," he said, in perfect English. I fell backwards. This must be the same one who'd punched me in the car. He really was a bastard.

The voices of children died away and I was tugged to my feet by my two companions, the mask pulled over my head, yanked up by both arms and forced to run blindly through the forest to where the vehicles were parked. I fell, was kicked, pulled up, fell again, kicked again and dumped into the boot of the car. The car moved off.

The journey dragged on interminably, hour after hour. The last stage was a long drag upward in first and second gear with many bends and twists and potholes in the track. Finally, the car stopped, the boot was flung open, my mask checked, and I was manhandled up a steep slope away from the track. This time, my mask wasn't removed, and I was immediately handcuffed to the trunk of a small tree. Sitting next to me, I sensed, were Sasha and Serge, and I think one other. I was conscious of this third presence, but he never spoke and seldom moved. It wasn't Sasha (2): I could always smell him. It was still daylight, Serge smoked incessantly, and offered me the occasional drag. I heard the vehicles below replenish their fuel tanks, and with a farewell toot of the horn from one, they moved away.

Chapter Thirty-one

We sat there for some hours. Sasha and Serge entered into a desultory conversation some distance away from me, but when they moved closer, I was able to pick out and understand certain phrases and sentences. Was this another conversation I was meant to hear and understand, I wondered? Sasha was saying that he had *no problem* with the ransom money of two million dollars. He was sure it would be paid. As for my own personal wealth, he was certain that one half hour with a pistol to my head would persuade me to co-operate. He and Serge then exchanged some kind of joke which made them laugh out loud. They were having a good time. The mosquitoes were biting hard, and although my face was protected by the mask, my hands and legs were quickly covered with bites. They were going for the bare flesh between my trousers and socks. I pulled up the remains of my socks as far as possible, but they still got up my trouser leg. The itching became almost unbearable, and, as had been the case at the cave, my hands, fingers and ankles reddened, and began to swell.

As soon as it became dusk, I heard the din of heavy vehicles moving up and down the track below us. There must have been dozens of them passing along that narrow dirt road. Once only, I lifted my mask for a brief second – and received the usual punch to the back of my head for my pains – but I caught a glimpse of a huge truck towing a covered trailer moving slowly and loudly down the winding road. It was a gigantic vehicle. My guess was that it was a timber-transporter. I was wrong, and learned later, much later, that these vehicles were used to smuggle armaments from Chechnya into Georgia.

We must have sat there for about four hours before darkness fell. Another hour or two passed before I realised that one of these trucks had stopped below us, slightly to our left, and had cut its engine. This had obviously been pre-arranged. I was pulled to my feet and propelled down the slope toward the now stationary vehicle. My captors were clearly in a hurry to get there. On reaching the truck I was lifted into the trailer, Serge promptly stuck my masked face down into some sacks and sat on my shoulders. I could scarcely breathe, but he was taking no chances of allowing me to see anything. The engine clattered into life, and the truck moved away, careered down a steep slope with the engine screaming wildly and entered a narrow tunnel. The noise was deafening as the blare of the engine reverberated against the walls of the tunnel and heavy metal objects crashed around within the covered trailer. All the while, Serge sat on me and made absolutely sure that I was unable to move from my face-down prone position.

The truck stopped, I was lifted out of the trailer and led into a small building, down a short spiral staircase, and dumped into the back of another truck. A short journey, about fifteen minutes, and the truck came to a halt. Again I was lifted out, and, this time, handcuffed to Serge. My mask was removed. It was very dark, but I saw that we'd been joined by a tall, gangly individual wearing the customary military uniform and balaclava mask and carrying a Kalashnikov. Sasha (2) had gone. Had he departed with the convoy of cars that had brought me from the cave? What were they going to do with me now?

The newcomer led the way, followed by Serge then me, with Sasha, as usual, bringing up the rear. We walked quite slowly up a gradual slope in a dried-up river bed. We had passed through a wooden gateway, over which hung a timber canopy bearing letters which I couldn't distinguish. It was like the entrance to an American ranch, as seen in the old western films. All that was missing was the cow-skull complete with horns.

As we climbed upward, I could make out the remains of concrete irrigation channels to the left of the track. We also seemed to be passing an expanse of water, as I could hear the squawks of ducks or geese in the near distance. Gradually and incredibly, the lights of a sizeable village came into view to our right. The houses, unusually, were lit by electric lights. There was also an electricity pylon, its stark silhouette stabbing into the dark sky. We passed within a few hundred metres of the village and the pylon, and I sensed the unease of my guards as the guy in front increased his pace. Sasha, behind me, cursed quietly in Georgian. If only I wasn't handcuffed to Serge, I could have made a run for it. I too cursed quietly under my breath.

After a spell of yomping, the landscape changed into a series of undulating hillocks and small plateaus topped by outcrops of stumpy trees and gorse bushes. I sensed that Sasha and his friends were looking for a place to bed down for the night – they frequently stopped to confer – but the proximity of the village seemed to be a deterrent, and we continued to climb slowly onward and upward, away from the village.

It had become quite cold, with a chilling wind blowing across the barren landscape. I was by now completely knackered; my footwear had long since given up the ghost so that the only remaining part of my shoes was the heel, which somehow still remained attached, the soles simply flapped. My feet were very sore and badly cut. My guards zigzagged their way across the moor. The man in front seemed to have no set objective: he was randomly searching for a place to hide for the night. I sensed the patience of Sasha was wearing thin. Whenever I fell, which was often, I was given an encouraging cuff to the head by Serge. He and Sasha conferred once more and decided to bear to the right, instead of moving directly upward. We stopped briefly at a stream, from which I was allowed to drink, before proceeding on what appeared to be a more permanent road, a dirt track but wider and reasonably well maintained. The track then turned abruptly left and I smelled animals – farm animals.

We moved between buildings on both sides of the track. It was very dark and the outlines were vague, but there was a series of bricked buildings to the left and right, punctuated by small open plots in which animals were kept. I heard the sounds and smelled the odour of pigs; I heard the lowing of cows and made out the silhouette of a horse to my left. Dogs barked constantly, their voices trailing off as we continued up the lane.

I counted four dogs. Leaving the buildings behind us, we moved into a more open landscape. I was made to sit on a grassy bank, just off the track, and turned around so that my back was toward my captors. They talked quietly among themselves.

A few minutes later and the gangly one walked past me, heading down the lane toward the farm buildings. He returned after about half-an-hour, accompanied by a short thick-set man dressed in civilian clothes, wellington boots, and wearing a balaclava mask. He hesitated and stared at me curiously as he moved past me, before entering into a conversation with Sasha in Georgian. I was unable to hear what was said, but they came to a decision pretty quickly.

I was hauled to my feet by the newcomer, who I took to be the occupant of the farm, and Serge. They placed a mask over my head and led me, firmly held by both arms, slowly down the track toward the buildings. About fifty metres down the track, we turned to the right, through a gate. A short walk on wet grass and we stopped abruptly; I could hear chickens clucking nearby, then the clinking of metal upon metal. My mask was pulled off and I stared down at an opening in the ground. The farmer holding a torch was climbing down a wooden ladder. Serge pushed me on to the ladder, and gestured to me too to descend into the hole.

For the merest fraction of a second, I panicked at the sight of the hole in the ground, and thought of making a break for it. But where could I run to? All around me was darkness, and my other two guards were not far away and had torches. They'd certainly quickly find me and another beating would surely ensue. Also, I was mentally and physically exhausted. I needed to sleep, anywhere, and I couldn't run. My shoes no longer existed, the soles of my feet were raw and my legs wouldn't carry me for any distance. So far I'd held it all together. Don't panic now. This is a stop-over; they will move me on tomorrow. Go with the flow and wait for a chance in daylight. The village isn't very far away. I forced myself to behave rationally and ignored the hammering in my chest and the churning in my stomach that forecast a panic attack. I took a deep breath as I put my foot on the top rung of the ladder and thought of Lisa and my unborn grand-child. Don't do anything stupid now.

Me – aged 6

With my parents – aged 13

After playing tennis with Mair – aged 17

Lisa, Rod and Pip – Christmas 1978

Family holiday in France - 1982

Rustaveli Avenue, Tbilisi

Barnov Street, Tbilisi -
my apartment is on the right

Eka

Lisiko

Ilia (far left) – my translator and his family

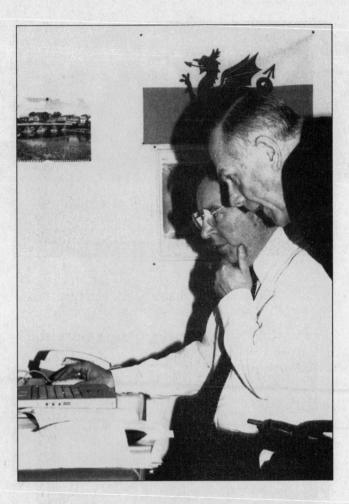

With Tim Hooper (Deputy Project Leader) in
Tbilisi, 1999

Birthplace of Stalin, Gori, Georgia

My apartment in Baku, Azerbaijan

Diana, Tbilisi - 1996

Diana with
Danny in
Georgia

When I reached the bottom of the ladder, the farmer was lighting a candle which he placed on a small table to the right of a cot. I was in a small cellar, about two metres by one and a half; the walls were covered in slime and cobwebs, and water dripped from the ceiling. He pointed to the cot which almost filled the available space, and said in English, "bed" indicating that I was to lie on it. The "bed" consisted of plastic sheeting filled with straw over a crude timber frame; a smaller plastic bag, similarly stuffed was to be my pillow. He held up three ladies' dresses; these were my bed-clothes. I sat on the cot and he placed a chain, which led under the wall next to the bed, around my neck and secured it with a large padlock. Initially it was too tight and I couldn't breathe. I struggled, pointing to the chain. He loosened it and I could breathe more easily. He pointed to the candle and said in English, "light". He pointed to a bucket with a metal lid on it to the left of the cot, and said "toileti." There was a match-box on the table next to the candle which he indicated, making a striking motion with his hands. He then said bizarrely, "bye-bye," and disappeared up the ladder.

The ladder was withdrawn upward and I heard the sound of a wooden trap-door being closed and the metallic clink of a key and lock. I was alone in the flickering candle-light; the only sound was the clucking of chickens above me.

I badly wanted to urinate. The chain around my neck led downward to the base of the stone wall to the right of the cot and underneath the wall, but there was not sufficient slack to enable me to stand up and reach the bucket. I yelled loudly, and continued to shout for about fifteen minutes.

Directly above the table was a small hole in the wall measuring about one foot square. Presently, I heard the sound of footsteps coming down a wooden stairway in an area behind the stone wall and the light of an electric torch shone through the hole in the wall. I rattled the chain and shouted "I can't piss. I cannot reach the bucket." Muffled whispers from beyond the wall, the sound of a key turning, and the chain was gradually extended by about six inches. I was just about able to stand, crouch, reach the bucket and urinate directly into it. The footsteps receded and all was quiet.

A few minutes later, more footsteps descending the staircase behind the stone wall. By stretching the chain to its limit, I was just about able to peek through the nearest corner of the hole in the wall, and make out the silhouette of the short, thickset character – the farmer – carrying a torch and moving toward the hole. I also glimpsed what appeared to be a bed-sheet, draped over part of the floor next door. A plastic bottle containing water was dropped through the hole in the wall; a bowl of steaming soup, a thick piece of bread, an apple and a plastic spoon, were placed on the sill. The farmer said "bye-bye," and went away.

I was seriously knackered, but also ravenously hungry. I ate every morsel. When I'd finished, I placed the empty bowl on the ledge of the hole and blew out the candle, a small inch-long stump remained. Complete darkness. Minutes later, the farmer returned. This time he had someone with him. He removed the empty bowl from the ledge, and entered into a whispered conversation. A heavy metal object was pushed toward the stone wall, which blocked my view through the hole. A half hour later, again footsteps on the staircase next door and the light of a torch flickered through the hole in the wall. A packet of cigarettes was placed on the ledge, and I heard the voice of Serge say in English, "Peter, you want?" I replied, speaking slowly, "Serge, I want… go home. Home, you understand?"

There was no response, but I knew Serge was standing there, as the light from his torch still flickered through the hole. After some minutes the light disappeared, I heard his footsteps climb the staircase, and a door close. The only sound was the clucking of the chickens above, and the steady drip of water from the ceiling. "They'll move me on tomorrow," I thought. "This is just a stop-over." It wasn't.

Chapter Thirty-three

I lit a cigarette and what remained of my candle and tried to take stock. I estimated the trap-door entrance to my left was about three metres above me. Three sides of the cell were made of brick, but that to my right was composed of blocks of large rough-hewn stone cemented crudely together. The ceiling was about two metres above my cot and was of concrete slabs from which water dripped steadily. Everything was filthy. The brickwork was crusted in layers of ancient caked soot, the shaft-like entrance to the hole looked as if it had been, in the distant past, a chimney, leading down to an old fire-place at its base. The stone wall to my right was pierced by the small hole through which I'd been fed, and was covered with spiders' webs, slime, and all kinds of hanging detritus. The ceiling was similarly adorned; the water that dripped constantly from it smelled foul, and was mixed with excrement from the chickens housed above. A large army of slugs was moving along the brick wall behind me, and an inch-thick layer of candle wax covered the small table to my right on which the candle had been placed. Someone had evidently been here before me. The place smelled of sweet, rotting flesh.

The chain around my neck led underneath the rough-stone wall to my right through which a hole had been gouged. I examined the chain intimately in the thin candle-light. It was old, but the links were massive and robust. I tugged at the chain as hard as I could but there was no sign of any "give". It was well secured.

The bucket – my toilet – was corroded and rusty. I held the candle-stump over the bucket with the lid off, and saw that a square hole had been cut in its bottom. This matched a similarly shaped hole which disappeared under the raised wooden platform on which the bed rested. There was a three-inch gap between the bottom of the bucket and the true floor of the cell. A mix of slugs, flies and various crawling insects occupied the base of the bucket and were happily creeping up its inside walls. The lid was not a good fit.

I examined the three garments that served as my bed-clothes. They obviously belonged to a short fat lady, presumably the wife of the farmer, and were all outer garments, made of a woollen material in plain black. The cell was very damp and cold, the sweet smell cloyed, my breath misted in the chilly air. I wrapped the garments around me, took off the remnants of my shoes, blew out the candle and, completely exhausted, I quickly fell asleep. Before doing so, I wondered once again where they would take me tomorrow.

I was awoken by the sound of a cockerel crowing loudly above me. Jolting sharply from a deep sleep into a sitting position, the chain around my neck tightened painfully. I could move forward only slightly, cold and wet, I could see nothing but an inky blackness. The only sound was the cockerel's cries – echoed by another in the distance – and the scratching of the chickens on the trap-door entrance. They obviously sensed the presence of something interesting beneath them.

I experienced an immediate and overwhelming sense of despair. It was a physical pain, a deep throbbing pain as opposed to a sharp stab. Although I had been roughly treated by my captors over the past weeks, and had been subjected to some pretty brutal beatings, at least I'd had company, and they had shared with me some of the hardships and deprivations. Now I was alone, tethered and in complete darkness. I felt abandoned. As the ache continued, I tried to reason. "There's no way that any human being can leave any living creature, a cat or dog or indeed any animal, in this small cell, tethered by the neck, unable to move, and without light, for any length of time: no way."

This situation was definitely temporary. They were surely keeping me in a secure place for a few hours, or at most a day or two, while they rested, before moving me on to a different location. Logically, I thought, if they'd wanted to kill me, they'd had plenty of opportunities. Simply shooting me in the head and dumping my body in the forest would ensure that I wouldn't be found for a very long time, if ever: long enough certainly for them to make their escape. They must surely still have had some hope, or even information, that the ransom would be paid. Why otherwise had they fed me? Why otherwise had they ensured that I was never able to see their faces? They must want me to live, and more, to never be able to identify them.

"Come on Shaw, get a grip! You're not dead yet. At least you're not being beaten now. Just take things step by step." I lit the stump of the candle.

Luckily I've never had a fear of insects, or mice or rats, or any of the small beasties that induce fear and panic in many people. Also, I've always taken the view that all living things have a right to live. It's an entitlement and not a privilege and I abhor cruelty to animals in any form. Except flies, I hate them and I've never had any qualms about swatting flies.

Flies were not the problem that first morning in the hole. The problem was slugs. There were dozens of them – on the bed, on the walls around me, and in my hair – black and brown and all sizes. I picked each of them up delicately, and threw them through the hole in the wall. It was the only thing to do. I didn't want to kill them: just get them out of the hole.

A short while later, there was the clump of footsteps descending the staircase in the space next-door and the light of a torch flickered into the cell. The voice of the farmer said, "Water; toileti."

I took this to mean that I was to pour the remains of the water I'd been given the previous night into the bucket. I did, and handed the empty plastic bottle to the two hands that appeared through the hole. In return, I was given two bottles of water, a half-candle, some matches, seven thin Russian cigarettes and a cigarette lighter. This was followed by a roll of cheap toilet paper, a bar of soap and a plastic bowl containing rice pudding, a plastic spoon and an apple. All these goodies were provided with a deliberation that suggested that my benefactor was having difficulty in bypassing the metal obstruction placed to block my view through the hole in the wall.

Then, a strange crackling sound: he was trying to tune in a radio. Eventually he seemed satisfied, and a male voice was apparently reading the news. The language used was definitely not Georgian or Russian. Eventually I twigged: the radio voice was speaking in Turkish – or Azeri. How come? With a final instruction to me – "Water, toileti," – the flickering torchlight disappeared, the footsteps receded and he was gone.

I lit the candle and ate the rice pudding slowly. Although my host had uttered only a few words, he had a very distinctive voice, light but with a soft, husky intonation. He somehow reminded me of the singer, Mel Torme. I had seen his hands in the torchlight. They were large and gnarled, very much those of a working man, with short stumpy fingers and dirty finger nails. His arms were thick, muscular and covered in black hair. The toilet paper, etc. were very welcome, but the realisation dawned on me that the intention must surely be to keep me in this hole for days, or longer, not hours. Why otherwise would I be given these supplies? Panic grabbed at my stomach and I gagged on the rice pudding. The voice on the radio finished speaking and was replaced by music – Muslim music and prayers. I've nothing against Muslim music as long as it's in small doses. The wailing and chanting droned on, and on, and on.

What are these bastards doing? I wanted to weep like a baby, but stopped myself. That would simply be self-pity. Panic turned to fear and notched downward; fright turned to anger. That was better; I could cope with that. The anger grew inside me, and I threw the remaining contents of the plastic bowl through the hole in the wall. At full stretch, I could just about reach one arm through the hole and feel for the metal obstruction. I shook it as violently as I could, and the radio toppled off it with a crash and fell silent. Bloody good job too. I blew out the candle and lay back in total darkness. Still the chickens scratched, but better that than the bloody wailing. I felt a little better.

But thinking was a problem; I couldn't stop doing it. My thoughts roamed over and over the same old ground. Who was doing this to me? Disgruntled customers, politicians, could any of my colleagues in the bank be involved? No way, surely! The Georgian police must be in on it. The police – or gangsters dressed like them – had assisted Sasha and his gang in the kidnap. Who would stand to gain politically by kidnapping me? Certainly those in the Ministry of Agriculture with whom we'd been battling for years, and others. The "dark forces" as Brussels called them. They wanted to give loans to friends, relations and colleagues which would never be repaid. Within a year, the bank would be bust. Was my kidnapping linked to the tendering process which had been due to be held in Brussels on the 20th June? Were the enemies of the bank trying to stop this from being held, leaving a vacuum to be filled by the "dark forces"? Surely the EC would not allow this to happen. Or was the motivation merely financial – the ransom demand? Obviously it hadn't been paid to date, or I would not be in this dank hole. It could never be paid.

How was my family managing? What did they know about the kidnapping? Were they even aware of it? At least my first wife and our children were self-sufficient: they all had good jobs and no financial problems. But how would Diana and Danny cope? Diana's only means of support now was me. She had no money of her own and no real job since Danny was born. How could she keep Danny in nursery school? Diana's mother and sister had no money, and existed on the income from Lena's dancing lessons. No one would starve but there was no money for anything else, certainly not school. Were they safe? My mind conjured up all kinds of appalling visions including Diana being kidnapped too, and beaten, or worse. Who was looking after them? Would the Embassy, or the Commission, have enough nous to help her?

What was going on, if anything, in the outside world? What could anyone do? Nothing, except maybe search for me. There was no chance of finding me here: wherever I was, it must be pretty remote. Is it possible that someone involved in my kidnapping would grass to claim a reward? Not likely! And where the hell am I anyway? The radio had played Muslim music. This was not in itself particularly odd as Azeri or Turkish radio programmes could be easily picked up in Georgia, but why not play Georgian programmes, if I'm indeed still in Georgia? Am I still making the news and my captors fear that I may be able to understand? The cigarettes I had been given were Russian but the packet had a Georgian customs mark. So what? The long journey could have taken me anywhere.

I determined to try and obtain information from the farmer, if and when he returned to feed me. In the meantime, my stomach churned and I needed to use the bucket. At least they had given me toilet paper. I counted the matches, there were fourteen. I lit the candle.

Chapter Thirty-four

I could stand up reasonably well if I stooped, and was just about able to reach the bucket. Although I poured a whole bottle of water into the bucket afterwards, and held the candle momentarily over the bucket to see the result, there were no signs of dispersal. There was no drain or channel taking the waste away. It would simply accumulate. Charming!

As the day wore on, I found that my cell was subject to very sudden changes of temperature and humidity. There were times when I felt extremely hot and clammy, but within minutes the temperature would plummet to an icy chill. It was almost as if the changes were being manipulated by my captors, who were somehow able to blow hot or cold air into my dungeon at will. I conjured up a vision of some diabolical figure sitting somewhere above ground, pulling and tugging on levers, inducing this subtle means of torture. I shook my head vigorously and dismissed the thought from my mind. Nevertheless, it was extremely uncomfortable, and yet it was still high summer. I counted the days since the date of my capture and I judged it to be mid-July. It was actually the 11th July.

My beard was quite long now. I hadn't shaved since the morning of the 18th June. It was dirty and matted as was my hair. I used half of the water in the one plastic bottle that remained to wash my face and hair. I had nothing to dry myself with, apart from my bedclothes, and these were already fouled by the constant drip of chicken waste and water from above. Still, I felt a bit better.

My finger nails were long and ingrained with dirt. I had no means of trimming them but was able to use a couple of spent matches to prise out the dirt from under my nails. My trousers and shirt – what remained of them – were filthy. I removed my socks, which were damp and smelled strongly of diesel, and stuffed them in a crevice in the wall to my right above the candle. The candle flame might eventually help to dry them out.

I was worried about my teeth. I hadn't brushed them since the day of my abduction, apart from rubbing them with my shirt-sleeve and rinsing my mouth with water following meals. So far, they had caused no problem, but I'd missed my usual six-monthly check when I was last in the UK, and a few days earlier felt a twinge of pain from a wisdom tooth. I must obtain a toothbrush from the farmer. How could I communicate this to him? The chain was too short for me to poke my head through the hole in the wall and gesture with my finger. What was the word for teeth in Russian or Georgian? I couldn't think of it and settled for *denti*. It sounded close.

The scratching of the chickens above was constant, but I could also pick up the faint murmur of machinery. It sounded like a chain saw, the type that would be used in cutting timber or lopping off branches. Someone was obviously working at something. Or was it the noise of a generator? Occasionally, dogs barked, usually some distance away, but one dog, somewhere close, above me and to my right, broke out into frequent spasms of hysterical yapping. Was it there to guard me, or raise the alarm should someone approach? Strangely, unlike the chickens, it didn't react to any noise that I made from within the hole.

At somewhere around mid-afternoon, the faintest glimmer of light angled itself into the cell from a chink in the trap-door above. For a few moments, I was able to see the parameters of the cell without the need for the candle. It was not a welcome sight, and simply emphasised the dank and filthy nature of the confined space in which I was being held. It also reminded me of my inability to move within it, tethered by the neck. The ray of sun lasted for about fifteen minutes, slowly dwindled away, and the blackness returned, but not before I glimpsed the shape of a dead animal, a rat, near the bottom of the cot. A deep cloud of sheer misery and despondency overwhelmed me. Black thoughts flashed across my mind, each of them more powerfully pessimistic than the other. I'll never get out of this hole! I tried to almost physically force these thoughts from my head. Think positively. You're alive and you're not being beaten any more. Get a grip. My thoughts swung like a pendulum, ranging from total belief in, and anticipation of, an early departure, to total despair and hopelessness. I forced myself not to break down, and lit another cigarette.

Hours later, the sound of a door opening and closing in the area next door, footsteps down the staircase and the beam of a torch through the hole in the wall. The voice, with the words, "Water, toileti."

I complied, and gave the empty bottles to the hands that appeared through the hole. The farmer didn't react to the radio having been toppled from its perch. I heard him pick it up and fiddle with it, but he made no remark. He took the empty plastic bowl and spoon from the ledge, and replaced them with a bowl of steaming soup, some bread and an apple. He went away for some minutes and returned with the plastic bottles full of water. He then handed me a plastic cup filled with hot water which contained a few specks of tea, and pushed a plastic bag containing sugar through the hole. This was followed by a small plastic plate on which was a piece of home-made fruit cake. I wasn't hungry, but somehow this gesture of generosity – for such I took it to be – lifted my spirits. At least, I'm not being starved to death. My matches were then replenished, but not my cigarettes.

I felt encouraged enough to ask him the questions I'd rehearsed. I said in English, "Georgia? This is Georgia, yes?"

He hesitated then said, "*Niet*, Azerbaijan." Adding, "Azerbaijan, good." And as if by way of an afterthought, "Georgia good, too!"

So, at least he could speak a few words of English. I said, "Peter Shaw – go home, yes?" A long pause, and then he said, "*Niz Naiu*" – "I don't know," in Russian. I tried again, "Please, toothbrush? – *Denti, denti*?"

No response. I repeated the word toothbrush three or four times. There was no acknowledgement, and within seconds the torch light disappeared and his footsteps receded up the staircase.

I lit the remaining stump of the candle and began to eat slowly. The soup wasn't bad. It contained large chunks of fatty pork, which I forced down, followed by the bread and tea. I left the apple until later. As night fell, the temperature dropped but remained stable. There were no longer the huge swings which made me sweat one minute and shiver the next. I wrapped myself in the damp smelly bedclothes, blew out the candle and tried to sleep, but failed. Thoughts again – Am I really in Azerbaijan? For some reason this possibility upset me. Why? Whether in Georgia or Azerbaijan I was a long way from home. What's the difference? Somehow I felt more secure in Georgia, and I missed not seeing Sasha. Why? He's a bastard. Why do you want to see him?

It was a long night, the first of many in the hole.

Chapter Thirty-five

The morning and evening feeding sessions became routine, always accompanied by two bottles of water, one of which I emptied into the bucket. With breakfast came the turning on of the radio – the Azeri programmes – which followed the same format: first the news, read in Azeri and then Russian, followed by interminable mosque music and prayers. Then, a short burst of western pop music followed by more Muslim music, speeches and prayers, all completely incomprehensible, and extremely wearing. The radio must have been placed on the floor of the adjacent room, as all my efforts to rock the metal cabinet and dislodge the radio were now ineffective. The news was broadcast at regular hourly intervals during the day, culminating in a lengthy summary at, I guessed, 6.00pm. The evening feeding session invariably took place at about 7.00pm when the radio was switched off. Every few days, the battery wore out, but was replaced, without fail, the following morning. I looked forward enormously to the few hours of silence the passing of the battery afforded.

The short period during which western pop music was played brought no relief. Clearly the radio station did not possess an abundance of western recordings, and there was a great deal of daily repetition. The staple diet was Celine Dion singing the "Titanic" theme, "Ave Maria" and a few others, and Ronan Keating's "If Tomorrow Never Comes." Hardly inspiring stuff! Even the occasional introduction of hit songs of Bryan Adams, Louis Armstrong and Roy Orbison were always from their repertoire of sad songs. It was as if the tunes were purposely selected by the programme controller to provide the listeners with a complete appreciation of the sadness of life in the western world. They certainly depressed me: not one jolly tune was aired. I wondered why my gaolers played the radio at all. Was their aim to convince me that I was indeed in Azerbaijan, and therefore completely beyond the reach of the

Georgian authorities? Or was their intention to exacerbate my sense of isolation and helplessness, or simply drown out any outside noises that might give me a clue as to my whereabouts?

In fact, I was able hear sounds from outside in addition to the regular hum of the chainsaw, or generator, the clang of hammer upon metal, and the intermittent barking of the dogs. Occasionally, in the evenings, I heard the sound of a child's voice. It was the voice of a young girl; I guessed a grandchild of the farmer. It seemed as if she was aware of my presence somewhere below ground, as I clearly heard her say my name, "Peter," followed by indistinct tones of admonition from the farmer and sometimes a female voice, perhaps that of his wife. I couldn't understand how my being held prisoner in this filthy hole could, in any way, be communicated to a young child. Surely she attended school, and would inevitably talk to other children with whom she would share this information. Clearly no one cared. My captors felt very secure.

I tried consistently to engage the farmer in some kind of conversation during his morning and evening visits. I rehearsed a simple phrase in Russian or Georgian, such as, "Where am I?" and "When can I go home?" The only response was either, *"Da, da, da"* – "Yes, yes, yes" – or *"Niz Naiu"* – "I don't know." Yet, I was convinced that he understood some English, or had access to someone who did. During the first week of my incarceration he presented me with a toothbrush and toothpaste. This, I assumed, was in response to my earlier request. The toothbrush was old and flattened with use. Nevertheless, it was a welcome gesture, and I used it every day, in addition to rubbing my teeth with my shirt-sleeve.

A few days later, in response to chattering my teeth in an effort to communicate that I was feeling the cold, he threw an additional garment into the hole. This was a large waterproof gentleman's overcoat, well-worn with holes in the material, but very welcome. By tucking my head under the coat, I was able to keep some of the drips from the ceiling off my face and hair, although it did little to alleviate the chill of the night, or the intense fluctuations of temperature and humidity during the day.

I hadn't seen or heard anything of the two Sashas or Serge. Somehow I found this unsettling. Had they left, and was I now in the custody and control of a separate, possibly Azeri, gang? Was this part of a pre-arranged plan by which a Georgian gang kidnapped me, and a separate gang took over and kept me hidden away for an indefinite period, or until the ransom was paid? Totally incongruously, I felt the need to do something to discover whether they were still around or not. On a couple of occasions, I sensed that someone had crept into the cellar adjacent to me during the night and was listening to me. Why? I had no idea, but I'd caught a glimpse of some blankets on the floor of the cellar on the first night of my incarceration. Were the blankets being used by a *watcher* or was my imagination working overtime? I knew that Sasha's gang was aware that I had a dicky stomach. They had shown little sympathy in the past, but surely no harm in trying again. It might even get me out of the hole.

I yelled and screamed loudly as if in considerable pain. It brought a result quite quickly: footsteps rapidly descended the stairs and the light of a torch shone through the hole in the wall. I pulled my knees tightly up to my chest and shouted repeatedly the words "stomach" and "pain," as I writhed and contorted in affected agony. The farmer mumbled something and disappeared. I continued to moan and groan in the darkness intermingled with the occasional sharp yelp of pain. A half hour passed then footsteps, the torch-beam and the immediately recognisable voice of Sasha, saying quietly, but menacingly, "Problem?"

I screamed in response, "Stomach pain. I need to walk," and continued to writhe and groan, holding my knees to my chest. They spoke together quietly for a few minutes, and went away. The farmer returned with two tablets wrapped in foil, which he placed on the ledge of the hole, and disappeared. Nothing was said.

Throughout that day, I kept up the pretence of being seriously ill, yelling and screaming my head off, but to no avail. There was no further visit from Sasha, and the farmer returned only to feed me at the usual time. There was no attempt at communication on his part, and no response to my efforts to talk. I didn't take the medication and, for the time being, gave up my attempt to feign sickness as a lost cause. I decided that there was really no point in "crying wolf" particularly as I might well require serious medical attention in due course. At least I'd established that Sasha was still around. Strangely, I derived a certain comfort from the knowledge that I hadn't been abandoned.

Chapter Thirty-six

As the days passed, I came to accept that my stay in the hole was not simply a stop-over *en route* to another destination. My transportation from the cave to my present location, wherever that may be, had been well-planned and well implemented; the promise made of my being freed – "no variant" – was simply a repetition of the usual ruse. As the understanding dawned on me that I could well be held prisoner in this terrible place for an undetermined time, perhaps forever, fear and panic gripped me in waves. I tried to fight it.

The same thoughts assailed me repeatedly. I was being fed and watered, and I was being kept alive. I had not been allowed to glimpse the faces of my captors. They had no intention of allowing me to identify them. If I tried, as I had, many times, I was beaten. Logically, this must mean that their intention was to release me – eventually. But this pre-supposed that the ransom money would be paid. It wouldn't – ever. And so I'd been taken to a place where I'd never be found and from which there was no chance of escape. My mind returned over and over again to my family in the UK, to Diana and Danny in Georgia, and to the mental anguish and torment which was undoubtedly being experienced by all of my loved ones. And I could do nothing at all about it.

Briefly, I contemplated suicide. I still had the two pieces of wire threaded into the loops of my trousers. I examined them by candle-light and considered whether they could be used to cut my wrists. If I timed it correctly by carrying out the incisions just after the evening feeding session, there would be a whole night for me to lie bleeding before they'd find me. Even if I failed to kill myself, surely some kind of medical assistance would have to be sought to revive me. That must involve my being taken out of the hole, even if only for a short period of time. I weighed up the pros and cons of undertaking this course of action. It might work. The problem was that I couldn't find my pulse. It all seemed so easy in the movies, where there was always a convenient knife and a bath filled with warm water. Unfortunately I had neither, and I couldn't even find the place to cut! Forget it!

I considered trying to throttle myself, using the padlocked chain around my neck as a garrotte. The chain led under the stone wall to its anchor in the adjacent room. The angle was all wrong, but I reasoned that, in a kneeling position if I leaned forward hard and long enough against the pull of the chain, then I may succeed in garrotting myself. I tried it once. The result was a loud roar in my ears together with, oddly enough, the noise of church-bells ringing loudly. When I began to black out, I toppled over sideways, the pressure was released, and I quickly recovered consciousness.

For the first and only time, I broke down and cried. When I recovered, I vowed, no matter what, I would never break down again. Nor would I ever consider suicide again. It represented a psychological decline into total self-pity and helplessness, and I realised then, at that exact time, that I had somehow to keep going.

I don't believe now that I was ever serious about taking my own life. Nevertheless, I ensured that those little pieces of wire were kept safely on the small wax-encrusted table at the side of my cot. Somehow they were symbolic of my ability to control my own destiny – at least to some extent.

Chapter Thirty-seven

There was no blinding light or flash of inspiration which led me into taking the decision to try to survive. Rather it was a gradual process that evolved from my increasing understanding that the hole was not to be a temporary halt. I was to be here for some time, possibly for the rest of my life, however long or short that may be. The only thing to do was to get on with it as best I could.

Over the following months I experienced immense mood swings: from long periods in the depths of utter misery and despair, to fleeting moments of joy. I am, by nature, an optimist. Nothing is for ever, good or bad, and a glass of water is always at least half-full and not half-empty. I'm the kind of odd bugger who can have a good time at a funeral. In fact, I've had some splendid booze-ups at funerals over the years. I relish life and rejoice in friendships, but I don't take it all too seriously. Perhaps my tendency to brush aside bad experiences and look for the positives helped me to come to terms with my situation underground. But I know that I fought to survive because I had to. There was no bloody choice.

I realised somehow that I had to reach a balance between my mental pain, which to a certain extent I could control, and my physical discomfort, about which I could do virtually nothing. When it rained, the liquid chicken waste fell from the ceiling in deluges and I became very wet and cold. As the bucket became well-used, flies and other insects became a real problem. I knew, that with no healing sunlight, bites would become infected and would inevitably lead to disease. I therefore covered myself, as best I could with my bedclothes and wore my smelly old socks as gloves to protect my hands. I learned to stay still when I slept.

I dreamed a lot: usually very pleasant dreams of past events in my life – the birth of my children, my daughter's wedding day, Christmas mornings over the years, camping holidays in

France. I don't know whether my brain was compensating for the harshness of reality by selecting only good memories on which to dwell when I dozed, but I never grew used to the shock of waking from a pleasant dream to the stark realisation of my situation. The contrast was unimaginable and desperately painful. Somehow I had to learn to manage the pain.

After a week or so in the hole, I found it very difficult to cope mentally with being awake during normal daylight hours. I imagined particular people, special to me, walking up and down High Street, Cowbridge, or Rustaveli Avenue, Tbilisi in the bright sunlight pursuing their everyday affairs; – perhaps a little sad, but dealing with their normal problems in office or home, in sunshine and in rain. Life goes on, but it was going on without me. I couldn't hack it. The images were too painful. And so I resolved to turn my night into day.

I was able to keep track of time by the radio broadcasts and by the feeding sessions. I marked off the passing of the days and weeks by making a mental note – at the end I found I was five days adrift, short of the actual. So, my supper became my breakfast and my breakfast became my supper. Initially, I wasn't altogether successful in achieving this. Even if I managed to fall asleep after the morning meal, I would invariably wake up around mid-afternoon, and spend long hours in the darkness listening to the noise from the radio. The evening feeding session became an obsession and if, as was sometimes the case, my gaoler was late in feeding me, fighting the waves of panic wasn't easy. When the arms eventually appeared through the hole, as they always did, I felt an immense sense of relief and gratitude. As the days passed, I was able to discipline myself reasonably well to existing in a different time-frame. The next challenge was to organise a means of filling that time as meaningfully as possible. I had to learn to live in this hole.

My mother brought me up to be fastidious in terms of personal hygiene. I remember our first holiday abroad, when I was twelve years old, in Switzerland of all places. My mam, totally untrusting of all things foreign, ensured that I layered the hotel toilet seat with reams of toilet paper before sitting on it. Thereafter, scrubbing of hands, not simply washing, was mandatory, and leaving the toilet without actually touching the door handle was a perpetual problem. I wondered what she would think of my toilet arrangements in the hole!

On waking up, I began my housework. The first chore was to collect the accumulation of slugs from the wall and dead bugs from my bedding and throw them through the hole in the wall. One day, I collected twenty-eight slugs; surprisingly, there were never any snails. This was followed by re-stuffing meticulously my plastic-bag mattress with the bits of straw that escaped during my period of sleep. I made myself search conscientiously in the darkness for every little piece and re-inserted it into the bag. It took a long time. As time passed, the plastic bag ended up in ribbons, unable to retain any straw, so this job became obsolete. I then took to stuffing my pillow, until that too fell apart.

I ensured that I always had a small reserve of water. Although the farmer never failed to replenish the plastic bottles, I had a permanent fear that one day he might either forget or, in a fit of pique, simply not re-fill them. Having established the reserve, I began a routine of washing my hands, face and hair, once every two days over the bucket. This served two purposes: the first to try and keep myself clean, and secondly, to ensure a constant supply of water to the bucket. I had soap, but I found it very difficult to hold the soap in one hand, the bottle of water in the other and wash myself. Inevitably, either the soap or the bottle slipped out of my hand with disastrous consequences. I subsequently used the soap very sparingly, only after using the toilet.

Each day, I spent time simply scratching with my finger nails at the layer of muck on my face which inevitably accumulated from the ceiling above. I deposited the scratchings in a neat pile on the table, before throwing them through the hole in the wall. I kept my fingernails and toenails at a reasonable length by rubbing them against the stone wall. I then used the stubs of the spent matches to clean my fingernails.

Gradually, I learned to exist for longer periods each day without using the candle. As I learned to control my panic attacks, I taught myself to live in the darkness. I ate in the darkness; I used the bucket in the darkness. I set about accumulating a small stock of four or five candle stubs. These I kept for emergencies, but once each week I used one stub to burn off my beard. Not an act of vanity, but rather the practical application of a useful tool. Inevitably, following eating, bits of food stuck to my beard. These attracted flies which increased in numbers as time went on. The flies bit the exposed skin on my face. By undertaking the weekly burn of the beard by candle, and by using cigarettes to burn away that bit of moustache that overlapped my upper lip, I reduced the length of the beard and moustache to thick stubble. A splash of water over my face completed the exercise. Whether it worked in preventing infections, I don't know, but I certainly felt better.

There was enough slack in the chain around my neck to enable me to undertake a few physical jerks. These took the form of push-ups and squats, the latter restricted to a half-crouching position, but better than nothing. Over the weeks, I aimed at a daily target of up to one hundred squats and sixty push-ups. The primary intention was to try and keep my body in some semblance of shape, but the exercises developed into something more mentally therapeutic. Whenever I became subject to a particularly black mood, I exercised: it prevented me from thinking. If I became suicidally despondent, I would launch into a series of especially punishing press-ups. This would leave me out of puff and totally knackered, but they stopped me from thinking.

As the summer wore on, animals and insects became more of a problem. At night – during my day-time – a population of rats scurried noisily under my bed and made for the contents of the bucket. As I've mentioned, I've never found any little beastie to be totally repugnant, although I was initially fearful that they would bite and inflict some nasty disease upon me. But they didn't. They had no interest at all in diversifying their culinary delights away from those which they found so easily underneath my cot. Apart from their noisy scratching, and the occasional patter of tiny feet over my legs, they left me in relative peace. I got used to them.

The flies were a different matter. I know not whence they came. I guess they followed the farmer at the twice daily feeding sessions, or managed to enter the hole through minute cracks in the trap-door. In any event, as time progressed they became much more numerous, no doubt in direct proportion with the level of malodour emanating from the bucket.

I developed a technique of lying in the darkness and calculating, by listening to their buzzes, how many flies had gathered in the hole. I'd try to ensure that there was no exposed skin, and kept my head well buried under the bedclothes. When sufficient had gathered, usually around ten, I'd light up the candle and watch, with something close to delight, as each of the flies in turn headed for the candle flame and self-destructed. The flies were of a particularly hard-cased strain, mainly blue- and green-bottles, and sometimes one or two would survive the first encounter with the flame. Without exception they returned for a second, killing, dose. I found the longer I waited in darkness before lighting the candle, the keener the flies became to zap themselves. I never imagined that I could derive such fun out of a few minutes of fly-killing. I looked forward to it every day.

Another daily challenge was to conserve as much as possible the morning supply of one half-candle to obtain the maximum benefit. I learned quite early on to eat very quickly and use the bucket as infrequently as possible. I grew accustomed to the fragile nature of the matches which broke very easily when striking them, and hoarded the match box inside the mattress to keep it dry. Each match was re-used several times by lighting the spent match with the cigarette lighter. In moments of acute depression, I relieved my despair by simply lighting the candle, if for only a few seconds. There was nothing to see apart from the four walls festooned with slime, spiders' webs, scuttling bugs and the ever-present slugs, but somehow it lightened my mood.

171

Another daily chore was cleaning up the wax from spent candles, using the handle of the plastic spoon to scrape the wax into a heap before depositing it through the hole in the wall. Quite early on, I broke the handle of the spoon and had to make do with the stump. Despite my repeated requests to the farmer, it was never replaced.

There was no grand scheme on my part to concoct a methodology for my survival, but these small acts of house-keeping certainly helped. They provided me with a daily routine, which together with my physical jerks, took up time. I had plenty of time. Also, I had to make a home for myself, despite the conditions, in this small hole in the ground. I had to manufacture a way of existing, which became sustainably acceptable. The challenge of building up a small reserve of candle stumps, spent matches and water imposed a level of self-discipline from which I was able to extract small benefits. I could burn off my beard; I could alleviate my black moods by lighting a candle stump for a few seconds; I could zap some flies; I could attempt to clean myself.

In other words, I convinced myself that I was able to exert a degree of control over my environment distinct from that imposed upon me by my gaolers. The jettisoning of slugs and candle wax through the hole in the wall were small acts of defiance. No doubt they caused little or no inconvenience to the farmer, but they were the best I could do. Also, I reasoned, in the extremely unlikely event of a stranger wandering into the area next to my hole, the accumulated debris would perhaps draw attention to the fact that someone was imprisoned behind the wall. The trick was to survive.

Chapter Thirty-eight

Memories are wonderful companions, and by golly, I needed them, but they were a mixed blessing. I found I couldn't dwell for long upon happy memories of recent events. A deeply black mood would inevitably set in. I worked out the threshold was about seven years ago, roughly the time of my daughter's wedding, and my meeting Diana. Any more recent happy events were just too damaging to contemplate.

I discovered I easily recalled people and events in my life going back to my very early childhood. Events I hadn't recollected for very many years. I remembered vividly, for example, going to a pantomime, *Puss in Boots*, in Swansea, with my mother and grand-mother when I was about four years old. It must have made a big impression upon me, as the following day I tried to take the family cat for a walk, using the clothes-line in the backyard of the family home, as a leash. The rope was wet, my hands slipped and the cat was hoisted off the ground by the pulley mechanism – by the neck! I was trying to be Dick Whittington, but instead nearly succeeded in strangling the cat. My mam fortunately spotted me in time and the cat was saved.

When I was eighteen months old I contracted bronchial pneumonia and was hospitalised for some weeks. I found I could remember the face of one particular nurse who spoke to me and comforted me constantly. The little boy who sat next to me in primary school was called Paul Kill. I hadn't seen or heard from him for over fifty years, but I remembered him clearly. I saw the faces of the kids I played with in the school-yard, and the faces of the teachers; I even remembered their names. I saw mental photographs of my grandfather and uncle having their daily bath, following their shifts in the coal mine, in the little tin bath in front of the old range fire-place. The voices of Bing Crosby and the Andrews Sisters, and Al Jolson – my Uncle Tom was a great fan – came back to me very clearly.

I found I knew the words to their songs. There were hundreds of similar images, and yet these were people I hadn't given one moment's thought to for decades, but the images were very real, and the events surrounding them took place as if yesterday. Strangely, many of these memories were tinged with sadness. The actors portrayed in my mental theatricals were frequently either dead or had suffered enormously. The scale of the events varied hugely from the Aberfan school disaster of 1966, to the death of my first dog, Lassie, when I was about ten years old. It was almost as if I was to blame for everything. Somehow I felt very guilty.

Fortunately, there were some more positive recollections. I love music, particularly jazz: something my father indoctrinated in me throughout my early life. I'm a great fan of Sinatra, Crosby, Ella Fitzgerald, Tony Bennett, Nat "King" Cole, Sarah Vaughan, Anita O'Day and many other performers of the Great American Songbook. I admire greatly the song-writers and lyricists of that era: George and Ira Gershwin, Cole Porter, Jerome Kern, Irving Berlin, Rodgers and Hart and many others. I also play the piano, another legacy of my dad, not well, but enthusiastically, and I'm blessed with a good memory.

I spent many hours of each day mentally transposing popular songs from the keys in which they are written into a different key. "St Louis Blues" (W.C. Handy) written in G major was transposed into E flat major, "What is this Thing called Love?" (Cole Porter) from A flat major into C major, "With a Song in my Heart" (Richard Rodgers) from C major to G major, and so on, with many tunes and key permutations – some totally outlandish. I'd then try and play them in complete darkness, envisaging the notes and chords, on the small table next to my cot. When I returned home and actually played them on my piano, they sounded bloody awful. But they took up a lot of time in the hole.

I remembered vividly the music we played as part of the very limited repertoire of the Pete Shaw Footwarmers, a group of apprentice jazz musicians I formed in my late teens; "St Louis Blues", "Dippermouth Blues", "Honeysuckle Rose", "In the Mood", "Sweet Lorraine", and recollected how really terrible we must have sounded. I have a large collection of recordings, and recalled, note by note, scores of jazz standards as played by the all-time greats – Basie, Ellington, Goodman, Artie Shaw, the Dorsey Brothers, the "Hot Five" and "Seven" recordings of Armstrong, together with dozens of tunes as played by the legendary jazz soloists. The voices of other great, if rather archaic, vocalists flooded back – Kathleen Ferrier, Paul Robeson, Gigli, Deanna Durbin, Binnie Hale, Richard Tauber, John McCormack and on, and on, and on. I surprised myself with the expanse, range, detail and clarity of my recollections, all previously hidden away somewhere in the subconscious.

I spoke, out loud, to my family relations and friends every day. As soon as I awoke and had completed my house-keeping chores, I selected a particular personality with whom I wished to talk. I then rehearsed mentally, and at length, that which I intended to say. The contents of my conversations were based upon incidents, experiences and interactions between that particular person and me going back over many years. The conversations lasted for two or three hours, usually containing a considerable volume of apologies from me to him or her. Having prepared the content and format, I'd then begin the conversation commencing with a brief description of my situation and an assurance that none of it was of my making. I then recalled mutual experiences, happy and sad, that we had shared, interspersed by apologies and explanations for my many misdeeds, actual or imagined. In fact I poured out my heart. I wished I'd done more when I had the opportunities.

It was not all sad or negative stuff. The dead people with whom I conversed always responded. I actually heard the distinctive voices of my father, my grandparents, my Aunty Nance and Uncle Tom, and others formerly close to me reverberating around the walls of my cell. I swear that this was not wishful thinking on my part. There's no question that the voice of the particular relation or friend actually spoke to me. They usually said words of comfort and the phrases used, the

175

accents, the emphases were definitely theirs, as was the tone and pitch of the voice.

My father's unmistakable Nottinghamshire brogue using his own term of endearment – "ducks" – and, "Nay, lad. Y' can't be doin' wi' this!" resounded in my ears. There was nothing ghostly or spiritual about this. There were no apparitions, but I felt the tangible presence of each individual actually in the hole, sitting alongside me. I drew immense comfort from the words they said, and from their presence. Not only relations, but friends too. Willy Webb, Russell Davies and Viv Williams, deceased colleagues and contemporaries of mine in Midland Bank, teased me and pulled my leg. They sometimes actually burst out laughing when we recalled some of our adventures together. They were a great tonic and kept me going in some of my darkest moods. My mother, my daughter and sons, Mair, and Diana, all of whom were very much alive, never responded to my long dissertations, but I knew that they were listening to me. My aunties, Iris and Shirley, were regular recipients of my communiqués, as were many long-standing friends.

Shirley in particular, who was, when a youngster, more a sister to me than an aunt, was someone I needed to talk with. We were extremely close in my formative years when I must have been a real pain in insinuating myself between her and her many boy-friends in the back-row of the Plaza cinema. Somehow we had drifted apart over the years. During this period, she suffered severe health problems, but I was never there when I ought to have been – too busy with the trivia of my own life to spare the time. I tried to make amends during my frequent conversations with her. I felt that she was listening and understood.

I am by no means religious. My attendance at church or chapel, for many years, has been limited to weddings and funerals. Of course I attended Sunday school as a young boy, and in my teens attended a Welsh Independent Chapel at Nantyffyllon – twice a day on Sundays – largely because all my friends attended, including my girlfriend and future wife, Mair.

Also I love Welsh hymns and four-part singing. In later life I degenerated into what can be best described as grudging agnosticism.

But, in the hole, I prayed a lot. I prayed at least three times every day. My preparation for prayers followed the same pattern as my conversations with relatives and friends. I mentally rehearsed the content and format meticulously before actually saying the prayer. The former always included a request for forgiveness of my many past sins, and incorporated an update on my thoughts and opinions on my existing situation. I believe this part of the prayer was simply a means of expressing my ever-changing views and emotions. By actually stating them out loud, and mulling them over in the same way as one would in conversation with a close friend, the sense, or nonsense, that made up my thoughts became clearer to me. My prayers were quite long, at least one hour each, and always ended with the request that my family, relations and friends – there followed a litany of names – be protected and cared for. The list of names never excluded my mam, Mair and Diana, Lisa, Rod, Pip and Danny, Shirley, Phil, Ken, Bev and Griff and Dil, but frequently included many more, according to those who figured within the scope of my memory-dredging exercise at that particular time.

I never asked God directly to save me, although I selfishly implied that if He chose so to do, then He'd find me a much reformed character in the future. I now doubt that to be the case, but of course, He moves in mysterious ways, and He was listening.

Chapter Thirty-nine

I'd had no contact with Sasha since the early days of my incarceration in the hole when I quite pointlessly feigned sickness. Since then, I'd convinced myself that I'd been passed on by my kidnappers to a holding group, probably Azeri. I reasoned that Sasha and his gang, by arrangement, were responsible only for the kidnapping and subsequent manoeuvres designed to avoid their identification and capture. They'd then handed me over to a more permanent group of custodians. Or, I wondered, had Sasha and his men truly expected the ransom money to be paid to them within a few days of my being grabbed? My mind cast back to the obvious delight with which they received the information imparted by Shevardnadze's broadcast on the day following my kidnap. Had their plans been thwarted, resulting in their being forced to deposit me somewhere remote and isolated and secure, maybe in Azerbaijan, while they made their getaway? For whatever reason, I assumed Sasha and his two henchmen had gone.

On 14th August – according to my reckoning – I received my evening meal as usual and completed my household chores. While I was in the process of preparing my daily conversations, my concentration was interrupted by a loud scratching from above, a rattle of keys, the creak of the trap-door being lifted, and the beam of torch-light flooded the hole. The unmistakable figure of Sasha descended the ladder, dressed in his usual military garb and masked. He was followed by two other military types, both masked, but unknown to me.

I sat up and stared blankly at Sasha. My mind whirled; was I to be taken elsewhere? Was I to be released? Was I to be killed? My heart thumped, but I tried to hide my emotions. Sasha launched into his usual spiel, "In ten days you go home. No variant!" accompanied by the usual arm gestures. "Bullshit!" I said under my breath.

A newspaper was thrust into my hands. Sasha squatted at the far end of the hole and produced a Polaroid camera. The others squeezed into the entrance to the hole; one sat on the bucket lid. I tried to turn the newspaper around to glimpse the language in which the headlines were written, and received a whack to the side of my head from the fist of the gentleman next to me. But I'd seen it was a Georgian newspaper, although I couldn't make out the date.

Sasha took three flash photographs of me holding the newspaper with both hands in front of me, pulling each out of the camera methodically before taking the next. He looked at the first with his torch to check on the progress of its development, nodded his head in satisfaction, stood up and disappeared up the ladder followed by his two companions. The ladder was pulled up, the trap-door replaced and locked and there was silence, apart from the chickens. The only words had been Sasha's.

My first thought was that although I'd trimmed my beard by candle-flame a few days earlier, Sasha had made no comment about the obvious lack of growth. He'd been very keen to deny me a shave when we were on the outside. Clearly he no longer cared; – no point.

I tried to gather my thoughts. Surely, this was positive! He'd come to take photographs of me which meant that he, or one of his colleagues, was in touch with someone outside who needed to be shown that I was still alive. The date on the front page of the newspaper was meant to illustrate that. Could it be that negotiations were still continuing in connection with the ransom money? No chance, I knew, but... As for the "You go home" statement, he'd said ten days this time, not five. Did this mean something? Hardly likely, but I counted down the following ten days meticulously. Nothing happened.

The second time Sasha visited me was on or about 11th September. It was in the early hours of the morning, long after I'd eaten my breakfast. Two pairs of footsteps descended the staircase in the area next door, the beam of a torch was directed into my cell, and two arms thrust through the hole in the wall.

In one hand was a photograph of me, in the other was a biro. The voice of Sasha rasped, "You sign!" He must have carefully rehearsed the words that slowly and laboriously followed, "I am in serious trouble. You must pay one million dollars. Please help me. You write and sign!"

I recognised immediately that the photograph and the words he wanted me to write underneath my image were to be forwarded to my family. My mind raced, clearly, if there ever had been any negotiations with the authorities, they'd broken down. These people were now turning to my family in the UK as a last resort. I said, "*Niet*! No way!"

Sasha went absolutely mad. He shouted and screamed at me in Georgian – mainly obscenities – and I involuntarily backed away as far as I could from the flailing arms that stretched through the hole. Fortunately he couldn't reach me. Eventually, he stalked away and I heard his voice, in heated debate with another, gradually fade away. A door closed with a loud slam.

Chapter Forty

I was given no food for the following five days. The water came as usual, but no food. This was bad enough but as nothing compared with the mental torment it brought about. The ransom demand had quite obviously failed. They were now shooting for my family. One million dollars! They may as well have asked for a billion. I had nightmare images of Rod, my older son, desperately trying to raise the cash by putting himself in hock for the rest of his life. I imagined Mair, Lisa and Pip trying somehow through the courts to obtain possession of my cottage in Cowbridge, and dispose of that, and my savings, in a frantic and useless effort to fulfil the demand. Even if by some miracle one million dollars could be raised, then these people would demand more. No integrity involved here. You can't deal with them. I prayed fervently to God that He would not allow my family and friends to be driven into taking steps that would ruin their lives forever. It would be better if I died.

Five days later Sasha and his companion returned, again in the early hours of the morning, with two bottles of water as usual, still no food. Sasha snarled out the same rehearsed request. Again I declined to write anything. This time there was no outburst from Sasha. They simply quietly went away.

I'd read about people who go on hunger strike of their own volition: inmates of the Maze prison in Ireland: some religious sects: anorexics. I'd always been ambivalent about that kind of commitment, having never felt the need to take such dramatic steps. I can now confirm that going hungry is a very uncomfortable experience, especially when it's not a voluntary act of self-deprivation and you have no means to end it. Logically, I assumed, there was no point in their starving me to death. There were easier means of disposing of me, and, if I was dead and gone, then there was no chance of their obtaining any money at all. My emotions swirled around in all directions, torn between a huge concern for my family, and my own increasingly desperate situation. Eventually I became tired of thinking at all and my brain simply numbed up. I stopped feeling anything.

Sasha returned three days later. This time I agreed to write something. I wrote, "I am in serious difficulty. They want one million dollars. Please help." I didn't sign or date the note.

I handed it back and waited to see the reaction. Sasha seemed to be satisfied. He simply grunted and departed. Within half an hour I was given a meal of meat, soup with bread, a chicken leg, an apple and radish, a piece of cake and some tea, together with two bottles of water. It was the best meal of my life.

Nevertheless, I felt guilty: as if I had let myself and, more importantly, my family down. I tried to convince myself that I'd managed to amend the words such that they could be interpreted as being directed not only at my family, but at any other interested party. It was simply a statement wasn't it? It didn't work; I still felt guilty. I continued to pray fervently, always including the request to God that He would guide my family away from undertaking anything on my behalf that would prove disastrous for them in the future.

I later learned that no one in my family, or anyone else in the UK, received that note.

Chapter Forty-one

Noises from outside intruded into my consciousness above the noise of the radio, machinery, hammering, dogs and chickens: the playful shouts of the little girl who seemed to visit every week-end. Occasionally I'm sure, she was joined by a little boy, a grandson perhaps? Sometimes, I heard the voice of the farmer's wife, laughing with them, or scolding them. It seemed totally bizarre. How could relative normality be so close and yet so distant? Frequently, during my day-time, I heard the sound of a gun firing. I assumed the farmer was hunting for foxes or rabbits, usually confirmed a few days later, by my soup containing a few pieces of rabbit meat. A couple of times I heard the distinct sound of drums being beaten: in particular big bass drums accompanied by distant, but clear, human voices, shouting. I assumed a festival, or a wedding party. I later learned that these were political demonstrations, a common occurrence, even in the Pankisi, at that time. Once, I heard the drone of aeroplanes in the distance, followed by individual muffled bangs. Later I learned of the Russian airforce attack on civilian targets in the Pankisi Gorge on the 23rd August.

But the sound I came to dread most of all was the sound of thunder. The noise began as a distant echo, gradually increasing in volume until it became a constant booming and banging above me. The rain followed: initially a pitter-patter on a metal roof somewhere nearby, which increased to a loud roar, like throwing pebbles on corrugated iron. The ceiling rapidly became waterlogged and the normal steady drip that was my constant accompaniment, increased to a deluge which fell on me, mixed with chicken shit. As summer became autumn, the storms became more frequent. I was never dry, and it became colder. My only source of warmth was the daily half-candle. As the weather deteriorated, I was forced to delve into the reserve of five stumps built up over many weeks. This was not good news, and I disciplined myself not to touch them other than in extreme emergency. During the period of my imposed fast, I hadn't maintained my daily physical jerks. As I became wetter and colder, I forced myself to resume these activities with ever increasing frequency. They helped a bit, but not for long.

Strangely, there was something positive in all of this. As my physical discomfort increased, and my efforts to alleviate it increased, I had less time for the depressing thoughts that had constantly assailed me. There'd been times, in the early weeks of my incarceration, when I'd almost hoped for rain and the ensuing discomfort, in order to stop my mind from working. My thoughts then turned instead to survival. I found I wanted to live. The more pain I felt, the keener I was to continue to exist. Increasingly, I focused on myself, pushing aside any concerns about my family or friends. I became the focus of my thoughts. It made me feel guilty, but I knew instinctively that if I were to survive, I had to become totally single-minded. I became very selfish.

During most of my time in the hole, I was able to brainwash myself into falling into some semblance of sleep. Having exhausted myself with family conversations and prayers, I would then repeat, usually out loud, the same phrase... "You will survive; you will go home. You will survive; you will go home. You will survive; you will go home. You will survive, you will go home." Over and over again, it really worked. Eventually I was able to convince myself, if only temporarily, that this was actually going to happen, accept it, and doze off. Of course when I awoke I had to start all over again. But I kept at it. I guess it was a form of self-hypnosis.

It was a constant struggle to come to terms with the physical and mental torture of my existence in the hole, but I had to win in order to survive. One of the major problems was the lack of light; having to live in complete darkness for more that twenty three-hours out of twenty-four was tough. But it's possible. As with a blind person, I guess the mind becomes accustomed to being deprived of that particular sensory function and compensates by maximising those that remain. After a few weeks, I could use the toilet without having to light the candle; I learned how to eat in complete darkness, and, of course, the blackness surrounding me was no impediment to my conversational and praying activities. The fact that I was tethered by the neck was a constraint, but apart from the physical discomfort – the links of the chain bit into my neck – it became nothing more than a bloody nuisance. After all, where could I walk? If there had been daylight, what could I see, apart from the bleakness of my narrow, fetid cell? Far more fun to eke out the term of each candle, and light up only to interrupt unbearingly depressing thoughts, or to zap a few flies. In short, I got used to living in the dark.

A problem I was never really able to overcome was the lack of information. I tried on innumerable occasions to glean information – anything – from my captor. In this I failed utterly. He simply wouldn't play ball. The most I was able to get out of him was the word "*suka*", which I've subsequently learned is Russian for "bitch." He called me that frequently. Without any information to the contrary, my mind constantly moved in the direction of the most pessimistic of outcomes. It was a constant struggle to retain some mental positivity, and prevent my thoughts falling into the black void. I found myself hoping that the farmer would say something; even very bad information would be better than my thoughts.

The other big problem was the loneliness. I guess I'm a gregarious guy by nature. I like traffic, I like crowds, and I like people. I much prefer living in my little cottage in Cowbridge town centre, than in my rather more salubrious former home in the quaint but quiet village of Llandough. Enforced isolation was particularly hard for me to deal with. It dispossessed me of an important part of my character in a fundamental way. This was very undermining for me. My thoughts turned instinctively toward those who had suffered in the past – Japanese PoWs of the Second World War and to the early Christian martyrs who died horribly in the Roman amphitheatres – how would I have coped in those kinds of situations. I couldn't imagine. But I always returned to the tenet that they suffered as a group, with companions. They were all in the same desperate situation together, and were able to comfort and encourage each other in their plight. They didn't die alone. I was in solitary confinement under the ground, isolated, in great discomfort and with no hope of escape. I cannot over-state the comfort I gleaned from the clear responses I received to my long soliloquies in the darkness, but I yearned for the presence of another human being. Being alone was my Achilles heel.

On one occasion, and one occasion only, in order to alleviate the despondency of one particularly bleak mood, I launched into song; I bellowed out the words of *Calon Lan,* a popular Welsh hymn, and later *Mae Hen Wlad fy Nhadau,* the Welsh national anthem. I suppose I wanted to show to anyone outside who could hear that I was alive and still kicking. I also felt the need for the companionship of my own voice. My efforts were clearly not appreciated. Not surprisingly, there was no response.

Chapter Forty-two

At home, events were moving swiftly. Michael Boyd of Landell-Mills had taken personal control of the situation in the UK. His first action, in co-operation with the Foreign and Commonwealth Office (FCO) and Scotland Yard, was to quickly convene an informal gathering of my professional colleagues within Landell-Mills and Agrisystems, my close family and FCO and New Scotland Yard personnel. This initial grouping was later formalised as the FACC Group – "Friends and Concerned Colleagues of Peter Shaw" – and subsequently met at least once each month at the FCO. Its sole objective was to get me out of captivity as quickly as possible and in one piece. The FACC group initially comprised of:

Michael Boyd (Executive Chairman of Landell-Mills and Director of the DCI group of companies).

My family – Mair, Lisa, Rod and Pip.

Tim and Jackie Hammond – Jackie acted as personal assistant to Michael Boyd. She also acted as secretary and coordinated on a daily basis with all other members. Jackie also kept a personal diary, updated daily, from which I intermittently quote. She became totally involved in the efforts of the FACC group to obtain my release.

Rob Macaire and David Drake of the FCO.

Detective Superintendent David Douglas and Detective Inspector Ron Holmes of New Scotland Yard.

Paul Craig – Managing Director of Agrisystems Ltd., the company I worked for during my last six months in Georgia.

Michael Mgaloblishvili, my Georgian co-director of the bank, was already in London and joined the group early on. He quickly recognised that my abduction may have had a political motivation and best results would be obtained by placing pressure on the government of Georgia, particularly President Shevardnadze. This immediately became the over-riding target of the FACC group.

In late June, acting on the strong recommendation of the FACC group, European Commissioner Chris Patten appointed Denis Corboy as Special Envoy to Georgia on behalf of the European Commission. This was a key appointment. Denis had been Head of the EC Delegation in Georgia from 1994 until his retirement in 1999. He had an intimate knowledge of Georgia and its politicians, the history of the ABG, and had been a good friend of mine and a very supportive boss. He quickly joined the FACC team and endorsed the view of Mgaloblishvili.

In early July, Detective Superintendent David Douglas and Detective Inspector John Crawford of Scotland Yard travelled to Georgia to assist the Georgian police in their investigations. They, inevitably, leaned on a few "sensitive" Georgian politicians which caused Denis to fire a warning shot. **(See Appendix 1).**

Chris Patten wrote a strongly worded letter to President Shevardnadze. He criticised the security situation in Georgia, and advised the President that there was to be no "business as usual" between the EC and Georgia for the time being. In other words, he threatened to postpone further aid from the EU until my release. This drew a sharp response from the government of Georgia. A spokesman denounced the Commission and stated that "Lawlessness in the country will become worse if we do not have the financial means to suppress it." He forecast rebellions in the provinces and national anarchy. A communiqué was sent by Romano Prodi, President of the European Commission to Shevardnadze describing my abduction as a "bad and shameful" event. There was no retraction of anything stated in Patten's letter.

At the same time, a series of meetings was being held in Georgia between Deborah Barnes-Jones, UK ambassador in Georgia and Jacques Vantomme of the EC Delegation in Georgia on the one hand, and Menagerashvili, Foreign Minister of Georgia, on the other. The latter confirmed that "Everything possible was being done to find and free Mr. Shaw." He also confirmed that President Shevardnadze had demanded "maximum effort at all levels." The message was that heads would roll if I was not speedily found and released.

Paul Craig, Managing Director of Agrisystems Ltd., (to which company I was then under contract) travelled to Georgia in July. Paul met with the Georgian National Security Council who confirmed that my car, and others used during the abduction had been recovered, photo-fits of those suspected of being involved had been distributed nationwide, and they were convinced that I was being held in or near Tbilisi. Paul concluded that "It appears there is a high level of commitment and genuine involvement in trying to resolve this situation as quickly as possible." Paul also met with ABG personnel – "no ransom will be paid" – and Deborah Barnes-Jones – "nothing is more important than obtaining Peter's release," and with Diana who was "completely at a loss to know quite what to do next." Paul immediately recognised that Diana might be the first point of contact for the kidnappers and that there was clearly a real need "to keep closely in touch with her and provide what support we can." A most welcome and, as it turned out, correct assumption.

Tim was determined to travel to Georgia despite the very real personal risks.

Jackie's diary:

11ᵗʰ July: Tim's in Tbilisi. I know he had to go. I'm worried to death but I feel proud of him. We've always said we'll support each other's decisions in life and this is so important to Tim. He's desperate to find a way in to the total mystery of why Peter's been taken.

Tim held a series of meetings with the UK Embassy, the EC Delegation, the US Embassy, the National Security Council (with Deborah Barnes-Jones), with ABG personnel and with Diana. Ever the considerate one, it was Tim who arranged, with the co-operation of the UK Embassy, for Diana and Danny to be placed into secure accommodation in Tbilisi, and to receive some money on a regular basis. He also arranged for the transportation of our commodious luggage, which had been thoroughly searched by the Georgian authorities, to the UK, and for the safe keeping of my personal effects – plastic cards, passport etc. – at the British Embassy.

President Shevardnadze issued a statement in his weekly radio address to the effect that "The situation with regard to Peter Shaw's abduction must be resolved quickly even if it costs the lives of Georgian law enforcers." He said he had received information that I was alive. This was confirmed by Narchemashvili, Minister of the Interior, who announced that an arrest was shortly to be made of at least one of those guilty of kidnapping me. No arrest was made, but similar statements were made frequently over the following months, either by the Ministry of the Interior or the Ministry of State Security.

The general view of the Georgian authorities was that a formal ransom demand would be received shortly after my abduction. After much deliberation – a tough decision to take – the FACC team, absolutely correctly, concluded that "none of the parties (within the team) had the financial resources to pay a ransom or indeed to employ private investigators and negotiators." Michael and Jackie abbreviated the reasoning within the team to the "3 Ps":

"Pragmatic – there was no insurance, and high sums that had been demanded in other kidnappings could not be physically raised.

Policy – FCO policy that no ransom be paid.

Peter – they knew how he would respond if asked – Peter wouldn't want his family and friends to bankrupt themselves in raising a ransom.

The objective set by the FACC was: the rapid and safe return of Peter in good health without payment of ransom.

The team did however agree to appoint an independent negotiator should a ransom demand be formally received. This turned out to be an important appointment.

Denis Corboy made his first trip, as Special Envoy for the Commission, to Georgia on the 16th of July. Over the following seven days he held a series of meetings with high ranking ministerial and government officials culminating in a meeting with President Shevardnadze on the 22nd of July. **(The report of Denis to the EC and the FACC group together with his accompanying file note is incorporated in Appendix 2).** Denis's report confirmed to Mike Boyd and the FACC team that their initial instincts, regarding a largely political motivation for the kidnapping, were correct. The way forward, confirmed by Denis, was to place as much pressure on President Shevardnadze and those close to him as possible, both inside Georgia and internationally. This they did with a vengeance. This approach was not totally endorsed by the FCO who preferred a much softer and more diplomatic strategy, avoiding the need to ruffle political feathers. Fortunately for me, the advice of the FCO in this context was ignored by the FACC team.

Chapter Forty-three

Diana was going through a difficult time. Within a few days of her initial lengthy grilling by the police, she was summoned to attend the unpacking of our suitcases and luggage held in a warehouse at the airport pending our intended departure. Fortunately, she had the foresight to telephone the UK Embassy, and the process of the police riffling through our belongings was witnessed by Embassy and EC Delegation personnel. Diana had the clear impression that they were looking for drugs, or something to incriminate me in some form of malpractice. Of course they found nothing.

On three further occasions over the following few weeks, she was grilled alone by a combination of the police and officials of the Ministry of State Security. One Dato Kashkamazashvili from the Ministry was particularly nasty and took great delight in describing to Diana the terrible conditions in which he judged I was being held, and the vile manner in which I was being treated. She was also bullied and accused several times of withholding information. Of course, she had no information to withhold.

On the 19th July, Diana received a text message in Russian, on her mobile phone. The sender stated that he was a member of the gang that had kidnapped me. He wanted to know the telephone number of Mair in the UK. Diana had been well briefed by Dave Douglas of Scotland Yard during his visit to Tbilisi but, quite naturally, she panicked. She telephoned Jackie Hammond (as coordinator for the FACC group) and, at Jackie's suggestion, the UK Embassy, who immediately contacted Scotland Yard.

Jackie's diary: *19th July. Di called in a panic; she was crying and it was difficult to understand her. She'd had a call and didn't really know what to do. I was able to help. The Georgian number that called her is still written on a now faded post-it note on our message board.*

In line with instructions received, Diana texted a message in return. She asked her caller to prove his credentials, and demonstrate proof of life, by providing the names of my two dogs. Only I and my family and close friends were aware that I had for many years owned two Labradors, Gus and Gil. Diana received a further six or seven telephone calls and text messages over the following days. In each the same instruction was given – to advise him of Mair's telephone number – and to each Diana made the same response. The conversations were sometimes heated, as the caller became aware that the authorities were in the loop. Veiled threats were transmitted to Diana alluding to her lack of co-operation: "These questions are not being asked by Peter's family but by the police. Do you not care about Peter's state of health?" Diana stuck to her guns.

When the Gus and Gil theme had run its course without response, she demanded of the caller to name my daughter's favourite meat. Only I and those close to me were aware that Lisa is a confirmed vegetarian. Then as suddenly as they'd started, the calls and text messages to Diana stopped.

The communicator the FACC team had selected was John Dexter. John was a senior management consultant who had worked for many years in Eastern Europe, Asia and Africa and was well known personally to Michael Boyd. I'd met John only once in the UK, and then quite briefly, but we'd got on well. He was supported by Tony Bishop: a fluent Russian speaker nominated by the FCO. Tony had worked closely with David Douglas and his Scotland Yard colleagues on many occasions in the past. Michael phoned John Dexter soon after breakfast on the twentieth of July, and asked him if he'd be prepared to come on board. He had no hesitation.

Dave Douglas would act as their adviser alongside the FCO Counter-Terrorism Policy Department. John rang Scotland Yard for instructions. He was advised to buy a new mobile phone dedicated to what they would call Operation Penrith, and to go to Scotland Yard for a briefing. The next day he took the train to London for a meeting with Dave Douglas and his team. A silent policeman took him up to Dave's office and left him on his own for five minutes. Was he being watched? Was the room bugged? On one wall was an organisation chart reminiscent of something from MI5 and, opposite, the uniform of a Chicago police sergeant – perhaps used in a shoot-out in which Dave had played a leading part? On the desk, an ashtray inscribed with grateful thanks from the Government of Colombia. Soon, someone with a cheery smile came in and offered a cup of coffee. It was DI John Crawford. The coffee arrived in a polystyrene cup, accompanied by a new face, DI Ron Holmes, and then Dave Douglas appeared to complete the party. During the next few months, these people became John's firm friends.

John's task would start by making contact with Georgia. He had to agree to have a tap put on his mobile phone, and he bought various pieces of recording equipment from an apparently innocuous electronics shop conveniently next door to Scotland Yard. Then he had to establish a link with the hostage takers. He had a mobile phone number. That was all. Their only contact so far had been the text messages to Diana. So text messaging would be his means of communication too.

The first message read: "My name is John. I want to help Peter. I am a family friend." Again twice the next day, nothing came back. Then, in the middle of a business meeting, the blue phone gave off its distinctive bleep. He read the message. "Do you speak Russian?" John replied: "Sorry, no I don't." Fifteen minutes later, the phone rang. John excused himself from the meeting. The call was coming from Georgia. "Hello, this is John," he said. The caller rang off. Almost immediately another incoming text: the same message, asking if he spoke Russian. He sent back: "Sorry, I don't speak Russian. May I speak to Peter please?"

By now his business colleagues could see he was on edge, and for some reason surmised that he must be having an extra-marital affair – an awkward complication he could have done without. An hour later, the same caller left the line open for three seconds whilst connected to John's answer-phone, but again said nothing. The following day, John repeated his text message at lunchtime and sent a new message at teatime: "Thank you for the message. I'm sorry I do not understand Russian. May I speak to Peter please?" After an hour the angry response came back: "Are you joking? Peter *times nou* (sic). Where is the interpreter?" John sent back a polite reply, to be met with: "I'm sick and tired of it! I demand an interpreter present. I don't speak English."

Dave Douglas and his colleagues had been advising on the wording of John's part of this bizarre conversation. Now it was time for closer collaboration. They agreed to wait until the Georgian evening and then play ball. "I will have a Russian interpreter available tomorrow at 13.30 BST (17.30 Georgia). Please may I speak to Peter then?" There was no response.

Next day, John arrived at Scotland Yard a little ahead of Tony, his interpreter. Up in Dave Douglas's office, Dave produced a tape recorder and wired it up to John's new blue mobile. The recorder lay on a small oblong coffee table alongside five polystyrene cups of hot coffee and various papers including a contribution from Dave: a sheet with big red letters proclaiming the responses John was supposed to make to the expected demands from the hostage takers. The guidelines were,

- always mention Peter by name,
- always show concern for his health,
- emphasise John's position as a friend of the family,
- ask for proof that the caller was actually holding Peter and that Peter was alive and well,
- avoid making promises,
- indicate a need to consult others,
- develop an atmosphere of uncertainty,
- establish a time for the next contact.

So began a long series of meetings trying to deal with someone they did not know. They gave him the nickname Boris: that seemed to make things easier somehow. Tony was called Anton. John and Tony would start a session by phoning him. Perhaps Boris would want to control times of communication and avoid giving away his position, for usually his phone was switched off. Then he would call them. Tony or John would respond and Boris would hang up. Why did Boris not speak? Here was the interpreter he had demanded, speaking perfect Russian, interpreting for John, the family friend. They spent hours wondering, guessing whether Boris had diverted his phone to avoid detection, analysing the detail of his communications, and thinking who he was and where he might be.

Suddenly, in one of these sessions, Boris sent his first substantial text in Russian: "Ask John and then reply. Have you been hired in from outside as an interpreter, or are you a person in whom John trusts to pass information in this matter?" Tony was able to finally send a carefully constructed reply. Then the threats began: the first on the 22nd July.

"Please give John our conditions. Peter and K have damaged our business to the tune of five million six hundred thousand dollars. We wish to regain our capital in exchange for Peter's life. Are you interested in Peter's life?"

John and Tony quickly realised that the amount mentioned was the sum total of the share capital of the ABG. Surely there was a link? Much later, another text: "If the decision does not lie with you, there is no point in dealing with you or carrying out your requests, because we shall get our capital in any event. If the answer is yes, then the solution will be favourable for us and Peter." There'd been a lull during this exchange, so they'd dispersed: Tony to Surrey, John to Hampshire. At Waterloo, John's blue phone rang briefly: it was Boris but he was cut off.

It was one of those very hot summer days when the rails buckle and trains leave late, and with so many passengers trying to phone home, the mobile network was jammed. No chance of getting back to Boris. At last the train left the station. Out in the suburbs the phone worked once more. John leant out of the carriage window to avoid the crush inside, while Tony gave him the Russian for his crucial next message, to puzzled stares from other sweating travellers.

The following Tuesday, they all assembled at the Yard. It turned out to be a frustrating afternoon: a combination of garbled texts, misunderstandings and furious responses while they were still working out how to deal with the last text but one. They gave up and suggested another attempt on Thursday. That day, John stayed at home and operated from there, with no better luck. He called Boris but having no response, he signed off, setting a rendezvous for the following Monday.

On the 5th August, back at the Yard, Boris called four times and sent four text messages. John and Tony tried repeatedly to explain to Boris that my family didn't have access to the kind of money of which they spoke, and emphasised the ordinary nature of my family and background. Boris became angry. "Tell us orally what you have in mind when you say that you have replied to our terms."

They tried to explain that they needed to know that I was alive. They requested Boris to ask me what instrument my father played. John and Tony knew my father had played piano. The response was, "Your messages are not reaching us. We are convinced that you think fit to have a joke at our expense with your Chinese messages and unserviceable phone. In order to obtain fulfilment of our demands, we have radical means available. Peter has requested that you tell his wife about his illness and imminent amputation."

This was worrying and depressing. The FACC group hadn't been able to establish good communications and had no idea whether I was well, or even alive. However, thanks to the efforts of the various police forces and government agencies, they were getting closer to my captors' lair – at least they were beginning to think they could estimate roughly where these calls might be coming from. John bought a large-scale map of Georgia.

They kept up a barrage of texts and voice calls for nine weeks, trying to discover how and where Boris was operating, whilst impressing on him the need for him to tell them about me and keep me safe. But they were not to hear from Boris again. The focus was moving from police, spies, technicians and negotiators to the politicians.

Jackie's diary: *22nd August. During the FACC meeting we had a call from Denis. Michael wrote on the bottom of my page, "the operation has started."*

Chapter Forty-four

Jackie's diary: *23rd September – it's now been 97 days – Peter dead or alive (not known), health (not known), location (not known), captors (not known), motive (not known), release date (not known). Our strategy to date has been compliant, co-operative, supportive, and innovative – but our results are zero!*

Local newspaper headlines in Wales blared:

100 DAYS OF HOPING FOR FATHER'S RETURN

They incorporated an interview with my daughter, Lisa, who, a few days earlier had given birth to my grandson, Ioan. Lisa wanted her Dad home safely and as quickly as possible.

Headlines of 26th September:

BODY FOUND IN INGUSHETIA IS NOT THAT OF PETER SHAW

The 30th of September:

GEORGIA: BANKER CAPTIVE STILL ALIVE?

This last reflected statements made, again, by the Georgian ministries who had apparently received information confirming that I was alive and being held in the Pankisi Gorge in north-eastern Georgia.

On 26th September, John Smith, my Member of Parliament, departed for Georgia. John was there to chair a NATO conference in Tbilisi, and to meet with President Shevardnadze, accompanied by Deborah Barnes-Jones. During his meeting with the President, John described the ordeal of my family, and the need for concrete information. John, like Denis, left the interview with the firm impression that Shevy knew more than he was prepared to say. The President did state, however, "with absolute assurance, that Peter Shaw is alive." John handed the President two letters, one from Mair addressed to the President's wife, and the other from Lisa addressed to the President. The latter read:

Your Excellency,

I am the daughter of Peter Shaw, the former director of the Agro-business Bank of Georgia, who was kidnapped in Tbilisi on the 18th of June.

It is now over three months since I, or anyone has heard from Dad, and despite repeated assurances from those in charge of the investigation to find Dad, we seem no closer to having him home than we did in June.

My two brothers and I, together with the rest of the family, grow increasingly concerned for Dad's safety. On many occasions we have been told that Dad's release would be imminent, and that he would be home soon, but every time our hopes have been dashed. Does anyone even know where he is?

As Dad's birthday and Christmas approach, we ask that you do all in your power to find Dad and to return him safely to us without delay. His grand-children miss him. His place is here with us. We trust your help in this will end this nightmare for everyone.

Regards,
Lisa Evans

John also handed photographs of Lisa and family to the President. Apparently he smiled, and through a translator said that "Ioan looks like his grandfather.

The 1st October:

EU WARNS GEORGIA OVER KIDNAPPING

On 5th October, the Georgian media reported that arrests had been made in the Pankisi Gorge of seven men suspected of being involved in my abduction. The FCO was unable to confirm news of the arrests. No charges were subsequently brought against those arrested. A few days later, a senior Chechen diplomat was arrested in Tbilisi, and accused of being implicated in my kidnapping. This he denied and was subsequently released through lack of evidence. It was suspected that his mobile phone had been the instrument through which the text messages received by John Dexter and Tony had been made.

On the 6th October, the long-postponed meeting of the EU/Georgia Co-operation Council took place in Brussels. During the course of the meeting, a senior EU diplomat threatened to further suspend all economic aid to Georgia unless the government of Georgia restored law and order to the country. Reference was made to the kidnapping of Peter Shaw and the murder of the German EC staffer, Gunther Beuchel, some months earlier. No arrests had been made. On the same day, the Georgian authorities announced that "Several people have been arrested in connection with Peter Shaw's kidnapping." This was later contradicted by Japaridze, Chief of the Security Council of Georgia. He did however announce that the authorities were "making progress with freeing the British banker."

On the same day, John Smith described to the FACC group at the FCO how he had met with UK ambassador Deborah Barnes-Jones in the garden of her private residence in Tbilisi, and conversed at length in the pouring rain; the only definite way to ensure a private discussion and avoid bugs. Denis described how he had met with the US Ambassador, during his last trip to Georgia, in a Perspex bubble at the US Embassy, which, he was told "was regularly de-bugged."

Throughout October, the pressure was maintained. The FCO provided the FACC group with a presentation on the situation in the Pankisi Gorge; the FACC group met with John and Helen Peters (John had been held prisoner for seven weeks during the first Gulf War), who were immensely supportive and encouraging to my family – "If he has a strong personality, he'll be OK." Denis Corboy met with Chris Patten and arrangements were made for his return trip to Georgia; Glenys Kinnock, my MEP, prepared to travel to Georgia and meet with Shevardnadze on the eleventh of November, armed with photographs and letters from my family; large numbers of posters bearing my mug-shot were plastered throughout Tbilisi; the Welsh press campaign for my release continued unabated; the American Chamber of Commerce in Georgia organised a meeting attended by a number of Georgian ministers, at which "all stood in support of a vast improvement in the security situation in Georgia, and the plight of Peter Shaw." David Douglas of Scotland Yard told the FACC group that he had "a strong gut-feeling that all will be well…"

Chapter Forty-five

October was a bad month for me. It rained almost every day, and the nights – my days – turned very chilly. It became more and more difficult to sleep at all, and my health inevitably began to deteriorate. Despite the cold, there were still plenty of flies, and they were biting like mad. The bites became infected. My right testicle became swollen, and sores in my groin exuded a bleeding pus; a fungal infection attacked my feet and between my toes. At some point in the early part of October, my gaoler began to supply me with a daily medicine bottle filled with vodka. I guess this was meant for me to drink in order to ward off the effects of the chill in the hole. I used it instead to dab on my various infections with a piece of toilet paper. It helped, but as my situation deteriorated, I realised that I could not possibly live through a winter in this hole.

I somehow had to come to terms with this. My method – if you can call it that – was a combination of self-induced brain-washing, by forcing an entrance into that part of the brain where untold numbers of happy memories are stored, and by mentally recounting examples of the many millions who had died bravely in far worse circumstances than mine.

The process was to initially mentally rehearse, and then say out loud, words to the effect:

"Who do you think you are, Peter Shaw? You've had a damned good life. You've enjoyed yourself thoroughly, worked hard and played hard during your time, and now you're going to die. So what! You have to die at some time. You've had fifty-seven good years. That's a lot more than many. Stop feeling sorry for yourself and get on with it!"

It sounds daft I know, but this mantra helped me to accept my fate.

I drew inspiration from figures in history: for example, a newfound affinity with Captain Scott of the Antarctic. Of course I'd seen the 1940's film starring John Mills as Scott, and as a schoolboy I'd read books describing his exploits and the great courage with which he met his death. I remembered his last written words – "For God's sake, look after our people." Somehow I found him to be hugely inspirational, perhaps because he was alone at the time of his death, as I was, and, like Scott, I was pretty bloody cold! And it was dark. And, maybe it was because ultimately he had failed in his objective of being the first to reach the Pole. In my depressed state, I viewed my life as having been a failure too. I did not, at the time, consciously try and work out why my thoughts fixed on him in particular, but they did. And I would try and die as heroically as he had.

This did not prevent me from including in my daily prayers the selfish request that I be allowed to die quickly, and as painlessly as possible. I asked repeatedly that I expire by the quick heart attack route and not suffer a long lingering death.

Mingled with these thoughts were my memory-dredging exercises of happy events of long ago and, amazingly, visions of the future. I saw myself opening the gate to my cottage in Cowbridge and struggling to unlock the front door – the key was always a problem; playing my baby-grand piano, too large really for my little dining-room; images of Diana and Danny on Christmas morning opening presents under the tree; the cats playing in the snow in the back-garden; buying the turkey and the all-important goose from the local butcher; the whole family at Christmas lunch, pulling crackers, wearing silly hats; Bing Crosby and "White Christmas", Alistair Sims and "A Christmas Carol", James Stewart and "It's a Wonderful Life"; a family reunion…

That was it! I vowed that *when* I returned home, I would organise a huge party for all the family: aunties, uncles, great aunts and uncles; and second cousins four times removed. The whole shooting match! I saw mental pictures of my mother singing "Catari" – a memory of Christmas parties of many years ago; of Shirley and Corris crooning "Unforgettable", of Aunty Iris belting out "Chicago", fox-trotting to Glenn Miller; Diana dancing with Danny, and always with me vamping along on the piano in the background. The fact that over half of the participants in the family Christmas parties of my boyhood had passed away long since, had nothing to do with it. Somehow they would all be there at the family reunion!

My thoughts were a mix of coming to terms with the inevitability of my death and managing that trauma, mingled with happy recollections, and imaginings of the future homecoming, beginning at Heathrow Airport and climaxing in the family gathering. I was in the middle of yet another wonderful re-enacting of my daughter's wedding celebrations of years earlier. It had rained, and I was cold, wet and pretty miserable; the rats had been particularly active that night and the little dog had been strangely quiet. I had my breakfast as usual and was in the process of cleaning up the remains of candle wax from the table. It was the beginning of just another day in the hole, when the trapdoor opened...

Chapter Forty-six

Into the darkness which had been my home for four months
came a beam of torchlight, followed by a ladder down which
descended Sasha with two henchmen following behind. As
usual, they wore balaclava masks, military uniforms and carried
Kalashnikovs. Sasha breathed heavily as he shone the torch
around my underground cell and visibly recoiled from the mess
and the stench; straw from my tattered mattress was strewn
everywhere; the contents of the bucket were over-flowing and
fetid water slopped on and around my bed. He stared at me with
unblinking eyes and said in English, "Peter Shaw, you strong
man." I said "Sasha, you cunt!" Fortunately he didn't
understand.

He tossed boots and socks, a military jacket and over-
trousers in my direction, and leaned forward to unlock the
padlock securing the chain around my neck. The immediate
relief was enormous: I hadn't realised how heavy the chain had
been. The other men hauled me to my feet and I struggled to put
on the clothes over my filthy rags. They tried to help me. Sasha
gestured that I was to climb the ladder.

This was not easy. My leg muscles refused to propel me up
the steps and I had to be pulled up by the arm by Sasha, and
pushed up by the two other members of the gang. Within
seconds I was standing – wobbly for sure – but actually
standing, on grass. I couldn't believe it. I could not believe that
I was really breathing fresh air again. I felt it on my face and the
bits of my exposed flesh; I sucked it into my lungs like a
vacuum cleaner. It tasted wonderful. It was a cold and very dark
night. I was standing in a field and heard the faint rustling of
trees around me, the loud clucking of the chickens and the
baying of dogs in the distance. I couldn't see a thing: everything
was blackness. But I was out of the hole and it was marvellous.
I really couldn't give a damn what they did with me now. I was
out of the hole.

Within seconds, I was grabbed by Sasha's friends, one to each arm and hustled across a field. Sasha walked ahead of us, while the others dragged me along behind him. They moved quickly for about ten minutes over grass, then on to a made-up road for some moments before bundling me into the back seat of a light-coloured car. The two strangers sat one to each side of me still holding my arms, their legs clamped over mine, my head forced down below the level of the front seats. Sasha drove up a rough dirt track quite quickly. As I bounced around, he exchanged a few whispered words with his colleagues in Georgian, which I was unable to understand. But I could sense their tenseness. The guy who held my right arm very tightly was shaking. I felt the vibrations through his hand, and his leg. I was not shaking. Why were they so nervous? I was out of the hole. That was good enough for me.

My mind was in turmoil now. I tried to think. Unusually, Sasha hadn't said anything about my going home. He hadn't launched into his "No variant" speech. This wasn't necessarily bad, surely? My gaolers had perhaps concluded, like me, that I couldn't survive the winter in the hole and were taking me to a warmer location, perhaps to a house or apartment with a fire. Or was I to be topped? Had they finally come to understand that the ransom wouldn't be paid and the only thing to do was to get rid of me? This was surely the most likely option. Strangely, I wasn't terrified. Sure I was frightened – I wanted to urinate – I knew that symptom of my fear well, but really, I was resigned to my fate whatever that might be. Anything was better than the hole. I said a little prayer and asked God to look after my people.

The car stopped after about fifteen minutes. I was dragged out, I heard the car doors close, and was hustled along a narrow dirt-track, a gradual incline, with one to each side holding me firmly by each arm. I was conscious that someone was walking behind us: that must be Sasha. I was beginning to feel my legs but couldn't walk at their pace. They were moving at a fair lick, I stumbled and was pulled and lifted along. It was still very dark but there were a few stars and the wind seemed keener and colder. I could see shapes, but no detail.

Suddenly, as if by arrangement, we stopped. There was no sign of habitation or lights from a village. There was nothing but a barren black heath. A few words of whispered conversation were exchanged, and my right-hand guard turned around momentarily to talk to the person behind us. I heard the sound of a weapon being removed from his shoulder and the metallic click of the bolt being drawn back. At that moment I knew I was going to be killed. I sensed rather than saw that there were some bushes to the left of the track. As he turned around to speak to the person to our rear, my guard relaxed his grip on my arm. Instinctively and without thinking, I lurched in the direction of the bushes, hit the ground, fell into a shallow ditch and rolled and scrambled away from where my captors stood. I will never know why I did that, a final fling of the instinct for self-preservation, perhaps?

Only a metre or so away, guns fired loudly; I saw brilliant flashes of white light against the black night background. I waited for the bullets to hit me, holding my arms around my head. My lurch into the undergrowth was surely only a gesture: they could easily strafe the bushes and kill me. Why were they not doing so? The gunfire lasted for only a few seconds. I lay in the gorse and listened incredulously to the sounds of footsteps departing down the track in the direction from which we had come. Were they going away? If so they would surely return. A breathy, deep gasping sound came from the direction of the track, continued intermittently for a few seconds and then stopped. I lifted my head out of the bushes and could just make out a shapeless dark mass on the track, and nothing else. There was absolutely no sound at all, apart from the faint whisper of the wind in the gorse bushes.

Odd, but I was still thinking, or at least I thought I was still thinking, quite clearly, but the situation was unreal. I couldn't believe that I'd actually lived through what I'd just heard and seen. Here I was sitting on a mountain side somewhere in the back of beyond, in a cold wind, in complete darkness, and alone. And I was alive. I actually said out loud, "Peter Shaw, what the bloody hell are you doing here?" It was somehow reassuring to hear my own voice. I sat there for some minutes trying to come to terms with the events I'd just witnessed. Surely they'd meant to kill me. But how could they have missed me? Obviously someone had been shot by mistake, but how could they have *missed* me?

I crawled slowly over to the dark mass on the track, felt for the cigarette lighter which was still in my trousers pocket, and flicked it on. The form on the ground was a man dressed in military uniform, masked, lying on his back, with arms and legs outstretched, surely one of those who had marched me to this desolate spot. I put my hand on his chest; there was no movement. He was clearly dead.

I felt absolutely calm, but numb, and distanced from this situation. All of this was happening to someone else, not to me. Think. Don't panic now, of all times. The thought flashed through my head momentarily that maybe I was free and no longer a captive. Could it really be true? I couldn't believe it, and just sat there, legs crossed, next to the body and tried to think. I had no idea where I was, and could see only a few feet in any direction. Should I remain there until it became lighter? No, it couldn't be very late, and surely Sasha and his gang would quickly realise that they had a man missing and come back and search for me. They must surely soon discover that they'd killed the wrong guy! That was surely the case. They might even be on their way back to find me now. I decided to move along the track. The footsteps had departed in that direction so I stumbled along the track in the opposite direction.

I don't know why I did what I did next. Some weird idea came into my head that I didn't want to wear anything military. So, having staggered along for a couple of hundred metres, I sat down and began to remove the over-trousers. Because they were elasticated at the bottom, I had to laboriously take off the army boots, then pull down the trousers and put the boots back on. This took some time, but I persevered. I also wanted to get rid of the army jacket, but I was shivering with cold now, so I decided to keep it on. I then continued, stumbling and falling along the track like a drunken man. After a few hundred metres more, the track split. The wider of the two seemed to proceed upward and around the side of the hill; the other ran diagonally down the hillside, but was muddy and badly rutted. I chose the latter. As I lurched down the track it became steeper and more and more difficult to negotiate. I fell often and got covered with mud, but kept on going. After about an hour, I sensed, rather than saw, the outline of some buildings, just a few metres down the path. To my amazement, I could also definitely see moving pinpoints of light in the distance: the headlights of vehicles moving along a road? Unbelievable, but was my muddy little path heading in the direction of those lights and a road? Could it be that I was really going to be free? I tried to quicken my pace. Falling down had never felt so good.

Hobbling along, I tried to work out what to do when I reached the road along which the traffic was travelling – if that was what I was seeing. I believed I was in Azerbaijan. I know very few words of the Azeri language, but, as in Georgia, the vast majority of Azeris speak Russian. I tried to rehearse what I'd say in rudimentary Russian if I was able to stop a vehicle on the road. I couldn't be far away from the Azerbaijan/Georgian border. I needed to get to the Red Bridge, the only border crossing I knew between the two countries. That's *"Krasni Most"* in Russian. Would I be able to persuade someone to take me there? How far was it? I had no money and looked like a scarecrow. Even if I got to the Bridge, how would I get into Georgia? To cross official borders in the Caucasus involved bribing the guards, even with the benefit of a passport and visa. I, of course, had neither, and none of the border guards would be able to speak English. Still, if I could get to the road I would manage somehow. Just get there.

Suddenly, voices; I crouched down. Had I travelled in a circle and ended up back in the arms of my captors? My heart dropped like a stone and I felt a desperate need to urinate. The voices became louder, they were drawing nearer to me and were speaking in Georgian. How could that be if I was in Azerbaijan? Then they began to shout in my direction. Despite the darkness, they'd obviously spotted me. In a panic, I stood up and tried to stumble away from the voices. Amazingly, one voice was shouting at me in English, yelling, "Who are you?" and "Sit down!"

This was incredible. I put my arms in the air and yelled, "Peter Shaw, Agro-business Bank of Georgia, Peter Shaw." A mumbled conversation and then "Sit down now," again. I shouted back, "Peter Shaw, Peter Shaw," and then, bizarrely, "Wales, Cardiff." Not too many Caucasians would recognise the word London in English leave alone Cardiff. I sat down cross-legged holding my arms in the air. I was scared shitless but there was no point in trying to get away. I couldn't move quickly enough to stand a chance. And one of them spoke English.

Out of the darkness came a group of seven or eight men. They approached me cautiously, crouching. They wore military uniforms and carried Kalashnikovs which were pointed at me. They were not wearing masks. One of them, in the front of the group shouted in English, "You are Peter Shaw?"

"Yes, Peter Shaw, Peter Shaw. I am Peter Shaw."

"Stay still. Do not move."

They ran toward me, gathered around me, mumbled to each other in Georgian and stared at me as if they couldn't believe their eyes. All at once, as if by a signal, they began to clap me enthusiastically on my back, pat me on the head, and took turns to shake my hand vigorously, babbling excitedly to each other in Georgian. One of them broke into a jig. My face must have been a picture. What on earth was going on? The one who spoke English put his face close to mine, as if that would assist me in the understanding process, and shouted excitedly, "You are Peter Shaw. You are famous. You are good man. We look for you for many months!" His head went up and down like a puppet, and he smiled broadly at me through yellow teeth and a black forest of beard stubble. He had a lovely face.

211

This was not right. It was all too much for me to take in. I wanted desperately to believe these people, but at the same time a nagging voice deep down inside was saying, "Don't believe them. If they are Georgian soldiers, what are they doing in Azerbaijan? They must be bandits or arms smugglers or drug smugglers. They cannot really be soldiers." I'd been so badly disappointed so many times; I refused to be taken in again.

Quickly, the English-speaking one, who seemed to be in charge, restored order, barked some instructions, and spoke quickly and breathlessly in Georgian into a mobile phone. I was given water, lifted to my feet and dragged down the path, stumbling and falling, the soldiers stooping and stopping frequently, as if expecting an attack. Another ten minutes and we came to an army jeep – I noticed no Georgian army markings. They bundled me into the rear-seat with two soldiers on either side of me, still patting me on the head, and smoothing my arms with their hands as if they'd found a much-loved lost dog. The driver put his foot down hard, and the jeep screamed down the track with me bouncing in the back seat. We stopped outside a large concrete building out of which a flood of soldiers rushed: dozens of them, all intent on shaking me by the hand, thwacking me on the back and shouting excitedly into my face. The soldiers holding me by each arm had great difficulty in getting me through the door of the building, baulked by the weight of people wanting to greet us. Yet I still couldn't believe I was safe.

I was taken into a small room off the main corridor, the door was closed to keep out the seething mass of uniforms. I was offered more water, cigarettes were thrust upon me and someone asked me questions, rapidly in Georgian, which I didn't understand. I simply shook my head and looked blank. I was in fact completely confused. My brain refused to accept what was happening to me. Then, out of the blur of sound, a voice spoke to me in clear English. It said, "Peter Shaw, Peter Shaw, we have found you at last!" I looked up and saw the face of someone I recognised. It was Irakli Alazania, Deputy

Minister of State Security whom I had met in Tbilisi at a function many months earlier.

I stared at him in complete and utter disbelief. Everything stopped, and then began to move again in slow motion; the voices around me faded away and then returned, slowly merging into one harmonious long chord. I could hear the cogs in my head turning as realisation dawned. I was free: I was actually free. And then I broke down.

Chapter Forty-seven

I blubbered like a two-year-old. Everyone tried to console me. Soldiers hugged me, put their arms around me, stroked me, patted me, and plied me with cigarettes, biscuits and mugs of hot, very sweet tea. Through a mist, Alazania was talking to me. I was not in Azerbaijan, but in Georgia: in the Pankisi Gorge. The Georgian army had found a trouser-belt in the Gorge months earlier, which they thought might be mine. It had been sent to Scotland Yard, and had been identified as a Marks and Spencer belt belonging to me. Elements of the Georgian army were in process of conducting a house-to-house search for me in the Pankisi Gorge. He explained that I had "escaped" and miraculously met up with a Georgian army outpost, and that I was a "hero". I shook my head. I was certainly no hero and continued to blubber away. Between sobs, I told him about the dead man who must still be laying on the ground a few hundred metres up the track, and he issued instructions to some soldiers who scurried off.

The remainder of that night is like a dream. I was vaguely aware of Alazania patiently trying to explain to me the great efforts made by the Georgian authorities to find me, the frustrations they'd experienced, where they'd found my belt, the combing of the Pankisi, but I wasn't able to make any sense of it. The small room filled and emptied successively with people wearing military uniforms mixed with people in black civilian over-coats, all running around making frantic telephone calls. No one seemed to understand that my tears were tears of joy, and my rambling words were small gestures of thanks to God for answering my prayers.

I tried to tell Alazania to contact my family, and repeatedly gave him Mair's telephone number. He simply reiterated, "Everything is okay, everything is okay. Don't worry. You are a hero," and continued with his telephone calls. I didn't want to be a hero. I simply wanted to talk with my family and let everyone know I was alive. I asked him to contact Diana. He simply said, "Everything is okay, Diana is fine. You are a hero. No problem. We go now."

Everything moved very slowly. I was gently lifted off the chair and led most carefully by many hands, with more back-slapping, to a waiting black Mercedes. I was deposited in the rear seat between two soldiers. Alazania sat in the front passenger seat and off we went, heading, this time definitely, for Tbilisi, a two and a half hour drive, followed by two other vehicles. We passed through the village of Akhmeta, proof if I needed it, that we were indeed travelling down the Pankisi Gorge, and then the town of Telavi. I was in a daze. It had all happened so quickly. I alternated between quiet sobs and whispered expressions of gratitude to the Man Upstairs. My soldier companions in the rear seat continued to stroke, pat and generally console me, although I was truly the happiest man in the world. I must also have been the smelliest man in the world.

The mobile phone of Alazania rang continuously throughout the journey. First, President Shevardnadze telephoned and Alazania passed his telephone to me. Shevardnadze speaks only a little English, but I clearly understood his message of congratulations and good wishes, and attempted to mumble something reasonably coherent in response. Then, a number of Ministers telephoned, some spoke in English, some in Georgian. Officials from the UK Embassy phoned; the Georgian Ambassador to the UK, the American Embassy... the phone was red hot. Between telephone conversations, Alazania continued to recount to me the intense efforts made by the Georgian and UK authorities in trying to find me. He also told me that the body on the dirt track had been found and identified. He was a bandit known as "Tashkent." He was sure that this information would quickly lead to the arrest of those who'd kidnapped me. I really couldn't give a damn then. I was still trying to come to terms with the fact that I was free and was on the way home.

As we neared the outskirts of Tbilisi, our car was stopped by a mass of people. We simply couldn't get through. I assumed that a serious road accident had occurred but Alazania explained to me that these people were journalists, all of whom wanted to interview me. As he was explaining this to me, the rear passenger door was yanked open, the soldier was pulled out, and a suited gentleman took his place. He proceeded to explain to me in perfect English that he was the Head of Communications in Georgia, and we must go immediately to the television studio. President Shevardnadze had so decreed. I tried to protest, but the President had given instructions and that was that. On reaching the city centre, Alazania pointed out to me the many large billboards that were plastered with an image of me surmounted by the words, in English and Georgian, "Peter Shaw, kidnap victim: Release Peter Shaw now!" I stared at them in disbelief. As our car parked by the steps leading to the television studio, a crowd of photographers and journalists descended upon us. Climbing the steps, flanked by Alazania, his driver, the Communications guy and the remaining soldier, I was greeted by the Ministers of State Security and the Interior who pushed their way through the crowd, and shook my hand vigorously. Cameras popped in my face accompanied by a barrage of incomprehensible questions.

Inside the studio dozens of people were waiting: journalists and many ministers and high-ranking government officials. Among the sea of faces I picked out those of Deborah Barnes-Jones and Jacques Vantomme. I have never in my life been so happy to see familiar faces. We hugged, kissed and cried; they were both kind enough to ignore the vile stench that must have wafted from me.

In a daze I was deposited before a television camera and I did my best to respond to the questions asked through an interpreter, although I now have virtually no recollection of what was said and how I responded. Still dazed and confused, I was whisked off to the Metechi-Sheraton Hotel accompanied by Deborah and Jacques, where awaiting me were Stuart McLaren and other Embassy officials, an English doctor, and a host of ministerial and security people. The hotel manager generously assured us that the bar in my suite was well-stocked and would be replenished if required. The filthy remnants I had worn for the past five months were disposed of and I was immediately and minutely examined by the doctor. He seemed to be keenly interested in my mental state but also undertook a detailed physical examination of me. His written report eventually included reference to "a healed longitudinal scar across the left parietal bone with a palpable depressed skull fracture; evidence of muscular wasting of arms and legs; severe candidiasis of both thighs and the anal region, and chronic fungal infection of all toes." His summary stated, "His captors have subjected Mr Shaw to a dehumanising experience… He is going to require intensive assistance to overcome this experience…" There followed a long list of recommendations. He was a very nice chap.

As far as I was concerned I was already on the way to complete recovery. I was the happiest man in the world. The penny had finally dropped that I was free and safe. I tried to appear calm and in control, but my heart was fluttering like a butterfly's wings and my stomach was dancing a tango. Everyone around did their best to pretend to be in control, but we were all very, very excited. Lots of corks were popped and congratulatory handshakes abounded. I know I chattered away all night: I couldn't stop. I was determined to make up for lost time. Gradually, with lots of hugs and kisses, the crowds dissipated until by the early hours of the morning there remained only Stuart McLaren and his Embassy colleagues. Deborah and Jacques had quietly departed to attend a meeting with the Ministers of State Security and the Interior. It was agreed that I should leave, with Diana and Danny, on the following morning's flight for Heathrow, but would I first co-operate with the authorities and attend a meeting with ministers before the 10.00am departure? I was of course very happy to comply.

I wanted to do four things urgently: telephone Mair and my three kids in the UK, hug and kiss Diana and Danny and have a proper shave and shower. In fact, I had two proper shaves that night, and three or four showers. As I was finishing the second shower, Diana burst into the bedroom. Unknown to me she had been collected by UK Embassy officials shortly after I had arrived at the hotel, and had been waiting in an adjacent room until the ministers and their followers had departed. It was really a dream come true. We hugged and cavorted around the bedroom floor in a flood of tears. Within minutes, Diana's mum and sister hurtled into the bedroom with Danny in tow; they'd been staying together in Rustavi that night, and they too had been brought to the hotel by an Embassy car – a black Mercedes with a Union Jack flying from the bonnet. I don't know what excited Danny the most – seeing his Dad, or the Merc with the flag flying! A few minutes later and Stuart managed to contact Mair and Lisa on the telephone. I was actually speaking to them. I couldn't believe it. They, together with Rod and Pip and many others would meet me straight off the flight the following day. I was, incredibly, really going home.

Just released

Arriving back in the UK

Meeting my grandchild, Ioan, for the
first time

In August 2006 Diana and I got married –
this was taken with Danny at our
home in Wales.

Chapter Forty-eight

Diana helped me to scrub off some of the accumulated dirt during my final shower that night, gave my tangled mane a quick snip, and cleaned and cut my fingernails and toenails. True to his word, the hotel manager had indeed replenished the bar, and my little Georgian family and I spent the remainder of the night crunching toast, slurping beer and chatting away with Stuart and his Embassy colleagues. I was on cloud nine and stayed there. I knew I was mouthing off something shocking but I couldn't stop myself from yakking away. Diana packed some clothes that the Embassy people had somehow managed to rescue from my Tbilisi apartment, Danny slept, and I recounted, as best I could, the events of the past five months to Stuart and his colleagues.

Before I knew it, 8.00am came and I was driven to a meeting at the British Embassy with the Minister of State Security, accompanied by Deborah and Jacques. My recollections are a little fragmentary but I remember the meeting was interrupted by a phone call from President Shevardnadze to Deborah conveying an "I told you so" message and passing on his good wishes to me and my family. I also recall the Minister of State Security opining that my kidnap was an "inside job"; someone in the Bank was involved and he had a pretty good idea of who that person was! He was also of the view that the "Hand of God" was involved in my escape and strongly suggested that I should attend church in future – a suggestion with which I was happy to concur.

After about an hour, I was whisked off to the airport in the Embassy Mercedes accompanied by Deborah and followed by Jacques with Diana, Danny and Diana's mother and sister. Another Merc contained the Minister and his entourage followed by more Government officials and security guards. At the airport VIP lounge, another meeting, this time with the Minister of the Interior and his colleagues, at which I again recounted the events of the past five months. The meeting lasted nearly two hours and the flight was delayed accordingly.

Outside, a host of journalists and photographers were gathered, and the staff – over forty of them – of the ABG, many of whom had travelled many miles to say good-bye. It was an unimaginably emotional moment. Ilia, my faithful translator was in tears; Lisiko, Dato and Eka who had been with me since the beginning of my time in Georgia, and many others, were simply speechless, but their eyes said it all. There were so many things I wanted to say to these wonderful people but the flight was waiting and a few garbled words and hurried kisses had to suffice. Then, a tearful farewell to Diana's mother and sister – we made them promise to join us in Wales for Christmas, which they did – and within minutes we were sitting in business class, no less. Diana and Danny sat together with a free seat in between, with me across the aisle with Stuart of the Embassy who accompanied us to Heathrow.

Chapter Forty-nine

It was an indescribably emotional moment for me as the plane taxied away from the sea of faces and waving arms framed in the window of the departure lounge at Tbilisi airport. I forced back the tears and tried to collect my thoughts. Everything had happened so very quickly. I was vaguely conscious of my leaving unfinished business in Georgia. I wanted to do more to help the Georgian authorities to find and arrest the people who had been responsible for my abduction. I didn't feel particularly vindictive: I simply wanted them to be found and punished. But most of all I felt a sense of incredible joy and gratitude. Not only was I going home, but I was going home with Diana and Danny. I had conditioned myself, in the hole, to come to accept that I would never see Diana and Danny and my family in Wales again. Never see my cottage in Cowbridge, never see the sea, never see the mountains, never see my friends, never feel Welsh rain, never see or feel any of the things I held dear again. I had come to accept that I was going to die. And yet, here I was, sitting in splendid comfort in an aeroplane that was taking me, and mine, home to Wales. I was really alive – *and going home!*

The flight captain apologised over the public address system for the delay in departing from Tbilisi and announced that a VIP was present on this particular flight. I looked around me to see who this could be, and all of the passengers burst into spontaneous applause. The VIP was me! The stewardess came along and offered me the air crew's congratulations and a magnum of champagne with the compliments of British Mediterranean. I stammered a thank you.

Stuart tried to explain to me the efforts that had been made by so many people to obtain my release, and prepared me for the kind of reception that I could expect on arrival at Heathrow. I listened in complete amazement and utter disbelief. Was this actually happening to me? Had all these things been done for me? As I tried to take in this welter of information, dozens of people came to my seat in turn, shook my hand and offered their congratulations and best wishes for the future. It was an amazingly emotional experience. Diana had a big beam on her face throughout the flight and Danny chattered and dozed off in turn. As we crossed the Channel and approached Heathrow I could hardly contain myself at the prospect of seeing my family: a family which now included my new grandson, Ioan, who I would see that day for the first time.

We were first down the steps and immediately ushered into a waiting limousine by a very nice lady from the Foreign Office. She explained that television cameras, journalists and photographers in some numbers were awaiting my return and would I mind spending five minutes with them. She apologised for this and was conscious that I must be very tired and in no mood mentally to go through another ordeal. In my totally euphoric mood, I simply nodded at her and shook my head in disbelief.

But first, my family – they were all there – Mair, Lisa and husband Gavin with my three grand-children, Megan, Manon Haf and little Ioan, the image of his grand-father; Rod, Pip and a host of others from the UK Foreign Office, the European Commission, the Georgian Embassy in the UK, Scotland Yard, the contractors Landell-Mills and Agri-systems. The champagne flowed as did the tears of joy and relief. It was all a little too much for Danny who found it difficult to cope with the hordes of people and the high-octane emotions. He dissolved into a flood of tears and was inconsolable until a bar of chocolate and an ice-cream appeared; all was then well. Diana joined in the celebrations – she had been to Wales on two occasions before and knew my family well – and was made welcome again in typically Welsh fashion. Explanations were given and information imparted, all in a rush of words and emotions. Everything was jumbled and confused and indescribably joyous.

The lady from the Foreign Office reminded me of the need to give a short interview to the media who were gathered in an adjacent room. She asked me to say only a few words and then say good-bye in Welsh. I suggested that we should just "wing it."

The door was opened and I almost collapsed in shock at the number of media people in that room. All were shouting questions and popping cameras in a frenzy of excitement. Although Stuart had warned me during the flight, I'd never expected this. I tried to respond to the questions asked as best I could and gave a brief description of the major events of my five month in captivity. Finally, I stated absolutely truthfully, that "There is a God" and I believed that "our Friend Upstairs" had been very much involved in my "escape" during the evening of the 6th November, and that I owed Him a huge debt of gratitude. I truly believed, at that time, that the people who took me out of the hole had done so to shoot and kill me. The fact that I escaped unhurt and the "wrong person" was killed, I put down to an Act of God with a small dose of Georgian ineptitude thrown in.

I finished up with an emotional spiel on the value of family and friends – a value that we all too often take for granted until reminded by an experience such as mine – and confirmed my commitment to never undervaluing those precious people ever again. I then grabbed Ioan and gave him a hug and left with a final acknowledgement to the journalists – "Diolch yn Fawr i Gyd" – Thank you all very much indeed. And I meant it.

The very kind and gentle Detective Superintendent David Douglas of Scotland Yard drove Diana, Danny and me to Lisa's family home in Creigiau near Cardiff, where we were to meet up with the remainder of my family. As our little cavalcade of three cars approached the "Croeso I Cymru" – "Welcome to Wales" – sign just over the Severn Bridge, David's phone rang and he handed it to me. It was Lisa yelling the rugby chant, "Wa-ales, Wa-ales, Wa-ales." I knew then that I was home.

Chapter Fifty

It's very difficult even now some years after the event, for me to really appreciate the huge efforts made by so many people to secure my release. Throughout my time in captivity, media pressure upon my family was quite relentless. Newspaper headlines variously read:

FATE OF KIDNAP VICTIM UNCERTAIN

MYSTERY OF KIDNAP MAN

KIDNAPPING SPARKS TALKS WITH GEORGIAN LEADERS

WELSH BUSINESSMAN KIDNAPPED

BRITISH BANKER KIDNAPPED BY GANG AFTER GUN FIGHT WITH POLICE

BRITON HELD HOSTAGE IN A COUNTRY WHERE LAWLESSNESS RULES

SCOTLAND YARD AID HUNT FOR KIDNAP VICTIM

A typical report, written by an experienced foreign correspondent of a national newspaper of the twenty-second of June, read:

"In Georgia, where police corruption is endemic and the law is widely viewed as the imposition of an alien power, the search for the Briton kidnapped by gunmen on Tuesday has been stepped up. But the fact that the Georgian police are leading the search for Peter Shaw, 57, may compound the Welsh banker's problems."

Very true, but hardly of great comfort to my family and friends back home.

Mair didn't leave her home for over a week following the kidnapping. Luckily, Lisa, my daughter lives only a few miles away and they provided mutual support to each other in the glare of media attention. The local police were superbly supportive, and relations and friends rallied around. My mam, elderly and frail, fortunately didn't fully appreciate the enormity of the situation. Her two surviving sisters, both living in South Wales, were able to provide the appropriate reassurances – "Peter has been delayed. He'll be home shortly." "Peter is taking a long holiday with Diana and Danny. Don't worry; he'll be home in a week or two."

Elements of the Georgian media had a great time. I was variously accused of having stolen millions of dollars from the European Commission or from the Government of Georgia. In fairness, others sprang to my defence: "These rumours are totally incorrect!" said a leading Georgian lawyer. The Head of the National Bank's Department for Supervision and Regulation stated that he didn't see "any connection between the activities of the bank and the kidnapping of Mr. Shaw." A Brussels EU diplomat was quoted as saying "He is one of us." It was recognised at home that these stories were totally unfounded and purposefully malicious. It was all part of the Georgian political game. Nevertheless, my family members were very hurt. Misha Mgaloblishvili tried to explain his countrymen's convoluted mental processes at the FACC meeting of the first of July. I quote:

"The strategy of the Government of Georgia will be to make every effort to obtain Peter's release. This will be very much a reaction to pressure applied by the EU, the World Bank, the Soros Foundation etc., in threatening to turn off financial aid. Over a period of time, certain factions within the Government, by rubbishing Peter and besmirching his name, will be able to say that this is not an easy job, and that his nefarious activities, never substantiated, will justify their non-performance in finding and freeing him."

In every other kidnapping in Georgia, most Georgian press accounts suggested the victims were somehow responsible for their own misfortunes. My experience was no exception. Other Georgian media reports in late June incorporated statements from the Ministry of State Security and the Ministry of the Interior in which the view was expressed that "existing or former members of some official structures in Georgia may have been involved in the attack... it bears the hallmarks of their involvement." On the 7th July, the Minister of State Security issued a statement to the effect that the Georgian authorities knew at least two of those who were responsible for kidnapping me. Arrests were to be made imminently. No arrests were made.

On 12th July, the Delegation of the EC in Georgia issued a press release in support of my activities in Georgia **(See Appendix 3)**. This put a spoke in the wheel of the rumour-mongers.

During August, a series of letters was sent to President Shevardnadze by President of the European Commission Romano Prodi, by Vice-President Neil Kinnock, by EC External Affairs Commissioner Chris Patten, by UK Prime Minister Tony Blair, Foreign Minister Jack Straw and President of the European Parliament Pat Cox. They all asked serious questions of Shevardnadze's Government with regard to the Georgian security situation, linked specifically to the kidnapping of Peter Shaw.

Michael Boyd's colleagues on the board of the DCI group of companies included several hugely respected international luminaries such as Dr Garret Fitzgerald, former Prime Minister of Ireland, and Lynda, Baroness Chalker of Wallasey, who had been Minister of Overseas Development in the Thatcher Government. All networked enthusiastically and very effectively.

Peter Sutherland, Chairman of British Petroleum was contacted. BP was heavily involved in financing the construction of a major oil pipeline stretching from Baku in Azerbaijan, through Georgia, to the Turkish port of Ceyhan. Negotiations in connection with the direction of the pipeline, and its subsequent funding, had taken years to come to fruition. The final decision to lay the pipeline through Georgia was of immense political, financial and social significance to the country. Shevardnadze had loudly proclaimed this to be his own personal coup, and had lauded the many benefits to be enjoyed by the population as a whole. He was hugely discomforted when questions were asked of him and his government by senior BP officials, and others involved in the proposed construction, regarding their personal security and that of their contractors. The plight of Peter Shaw was frequently and pointedly mentioned in this context.

The Chairman of the board of DCI was the well-known Irish entrepreneur Trevor Bowen. Trevor was also director of the company, Principle Management Ltd. which managed the pop group U2. Bono, lead singer of U2, wearing his global poverty alleviation hat, had on several occasions met Mr. Paul O'Neil, then US Treasury Secretary. Mr. O'Neil happened to be in Georgia on a mission during August 2002. He was contacted by Bono. Mr. O'Neil held a number of meetings with President Shevardnadze. Apparently my name was mentioned – at the bottom of the agenda no doubt – but nevertheless, mentioned.

The US government had for years been a major benefactor to the Georgian government. Their embassy in Georgia quickly expressed "grave concern" with regard to the security situation in Georgia and provided the government with a long list of physical attacks on American citizens in Georgia in recent years. This criticism was delivered at the same time as the European Commission froze ongoing aid and postponed indefinitely any future meetings with the Georgian government.

The ABG financed the installing of large coloured posters on hoardings throughout Tbilisi portraying an image of my ugly mug with a caption, in English and in Georgian, which read "Peter Shaw – Kidnap Victim." These posters were strategically placed on routes throughout the city taken each day by

President Shevardnadze and his cavalcade of protectors. The point was to ensure that wherever Shevardnadze was going, and with whomsoever he was meeting, the plight of Peter Shaw was part of every conversation and intruded into his and his Government's daily activities. And if he ever needed to be reminded, the face of Peter Shaw stared at him from every billboard lining his route home.

The American Chamber of Commerce, an important pressure group for reform in Georgia, chaired by Fady Adsey, a prominent Lebanese businessman, wrote a stinging letter to President Shevardnadze on 7th August **(See Appendix 4)**. A few days later, the Georgian Minister of the Interior confirmed that he "had received information that Peter Shaw is alive," and "arrests are imminent." Later that month, the UK Foreign Office sought validation of this statement. Confirmation was received, but no arrests were made.

The Shevardnadze government was also under pressure from Russia. The Putin administration had long accused Georgia of harbouring Chechen terrorists in the remote Pankisi Gorge in north-east Georgia. Shevardnadze responded that his government was merely providing succour and aid to genuine refugees who had crossed over the wild mountain passes into the Gorge from their devastated homeland. Russia didn't believe it and showered a few bombs on the Pankisi Gorge. I heard the explosions from my underground prison on 23rd August.

The US government took the side of the Georgians, fearful of Russian ambitions to expand their influence into Georgia. The Americans provided one thousand troops to train the Georgian army and bolster their ability to oppose any Russian military activities.

The Georgian government mobilised troops into the Gorge to contain further hostilities. Shortly afterwards, Georgian troops found the belt in the Gorge which was identified as belonging to me. The authorities concluded, correctly as it turned out, that I was being held in the Pankisi Gorge.

On 19th August, Denis Corboy again travelled to Georgia. He held a series of meetings with ministers, ambassadors and with President Shevardnadze. The latter told Denis that he "felt that Peter Shaw is alive". He offered no explanation for this, but Denis left the meeting with the firm impression that "Shevy knew more than he was prepared to openly state." **(See Appendix 5)**

My local newspaper, the *South Wales Echo*, launched a "Send Peter Home Now" campaign **(See Appendix 6)**. On 7th September, Glenys Kinnock, my MEP, who had throughout remained close to my family and provided immense support, announced her intention to travel to Georgia and seek a meeting with the President "if appropriate and wise". "I find it so awful that he could be suffering for just doing his job. He was working with the European Commission to help Georgia, and this is his reward. It is completely unacceptable," Glenys said. At the same time, the Georgian Ministry of the Interior announced that my whereabouts were known and the Georgian army was to launch a rescue mission. These reports were later denied and no rescue mission was launched. A few days later, the BBC reported that a contingent of the US army sent to Georgia was to help in the kidnap hunt.

Chapter Fifty-one

John and Tony, with expert support provided by the FCO, had been trying to analyse some of the characteristics of the sender of the text messages.

Boris was deemed to be reasonably well-educated and (his Russian was) grammatically correct in all respects. His vocabulary was natural and his style appropriate to his assumed purpose, being relatively intelligible and even verging on literary elegance. Initially his messages contained some jokiness – *"Send us messages as text because, as you should know, the phone system is bad here!"* And, when texting in English he threw in: *"You must be joking!"* He was also a little cocky, for example, *"We'll get our money back in any event – in one way or another."*

As time passed, he exhibited a tendency to bully and a willingness to threaten: *"I'm sick and tired of it. I demand an interpreter,"* and *"Unless you are playing games with us..."* He accused John and Tony of hiding behind "Chinese" – deliberately obfuscating – messages, and of using a malfunctioning phone. He asked them several times *"Are you bothered about Peter's life?"* Further conversations revealed a touch of mental sadism too; even Boris's amputation threat had a certain refinement. It was neither brutally explicit, nor an ultimatum which a cruder soul might have favoured. Boris preferred an oblique hint leaving John and Tony to fill in the dots. He gave it an extra twist by purporting to make it a message from me to my "wife". The analysis suggested that, with the initial jokiness and cockiness, Boris was deriving some enjoyment from the game.

The conclusion was that Tony and John were not dealing with a muscle-bound, ill-educated thug. He had some refinement of thought, some clear calculation too, but also some inconsistency, flashes of temper, volatility and perhaps some mental cruelty. Of course, they were not aware whether the above described the drafter of the messages, or the keyer and sender (if a different person), or whether the texts were ever a "committee draft." The occasional speed of response suggested that this was unlikely.

Scotland Yard expected that Mair would at some time receive a phone call from the kidnappers. She was thoroughly briefed on how she should react to the calls, and provided with a hand-out detailing the type of demands she might receive and how she should respond. She was also provided with recording equipment. Fortunately it was not required. Still, Mair lost a lot of sleep. She remains convinced that her telephone was bugged. Perhaps we'll never know.

Chapter Fifty-two

Since my return home I've tried to piece together, with the help of many others, the bits of the jigsaw puzzle in order to make a whole. The result is still incomplete, and will probably remain so.

Why was I kidnapped and who was responsible? I've certainly had enough time to ponder on this during the period of my incarceration, and subsequently. It could have been an inside job, as opined by the Minister of State Security on the morning of my departure from Georgia. He believed that there were several ABG bank employees involved and that one of them made calls to Diana in Georgia and John and Tony in the UK. He offered no substantiation of this and I doubt it. Could the culprits have been disgruntled customers who had been refused loans? Hardly likely. Breaking legs would be more in keeping with the Georgian way.

Could they perhaps be the directors or shareholders of those banks who had accused me of causing their "bankruptcies" during the RARP1 project? They had certainly done their best to blame me through the media at that time, but the purpose then was simply to shift the blame. These people had effectively stolen money from the project's capital. We were able to recover only a tiny fraction through the courts of Georgia. They had already benefited and no good purpose would be served by kidnapping me. They had all the loot they wanted. Surely they could not want more? Or could they simply want revenge? Then why wait three years to do it?

Those who organised the crime may have wanted me out of the way to allow them to have their wicked way regarding the future operation of the ABG. They wanted to hijack the bank and manage the lending book in a way that would ultimately benefit themselves, their friends and colleagues and their particular political faction. The Bank's capital – very modest in Western terms – of five million six hundred thousand US dollars was a hugely attractive incentive to some Georgian politicians and government officials in a country where a senior government minister, for example, was paid a salary of two hundred and fifty dollars per month, and that intermittently. Perhaps they've now had their way!

Politically, who would benefit? The Ministry of Agriculture – the so-called project recipient – and many of the senior officials within the Ministry had long borne a grudge because they were no longer the sole government representatives on the Senior Boards of the ABG. Policy management was shared between various ministries, and the EC representatives. This was not my decision, simply the wish of the government and the EC, but I was the Project Team Leader and therefore the easiest one to finger and blame.

Also, the Ministry of Agriculture was totally opposed to the co-operative banking privatisation route. The last thing that they wanted was to see the ownership of the ABG being shared among many thousands of small farmers and agri-businesses. The Ministry would never be able to control or manage the bank thereafter. The tendering process was due to take place on 19th and 20th June in Brussels. Did the Ministry perhaps believe that I would influence the decision of the EC selection board and point them in the direction of co-operative banking? It was well-known that I was a strong advocate of the co-operative banking route. Was I therefore taken out on 18th June to ensure that I did not participate in the meetings in Brussels?

Finally, there was the question of a ransom. It matters not how badly formalised or poorly-networked the ransom demand was, it certainly existed. To those who actually carried out the kidnapping and held me in captivity, it was the main, if not the only, motivation. The fact that the Polaroid photographs and the hand-written note were not received by the European Commission, the UK government or by my family, doesn't mean that they were not received by those at the top of the Georgian government.

I believe it was the Georgian government that eventually negotiated my release. No doubt, some money was exchanged

236

(but nothing like two million dollars) and political favours were granted in exchange for my release. A major factor in achieving this was the huge amount of pressure exerted by the FACC team, their connections, and Denis Corboy (the *Special Envoy* of the European Commission) on Shevardnadze and those close to him. He was considerably embarrassed and harassed by the constant drip of questions asked and doubts cast by existing and potential investors in Georgia, and the refusal of the European Commission, and other donor institutions, to carry on "business as usual". At some stage he sought to end it, and those close to him were instructed so to do.

Jackie's notes made three years after my release:

I'd never met Denis (Corboy) in person but held him in high esteem from the conversations we had over the medical evacuation I'd dealt with previously from Georgia. It was such a triumph when Brussels appointed him Special Envoy – I really thought Denis was the key to your release and I still feel that today. With the support and momentum of the Group, Denis continued to apply pressure at every opportunity. Looking back, the strategy of the Group was to be active, apply political pressure, provide mutual support, be prepared and be patient. Frustratingly we were advised to keep a low press profile.

I was soon talking to Denis on a daily basis – he would talk to me at length of what he had gleaned. Denis has such a powerful yet quiet tone – he commands attention and has a natural presence. I felt comforted. It was very rare for Denis to be at all despondent, but there were times when he felt "very discouraged" and looking back now very accurately said on one occasion, "I have a feeling we are in for a long haul."

I always took down our conversations verbatim so that I didn't misunderstand any part. I remember once being out for a walk with Ella when Denis called. The only thing I had to write with was a lipstick which I wore down to a stump scribbling notes on a paper towel.

Like Jackie, I believe that Denis was a Very *Special Envoy*.

Another scenario and perhaps the most plausible explanation – picture the scene. There was an inter-factional battle going on within the government of Georgia at that time, as to who controlled the very lucrative armament smuggling trade emanating from Russia, organised by Russian military commanders. The trade had been going on for many years by which Russian armaments were smuggled out of Chechnya via the Pankisi Gorge, paid for in part by contraband in the form of drugs, routed through Tbilisi airport, and eventually utilised in the Middle-East and elsewhere. Some have been found as far afield as the Yemen. There were also sales of Russian arms to Chechen rebels. Such illegal trafficking was carried out on a large scale and would have had to involve many people who were high up in the Georgian power ministries. Shevardnadze had in early 2002 sacked a number of key ministers who had managed this trade. Subsequently, internecine rivalry had escalated within the government factions about who would fill the vacuum.

Denis Corboy, acting as Special Envoy, met regularly with Shevardnadze and members of the government. He came to the conclusion, at an early stage, that the trigger for my kidnapping was, initially, control of the Bank. As time passed and the deluge of international criticism of the Georgian government increased, I became more valuable and was used as a pawn in the dispute over control of the Russian arms traffic through Georgia. Certain ministers were subsequently re-instated within the Georgian government as part of the arrangement leading to my release.

Denis continues to travel to Georgia as Director of the Caucasus Policy Institute and to support the charity for handicapped children there which was founded by his wife. He tells me that discussing these events with former ministers who were in the Shevardnadze government at the time, they tend to confirm this theory as to why I was kidnapped and the nature of the price paid for my release.

The huge trucks I glimpsed while waiting for nightfall,l and before being forcibly transported into the Pankisi Gorge, and which I guessed to be timber transporters, may have been used for armament smuggling. Additionally, some of the contents of the text messages received by John Dexter and Tony Bishop seem to support this theory.

Of one thing I am certain. I did not "escape" during the night of 6th November 2002. I was released, and the manner of my release was engineered by the Georgian authorities.

I've also learned that two of my kidnappers have been identified as having been shot and killed in gun battles between the Georgian forces and Kist renegades in the Pankisi Gorge. I am told that the "farmer," a Kist named Monogarashvili, was killed by a bomb planted in his toilet by a rival gang-leader! All very convenient, but perhaps true.

The widow of Tashkent, the man who was killed during the evening of 6th November and later apparently identified by the Georgian police as a member of a well-known criminal gang, appeared on Georgian television shortly after my return to the UK. There are two versions of what she said. The first is that her husband was a police informer who had infiltrated his way into the gang. His true identity had been discovered by my kidnappers and he had been shot and killed in revenge. The second version is that he had been asked by his accomplices to accommodate me during the winter at his home in the village of Akhmeta in the Pankisi Gorge. They realised that I would not last through the winter in the hole. He refused to co-operate for fear of endangering his family, and was shot and killed in retribution.

The official Georgian version is that I was rescued by a group of Georgian soldiers who ambushed my captors on that fateful night. They say a gun battle broke out, during which one of my captors was killed. They say they found some fifteen spent cartridges about fifty metres away from where the body of Tashkent was found. This is absolute nonsense. I was there, in the bushes, and the only gun-fire came from my immediate vicinity. There was no Sheriff's posse rescuing me from the outlaws that night.

Nevertheless, I have no doubt that a series of miracles took place that night, and the Man Upstairs was certainly heavily involved. But I wonder whether He organised it all. I was taken out of the hole to a place quite close to where a Georgian army depot had been established. Inevitably *I met up with some of them*. Among that group was a *private soldier* who spoke excellent English: not common in the Georgian army. I was taken from where they found me to the Georgian army headquarters in the Pankisi, where there just happened to be the *Deputy Minister of State Security*, hardly a place where he would spend his normal Tuesday evenings. All in all, a remarkable sequence of coincidences!

Chapter Fifty-three

People frequently ask me what lasting effect the five months I spent in captivity, particularly the four months in the hole in the ground, has had on me, and whether the experience has affected my personality. I can honestly say that the only permanent impression made is a positive one. Physically, I was in pretty poor condition when I arrived home, but the ministerings of my local GP sorted out the various fungal infections and abscesses pretty quickly. My teeth caused me more severe problems and it took twelve months of intensive dental care to finally resolve the results of enforced neglect. Also, I found it very difficult for the first few weeks to sleep in my bed – far too comfortable – and found it easier to curl up on the bedroom floor; much to the amusement of Diana and Danny.

I was offered counselling but declined. I was sure that the close and caring attentions of my family and friends would put paid to any lingering difficulties in that department; and I was right. Sure, in the early days I had nightmares, still do, and wake up occasionally even now in a cold sweat, when I dream of being trapped in a dark enclosed space and remember the bootings and beatings to which I was subjected. But then I look around me, realise where I am, and thank the Lord for depositing me safely in my warm bed, lying next to Diana, with Blacky the cat from Georgia on top of the bed, and Danny tucked-up in the next bedroom. All safely ensconced in the little cottage that I thought I'd never see again. Interestingly enough, my fear of heights has increased since my release. I've no idea how this relates to my time in captivity, but my fear has certainly become a true phobia in recent years.

But I am certainly much more appreciative of those things in life which, I'm sure we all take too much for granted. I refer not only to central heating, light switches and toilet flushes, but most importantly I have a much greater appreciation of the meaningfulness of family and friends, all of whom I certainly took too much for granted in my former life. This is definitely not the case now. I'm not naturally demonstrative with regard to my emotions, but I keep Diana and Danny very close and meet with Mam, Mair and our kids every few weeks without fail. Similarly with friends, and if distance precludes regular get-togethers, then I phone or text regularly. I'm probably a bit of a nuisance now, but I'm determined more than ever before to keep in touch. I hope and believe that I'm a much more patient and understanding person than hitherto, and truly, nothing fazes me. Yes, of course I become irritated with the call-centre culture when I can't get hold of the gas-man or the drain-man, but, when real problems arise, I click automatically into a much more pragmatic mode. Because I know that I'm very lucky to be alive, and simply to be able to experience these small problems is a blessing. I have no doubt about that.

To my shame, I have failed to honour the promises I made to God during the period of my incarceration in the hole, particularly in terms of becoming a regular church or chapel-goer. In my defence, I've tried on several occasions to find a suitable venue on a Sunday in which to say a small prayer and have a quiet word with the Man Upstairs, but I've failed. I cannot cope with guitar-strumming evangelists or ill-humoured theologians pronouncing upon outmoded biblical texts which, I'm afraid, mean nothing whatsoever to me. I pray a lot now, but not in church. But I certainly believe in the power of prayer. Prayers work.

I'm frequently asked how on earth I managed to survive the ordeal of being chained in a filthy, wet, dark hole for that four-month period, and stay relatively sane. I well remember the words of a wise and sensible lady, who was among the scores who phoned me in the early days following my homecoming. She forewarned me that this question would be asked of me frequently, and suggested a suitable response – "because you bloody well had to. You had no choice." And she was dead right.

Surprisingly, a few people have suggested that because many of my male forbears were coal-miners who spent many years underground in miserable conditions hewing coal for a living, then there may be some genetic imprint left on me which enabled me to manage my underground experience. This is of course a complete nonsense. True, it takes real courage to work underground, and it may be that I have inherited some small traces of their bravery, but no more than that. I believe quite simply that the instinct to survive is a basic human characteristic, which we all have in huge amounts. Perhaps I was a little lucky in possessing a vivid imagination, a strong physique and an inclination toward positivity which stood me in good stead in my time of need. These attributes may well have been inherited from my forefathers.

Finally, I am not, by nature, vindictive, and of course life goes on, but I would dearly love to see those responsible – those truly responsible and not paid fall-guys – be punished, and that part of their punishment entails their being individually incarcerated in a small, cold, wet, underground hole for a period of at least four months, without light, sanitation or communication, chained and padlocked by the neck, and with a bucket of chicken-shit thrown over their heads every day. I think that would be good.

Appendix 1

There is an important point which is difficult to explain and on this please trust my advice. The Georgian power structures are very complex with multi-layered links between roofs, clans, mafia businesses and including the top family. It would be a serious mistake to try to explore or untangle these structures. To delve into this would almost certainly further endanger Peter's life and other lives. Having New Scotland Yard (NSY) ask questions in relation to Mr T etc. has been entirely unhelpful and I hope that NSY is beginning to understand that this murky world is out of bounds for policemen. It is sufficient that they follow the police investigation in that Peter is being held by criminals who may soon ask for ransom etc., but that up there, and out of reach, there are political forces at work which could effect his release at a certain point. The reasons why this could come about, which hopefully it does, will probably never be understood. In my view, the key is M. S (Shevardnadze) and the clans related to the top family and their interests. The police are of course a necessary piece of theatre, and visits to them by NSY give the impression of a normally functioning state, which Georgia is not by a long shot.

Denis Corboy
Special Delegate of the European Commission to Georgia
24th July 2002

Appendix 2

"Mission of Denis Corboy to Georgia 16th – 23rd July 2002

The programme for the visit was jointly arranged by UK Ambassador Barnes-Jones and Head of EC Delegation, Torben Holtze who accompanied me on all scheduled meetings. With their agreement I also had private one-on-one meetings with the President, his Chief of Staff and others who might be able to help in understanding the circumstances surrounding Peter Shaw's kidnapping, and what steps might be taken to expedite his release.

Background

Georgia may not yet be classified as a failed state, but it is certainly a very troubled one. In the mid 1990's there were justified expectations that Shevardnadze would lead the country to a stable democracy, market economy and a gradual integration into European and International structures (PCA,CoE,WTO). This transition did not happen largely due to corruption, a failure to allow the reformers who won the parliamentary election in 1995 to be reflected in the Shevardnadze governments, and a corrosive overlapping relationship between law enforcement, criminal gangs, illicit drug and arms trafficking and, more recently, kidnapping.

You will recall that the former Minister of the Interior, Targamadze, was dismissed on the 1st November 2001, when Zhvania, the leader of the reformers and Speaker of Parliament, uncovered a plot to cause civil unrest leading to violence and a pretext for his arrest and the arrest of other reformers in the Parliament. Although new ministers were appointed, much of the overlapping relationships I have described continue to operate. To some extent there is a state within a state which complicates both the understanding and resolution of this particular case.

Conclusions

My preliminary conclusions are set out in the attached file note. Peter was selected by those who ordered his kidnap because of his high profile and the number of enemies he had made through his persistence in protecting the assets of the ABG Bank.

The motivation for his kidnap could be multi-faceted, but the primary one would appear to be political. The details of what we understand about the groups who conducted his kidnap and are now holding him are set out in the note for the file. At least four recent kidnappings would appear to be the work of the same groups.

My principal conclusion is that the only authority which might be able to bring about his early release is the President, and I will be advising that we continue to put pressure in this direction, both local and international. The telegrams sent by Ambassador Barnes-Jones reporting on my meetings have been copied to Cabinet Patten and it would not be appropriate to repeat their contents in this note. I attach a summary of conclusions and a programme of the visit. I will return to Brussels early on 23rd July and will report to Cabinet Patten and RELEX on arrival. UK Ambassador Barnes-Jones has indicated that she would appreciate it if I would also brief in London, which I am very prepared to do.

Denis Corboy

22nd July 2002

The file note to which Denis refers reads as follows, quoted verbatim:

1. The objective of the visit is through meetings with the highest officials to convey a message of growing concern with the continuing captivity of Peter Shaw, and during discussions to put pressure on the Georgian authorities to ensure a speedy release with due considerations for his safety.

2. No proof has been provided that Peter Shaw is alive but based on various statements, the indications are that he is alive. Various contacts by the people claiming to hold Peter Shaw have been made. So far none have been verified. One approach is now under active consideration.

3. There are few hard facts. Peter Shaw may be held by a different group than the one that kidnapped him. This group appears to be criminals possibly involved in previous kidnappings, while the first group of kidnappers may possibly be made up of people from, or linked to, the law enforcement agencies. The Minister of State Security claims that the people of the two groups have been identified and the police are trying to find them. The Minister of the Interior is more cautious claiming that the group or groups have been identified but the identity is only known of two people.

4. Although the Georgian authorities in the past have claimed that Peter Shaw could not have been moved out of Tbilisi, this may no longer be the case, since the group holding him seems to be operating outside Tbilisi in the areas to the north.

5. While the first group never made any contact asking for a ransom, the Georgian assessment is that the second group will most likely only release Peter Shaw if money is paid.

6. The Prosecutor General claimed that having scrutinized Peter Shaw's financial records and personal life, the Prosecutor General's Office had no evidence of any wrong doing by Peter Shaw and that he was a highly competent professional banking expert respected by many people. His bank records show a modest use of money, deposited into his account by regular transfers from the UK. The review of the ABG shows good banking procedures.

7. In the meeting with the President, I stressed the increasing concern in Europe, and the fact that this was shared on the highest level (Patten, Mr. & Mrs. Kinnock, Cox). The concerns had also been shared with US officials. Prior to the meeting the existing Italian Deputy Foreign Minister and the US Treasury

Secretary had raised the issue with President Shevardnadze. The President spoke about motives possibly being ransom or intentions to cause political damage to Georgia including the relations with the EU. He also said that there may be other motives. Asked if there was any proof that Peter Shaw is alive, the President stated that there is no concrete evidence but he felt that Peter is alive.

8. The Minister of State admitted the possibility that people of law enforcement agencies may be involved and this could slow down the solving of the case. He talked about a new drive to fight corruption and the links between officials and drug/arms traffickers. He stressed that the concerned Ministers would be dismissed if they did not solve the case. He appealed for the EU not to suspend its assistance, pointing to the possible consequences to Georgia's political, economic and social development which could lead to increasing criminality as a result. He nearly blamed the EU for making Georgia a victim, if the EU suspends its assistance. As a motive, the State Minister did not think that ransom was the main objective. The people behind the kidnapping were more interested in economic and political destabilisation of Georgia.

9. Overall conclusion, Georgian authorities do generally seem to be working intensively on the case. British professionals have said that the approach is along the right lines but of course only results will count. Although there is co-operation and co-ordination between the law enforcement agencies, one cannot exclude elements of competition and political motives which makes this case much more difficult to solve.

Denis Corboy

Tbilisi, 22nd July 2002

Appendix 3

Press Release the Delegation of the European Commission dated 12th July 2002

TBILISI 12TH JULY 2002. The kidnapping of Mr. Peter Shaw is of great concern to the European Commission as expressed in a letter of 24th June 2002 from Commissioner Patten to President Shevardnadze as well as in several meetings between the EC Delegation, the UK Embassy and the Georgian authorities. The concern about Mr. Shaw's well-being is growing with the length of his captivity. An early release is on everyone's mind.

Referring to a number of articles and statements in the Georgian press about Peter Shaw and his work during his stay in Georgia over the last six years, a lot of misinformation and allegations have surfaced.

Contrary to several reports, Peter Shaw was not a private businessman at any moment during his six-year stay in Georgia. Peter Shaw was paid exclusively by the European Commission as he was rendering technical assistance financed by the European Commission as a consultant to the ABG. The ABG was regularly audited by an international auditing company, Ernst and Young, as well as inspected by the Georgian National Bank. They concluded that the ABG was operating according to international banking regulations. Peter Shaw carried out his assignment in full compliance with the professional standards of the European Commission's technical assistance programme (TACIS).

The employment of Peter Shaw was established through a contract between the European Commission and a consultancy firm. This contract was awarded to the consultancy firm after a tender. This type of contracting is used extensively by the European Commission to employ experts worldwide for its co-operation with third–world countries (non-European Union countries). The experts are paid exclusively by the European

Commission. During his six years in Georgia, Peter Shaw has worked solely as a consultant for TACIS financed activities.

As part of the team running the ABG, Peter Shaw has contributed significantly to the prudent approach of the ABG to lending, with the result that repayment rates are almost 100%. The ABG has also been extended with 9 branch offices into the rural areas to the benefit of farmers throughout the country. It is to Peter Shaw's credit that the ABG has developed into a sound operational structure, providing an important instrument for the future development of the rural socio-economy as envisaged when it was established with the support of President Shevardnadze and the then EC External Relations Commissioner Van den Broek.

Signed: Torben Holtze. Head of the Delegation of the European Commission in Georgia

Appendix 4

Letter from the American Chamber of Commerce, Tbilisi, Georgia to President Shevardnadze of 7th August 2002

Your Excellency,

We would like to highlight the kidnapping of Peter Shaw, Director of the Agro-business Bank and member of the American Chamber of Commerce.

Peter Shaw was abducted in Tbilisi on the 18th June and his whereabouts are still unknown to us.

However, this is not the first time that a foreign national has been kidnapped in Georgia. Last year, two Spaniards, José Tremino and Francisco Rodriguez were abducted and held for more than a year, and Charbel Aman, a Lebanese businessman (business partner of Fady Adsey), and a member of our Chamber was kidnapped and held for 77 days.

Such crimes are a disaster for Georgia, a country in desperate need of foreign investment. We have no doubt that one of the goals of those responsible for such acts is to discredit Georgia, and undermine your credibility as president and the credibility of your government, particularly the Ministers of the Interior and State Security, who have been actively working to reform their respective ministries.

One of the main aims of the Chamber is to attract foreign investment to Georgia. However, in the light of the present security situation and the absence of the rule of law, we find ourselves unable to encourage any newcomers. During the past two years we have spent the majority of our time convincing our members and other foreign investors to stay in Georgia.

After the release of José Tremino, Francisco Rodriguez and Charbel Aman, representatives of the law enforcement bodies loudly proclaimed that they knew the identity of the kidnappers. However, until now, no one has been prosecuted or arrested for these crimes. We wonder why?

The Minister of State Security publicly announced that the identities of Peter Shaw's kidnappers are known to the authorities. It was also reported in the international press on 7th July that the Minister alleged that Interior Ministry officials were involved in the abduction. The Minister of State, Avtandil Jorbenadze has also publicly confirmed the possible involvement of official structures in the kidnapping.

Since the perpetrators of these crimes are known to the authorities, we urge you to take the political decision to put an end to the action of those criminals, whatever position of power or influence they hold now or have previously held. Such action should facilitate Peter's early and safe release, prevent further kidnappings and ensure the rule of law is upheld.

Those who close their eyes to such criminal acts can only be considered as accomplices. Unless there is a real will to end officially sponsored crime in Georgia, both the political and investment climates will undoubtedly suffer.

We trust therefore you will take the appropriate steps to ensure Peter's safe release.

Sincerely yours,
The American Chamber of Commerce in Georgia.

Appendix 5

Report of Denis Corboy to the European Commission and the FACC Group dated 22nd August 2002

1. The Ministers of the Interior and State Security have said again this weekend that they continue to be confident that Peter is alive and is being held in the Pankisi Gorge.

2. They believe they can bring about his release within the coming days.

3. Sustained diplomatic pressure on the President and the government of Georgia has been maintained throughout August.

The Ministers and the President told me that they have an informer who is connected to the group holding him, and for this reason, it is probable that their statements are correct.

From the record of previous kidnappings involving Chechen/Kist criminal gangs, I fear that Peter will have been badly treated.

The Shaw case has given us an insight into the seriousness and the depth of the crisis of governance in Georgia. The government seems incapable of dealing with criminality and organised crime (kidnapping is now a common event), corruption and kleptocracy is increasing amongst the highest officials, particularly those surrounding the President and his family, democratic standards have deteriorated, reforms have stopped, investment climate worsened etc. In these circumstances it is necessary to review programmes and see whether conditionality on good governance and internal security can be included. The security situation for ex-pats working in the Delegation, project leaders, consultants etc. is also under review. Some contractors may have to build this into their proposals.

I believe that one of the motives in Peter's kidnapping was to give a warning to European Union representatives that should they take a tough line, as Peter did, the same will happen to them. In the Shaw case, it was to maintain Brussels' control of the Agro-business Bank between now and its privatisation, and to protect the Bank's assets from being burgled. This he did, but will those who follow him have the same courage?

As soon as there has been any new development, I will contact you. On a daily basis, Ambassador Barnes-Jones, Head of EC Delegation Torben Holtze and I are in touch and share notes. If nothing happens in the next seven days, I suggest we need to review tactics. I will attend the meeting of the Task Force (FACC) at the FCO as soon as a firm date has been confirmed.

Denis Corboy

Appendix 6

We are writing on behalf of readers of the South Wales Echo to express concerns at the continued disappearance of Peter Shaw.

The kidnapping of our fellow countryman has not only caused considerable pain and distress for Mr Shaw's family and friends, but is damaging the reputation of Georgia throughout Wales and the world.

For the past two months we have been repeatedly told by government officials that the release of Mr Shaw is "imminent" and that his whereabouts are known to the police. Yet no sightings have been confirmed and we still do not even know if he is alive.

Meanwhile, government announcements continue to be unreliable, or at worse, misleading. Better information about this case is vital for the peace of mind of everyone who knows Mr Shaw and to improve the international standing of Georgia.

Mr Shaw is the latest in a long line of prominent foreigners to be abducted in Georgia. Some of them have been held in the Pankisi Gorge for more than a year. We would implore you to make sure that this does not happen in the case of Mr Shaw.

On behalf of the people of South Wales, we urge you to make the prompt release of Mr Shaw, and the hunt for his kidnappers a priority.

Yours sincerely,

South Wales Echo

PETER SHAW

Peter was born in Maesteg, Mid-Glamorgan on 15th December 1944 and was educated at a local primary school and Maesteg Grammar School. After leaving school in 1963 he worked for Midland Bank (now HSBC Bank) for thirty-two years attaining four managerial positions. In 1994 he took EVR and worked abroad as a free-lance banking and financial consultant, working mainly for the European Commission in Hungary, Czech Republic, Lithuania, Belarus, Ukraine, Azerbaijan, Estonia and Georgia. He spent six years in Georgia as Project Team Leader for the European Commission in the establishment and management of the Agro-business Bank of Georgia. He was given the "Individual Consultant of the Year" award in November 2001 by HRH the Duke of Gloucester on behalf of the British Consultancy & Contractors Bureau at No.1 Whitehall. In June 2002, two days before he was due to leave Georgia at contract end, he was kidnapped and held in captivity for a total of five months, for four months of which he was incarcerated in a tiny underground cellar, chained by the neck in complete darkness. He "escaped" in dramatic circumstances in November 2002 and returned to Wales with his Georgian partner, Diana and their three-year-old son, Danny.

Peter now lives in semi-retirement in the Vale of Glamorgan with Diana and Danny. He has three grown-up children, Lisa, Rhodri and Philip by a previous marriage, and three grand-children.

The History Of Pembroke Dock
A Town Built To Build Ships
by Phil Carradice

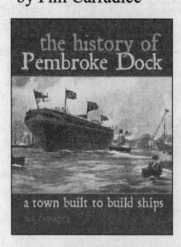

The story of Pembroke Dock is one of triumph and disaster, of hope and terrible failure. Nearly three hundred ships were built in the yards, including some of the most powerful ships in Queen Victoria's navy – as well as four famous Royal Yachts. Then in 1926, the dockyard was suddenly closed, leaving the town without reason for existence. What followed was a brutal battle for survival.

The history of Pembroke Dock is a fascinating social study, taking a community from its raw beginnings to full and accepted standing in the world. It makes compulsive reading for anyone who has an interest in history.

ISBN 1905170181 / 9781905170180   **Price £19.99**

Fully illustrated hardback

Beyond Belief – the real life of Daniel Defoe

by John Martin

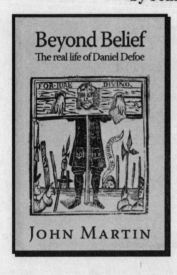

JOHN MARTIN is an Anglo-Irish writer who has investigated the mysterious and secret life of Daniel Defoe, the father of the English novel, whose books *Robinson Crusoe, Moll Flanders* and *Roxana* have sold in vast numbers throughout the world for nearly three hundred years.

He reveals for the first time the *real* life of a highly talented religious dissenter whose sometimes outwardly pious and holier-than-thou demeanour disguised another, different existence in the shadows. His complex life as journalist, government spy and secret 'Governor General' of the press, was paralleled by great personal confusion. A gay man, he was 'married' many times, with children by several women; he was always in debt; thirteen times arrested; pilloried; and twice bankrupted. This book demonstrates that his secret life was stranger than those of the pirates, courtesans, pimps and murderers who crowd his pages.

ISBN 1905170564 / 9781905170562   **£19.99**

Hardback - biography

THE CITY OF LONDON COOK BOOK

by Peter Gladwin

Celebrating the foods, feasts and recipes of the City of London.

The City of London Cook Book is a serendipitous combination of fact, gossip, humour and mouth-watering recipes and includes contributions by key figures including Prime Minister Tony Blair and London Mayor, Ken Livingstone. This unique compendium explores the food of the city: its traditions, recipes and obscurities. Top city restaurateur and chef, Peter Gladwin, reveals a world beyond normally closed doors: spectacular royal receptions, livery company feasts and boardroom banquets. Fascinating facts, quirky quotes, rare illustrations and fabulous food await your delectation.

All profits benefit the Lord Mayor's Appeal

ISBN 1905170386   Price £12.99   Illustrated hardback

www.londoncookbook.com

Fiction by the Queen of Welsh Crime...

Katherine John

This fast-paced action thriller is a multi-layered story that spans eight centuries, from medieval Germany and Prussia to present day Poland and the USA centred on the legend of the Amber Knight – a beloved relic that inspired generations until the Nazis stole it.

Created in 1232 during The Teutonic Crusade when the heroic knight, Helmut von Mau, died in battle at Elblag. When the town was burned, the amber in the treasury melted and was poured into Helmut's sarcophagus, covering his body and creating the Amber Knight.

Present day Gdansk.
Adam Salen, director of a museum trust, receives photographs of the Amber Knight, which disappeared in 1945, and a demand for 15 million dollars. His assistant, Magda, believes that, given a corpse, amber and armour the knight could be recreated.
Adam and Magda want the knight for the museum, but when a mafia hit-man is found dead on Adam's doorstep and more corpses are discovered in woods near Hitler's Wolf's lair, it seems like there may be truth behind the myth that death awaits every unbeliever who looks upon Helmut's face.

ISBN **1905170629 / 9781905170623 £6.99 paperback**